P9-AEV-829

SCALES, INTERVALS,
KEYS, TRIADS,
RHYTHM, and METER

Norton Programed Texts in Music Theory

SCALES, INTERVALS, KEYS, TRIADS, RHYTHM, and METER

A Self-Instruction Program

JOHN CLOUGH,
Slee Professor, State University of New York at Buffalo

JOYCE CONLEY,
The University of Michigan, Ann Arbor

W • W • NORTON & COMPANY
New York • London

Copyright © 1983 by W.W. Norton & Company, Inc.
Copyright © 1964, 1962 by John Clough
All rights reserved.
Published simultaneously in Canada by George J. McLeod Limited, Toronto.
Printed in the United States of America.
Manufacturing by The Murray Printing Company.

Library of Congress Cataloging in Publication Data
Clough, John (John L.)
   Scales, intervals, keys, triads, rhythm, and meter.
   (Norton programed texts in music theory)
   Previous ed. published in 1964 as: Scales, intervals,
keys, and triads.
   1. Music—Theory—Programed instruction.
I. Conley, Joyce. II. Title. III. Series.
MT6.C592S3 1983   781'.07'7   82–24630

W.W. Norton & Company, Inc., 500 Fifth Avenue, New York, N.Y. 10110
W.W. Norton & Company Ltd., 37 Great Russell Street, London WC1B 3NU

ISBN 0-393-95189-8

1 2 3 4 5 6 7 8 9 0

ABOUT THIS BOOK

The reader is assumed to know the names of notes in the treble and bass clefs and the names of keys on the piano keyboard. (A note and key chart appears on page xi for reference.) Otherwise, no special knowledge or musical skill is assumed.

The earlier version of this book, *Scales, Intervals, Keys, and Triads*, dealt with the rudiments of pitch and provided a brief introduction to harmony. In the present book, all of the material on pitch has been retained (and revised where necessary) and the treatment of harmony has been expanded to include triad inversions, principles of voice leading, and connection of I, V, and V^7. An introduction to rhythm and meter has also been added.

The original book was extensively tested at Oberlin College. New materials in this book were brought to final form on the basis of trials in classes at the School of Music, University of Michigan.

In the quarter-century since B. F. Skinner and his co-workers evolved the technique known as "programed instruction," refinements have been introduced and much has been learned about its usefulness for different kinds of materials. Here as elsewhere, however, the basic advantages are still the same: (1) each student works at a personal pace, no faster and no slower; (2) the student is continuously active and is called upon to apply each new fact or idea in a variety of situations; (3) an awareness of individual progress is constant since the student finds out, upon the completion of each task, whether it has been correctly worked out. In these respects, programed learning is akin to study with a private tutor.

TO THE CLASSROOM TEACHER

This program may be used for high school or college courses in elementary music theory. It is intended to provide a foundation for subsequent or concurrent work in one of the standard textbooks, and to serve equally well the needs of teachers who prefer not to use such a textbook. A second volume of programed instruction in harmony, taking up where the present book concludes, is now being prepared by the authors.

Most students will require fifteen to twenty-five hours to complete the program. Thus, in some courses it will be convenient to assign completion of the entire program within a prescribed period at the beginning of the course, say three to five weeks. Or it may be assigned in sections, provided that each set is done in its proper turn. (Two exceptions: Sets 10 and 11, and the corresponding questions in the test at the end of Part 2, may be deferred or omitted altogether. Part 7 may be done at any time.)

It can be reported that this book has done an effective job of teaching its subject matter. However, those who adopt it should be cautioned not to expect miraculous extensions of learning to areas not really covered in the program. For example, a student who has completed the program should know that five sharps is the key signature of B major or G♯ minor. But the ability to identify the key of a given passage in an actual composition is not dealt with in the program, since it ultimately involves a judgment based on aural, not visual facts. The teaching of this skill (not to mention countless others) properly belongs to the classroom teacher.

In order to avoid a large number of exceptions, and exceptions to exceptions, we have adopted a set of relatively simple four-part writing rules. If there is some sacrifice of fine detail in the interest of efficient pedagogy, it is made in the belief that the foundation provided here will support and find compatibility with more elaborate training available to the student through standard textbooks and classroom instruction.

TO THE PRIVATE MUSIC TEACHER

Few private teachers are able to devote sufficient time to basic theory. Many are keenly aware of their students' lack of knowledge of key signatures and other fundamentals. A self-instruction program in theory therefore seems a logical adjunct to private applied study. A good plan might be to assign the student one part of the program at a time and, following the completion of each part, to discuss its applications in a piece currently being studied.

This program was written with students of high-school age and older in mind, but it may also be undertaken by younger students who are musically and intellectually gifted.

HOW TO USE THIS BOOK

The program is divided into seven parts. Each part has several *sets*, and each set contains roughly twenty to fifty *frames*. Each part is followed by a test covering the material in that part. Frames are numbered within each set and separated from one another by horizontal lines. Each frame presents information, asks a question, gives a statement to be completed, or directs that a certain operation be carried out. Occasionally a single frame does two or more of these things.

To use this book, cover the left-hand side of page 1 with the masking card. Read frame no. 1 and write your answer in the book. Slide the masking card down just far enough to expose the correct answer to frame no. 1, which lies directly to the left of frame no. 1. Check your answer. Next read frame no. 2, write your answer, slide the card down and check it. The great majority of your answers will be right. When you do answer a question incorrectly, reconsider the question and try to find your mistake before going on.

Continue with frame no. 3 and on to the bottom of page 1. *Do not turn the page yet.* Insert the masking card *under* the left-hand side of page 2, which is a right-hand page as the book lies open. After completing page 2, follow the same procedure, setting the masking card in place for page 3 before turning the page. Continue through the book in the same way, doing each right-hand page in order. This arrangement of pages and method of placing the masking card will prevent your seeing answers accidentally while turning pages. When you have completed all the right-hand pages to the back of the book, turn the book upside down and work back through it to the front. Once again, your work will lie on the right-hand pages only.

In writing your answers to the completion questions, observe these conventions: A single blank line such as this _____ calls for one word; two blanks _____ _____ call for two words, etc. In a dotted blank . . . . fill in one word, or two words, or any number of words you think will properly complete the statement. Short blanks like this ___ are used when the answer is a letter (x, y, z), a sign ($\sharp$, $\flat$, $\natural$, $\times$, $\flat\flat$), a numeral (1, 2, 3 or I, II, III), the name of a note (C, C$\sharp$, C$\flat$), the word *yes* or the word *no*. Short blanks are also used for certain special abbreviations and signs introduced in the book. All other blanks are the same length, that is _____. If your answer is too long for a given blank, simply write your answer near the blank. Many frames require more than one answer, in which case each answer space may be numbered: (1) _____, (2) . . . ., etc. When blanks calling for a *series* of items are *not* separately numbered, the items may be written in any order.

Close synonyms of the given answer should be considered correct (for example, *little* instead of *small*). To save time in writing answers, abbreviations may be improvised (for example *sm.* for *small*), but *it is essential that answers be written, not merely thought.* Looking ahead at the correct answer without writing it is a fatal error. It leads to vague answers, guessing, and consequently to poor learning. Remember: *you will not be judged or scored on your performance in this book.* Your goal is command of the subject matter *after* completing the book, and the practice of looking ahead reduces your chances of achieving it.

Should you find a set especially difficult, review it before going on to the next set.

When two or more consecutive frames are separated by a dashed line, the first frame of the group contains instructions or examples that apply to the whole group.

A sheet of music manuscript paper should be kept handy—it may be needed occasionally as scratch paper.

ACKNOWLEDGMENTS

Work on the predecessor of this book, *Scales, Intervals, Keys, and Triads*, was begun as part of an Oberlin College project on programed learning supported by a grant from the Ford Foundation. The authors of the present book are grateful for comments and suggestions offered by students at the University of Michigan, and are especially indebted to Professor James Dapogny of the University of Michigan, who reviewed all of the new materials.

CONTENTS

The following illustrations, based on diagrams in *Rudiments of Music* by John Castellini, will serve as a guide to note and key names.

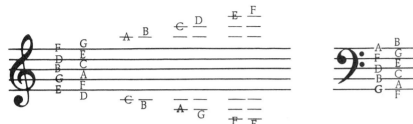

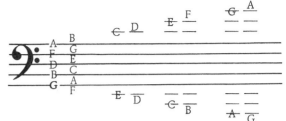

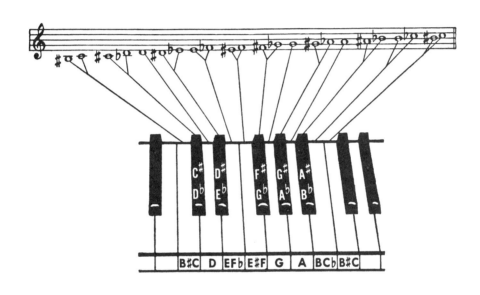

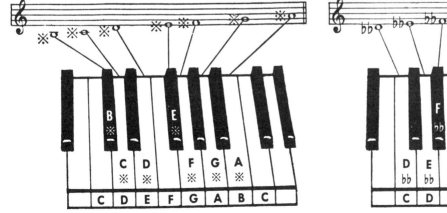

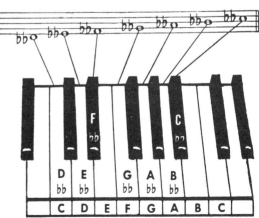

Detach the masking card from the back cover and place over the left side of page 1.

Set 1   /   THE SEMITONE

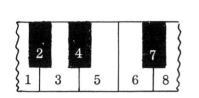

1

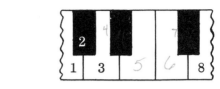

This diagram is a section of a piano keyboard. Complete the numbering of keys from the lowest to the highest.

2

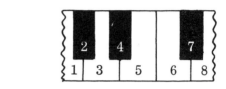

adjacent

Two keys with consecutive numbers are *adjacent*. Key no. 2 and key no. 3 are adjacent. Key no. 2 and key no. 1 are ___adjacent___ .

3

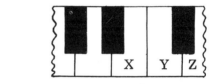

(1) X
(2) Z

Key **Y** is adjacent to key (1) __X__ but not to key (2) __Z__ .

adjacent

4   No two black keys are ___adjacent___ .

adjacent

5

x   y

The two notes in example **x** are played on adjacent keys. The two notes in example **y** are played on ___adjacent___ keys.

are

6

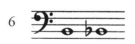

These two notes . . ___are___ . . . . . . (are *or* are not) played on adjacent keys.

are not

7

These two notes . ___are not___ . . . played on adjacent keys.

6. In simple meters, the top number of the meter signature gives (1) . . . .; the bottom number gives (2) . . . .

7. In compound meters, the top number of the meter signature gives (1) . . . .; the bottom number gives (2) . . . .

8. The note values that most commonly represent the beat in simple meters are:

☐ , ☐ , ☐ .

9. Beats in compound meters are most often represented by the note values:

☐ , ☐ , ☐ .

10. Meter signatures having a top number of 12 are _____ (duple, triple, *or* quadruple).

11. $\frac{6}{4}$, $\frac{9}{4}$, and $\frac{12}{4}$ are all (1) _____ meters having (2) ☐ as the note value of the beat.

12. For each of the following meters:
    1. Classify as simple or compound.
    2. Classify as duple, triple or quadruple.
    3. Notate the beat.

    $\frac{2}{2}$ (1) _____   (2) _____   (3) ☐

    $\frac{9}{8}$ (4) _____   (5) _____   (6) ☐

    $\frac{6}{16}$ (7) _____   (8) _____   (9) ☐

    $\frac{4}{4}$ (10) _____   (11) _____   (12) ☐

13. Notate the beat, the division, and the subdivision for the following meters:

    $\frac{6}{8}$ beat = (1) $\frac{3}{4}$ beat = (4)
       division = (2)   division = (5)
       subdivision = (3)   subdivision = (6)

14. Provide bar lines for the following:

    The example begins with a(n) _____ .

15. Provide bar lines and beams as appropriate for this rhythmic pattern:

yes	8	Are these two notes played on adjacent keys? _yes_ (yes *or* no)

(Students unfamiliar with the double flat sign (♭♭) should consult the note and key chart on page xi).

---

one semitone	9	The distance between two notes played on adjacent keys is one *semitone*. The two notes shown are played on adjacent keys. The distance between them is __one__ __semitone__ .

---

adjacent keys	10	*Half step* and *half tone* are synonyms for *semitone*, but only the word *semitone* will be used in this book. The distance between two notes played on __adjacent__ __keys__ is one semitone.

---

is	11	The distance between these notes ....*is*..... (is *or* is not) one semitone.

---

is	12	The distance between these notes .....*is*..... one semitone.

---

no	13	Are these notes one semitone apart? _no_

---

one semitone	14	These notes are ../ *semitone*. apart.

---

lower	15	The first note is one semitone __lower__ (higher *or* lower) than the second note.

---

lower	16	The first note is one semitone __lower__ than the second note.

The questions below will test your mastery of the material in Part 7. Complete the entire test, then check your answers with the correct ones on page 140. For each question that you miss, the corresponding material may be reviewed in the set whose number is given with the correct answer.

1. Draw these note and rest symbols:

    (1)   16th note

    (2)   quarter rest

    (3)   half rest

    (4)   half note

    (5)   32nd rest

2. Add the appropriate note values to the following:

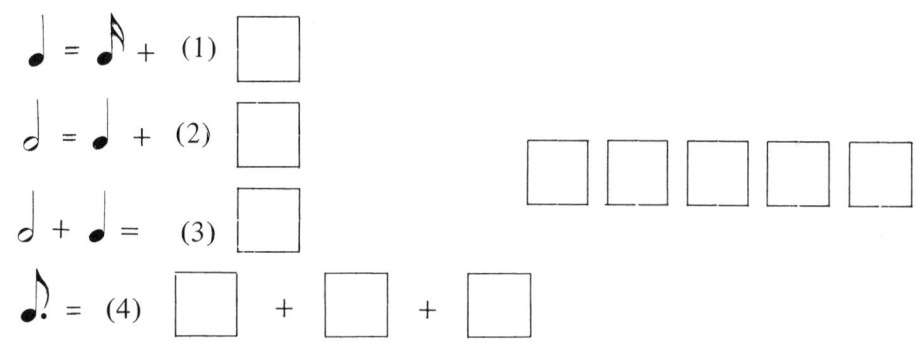

3. ▬ = (1) ____ *(how many?)* 𝄾 's.

    ♩ = (2) ____ ♬ 's.

    ♩ 𝄾. ♬♩. ♬𝄾 ♩ ♪𝄾 = (3) ____ ♩'s.

4. Divide the following note value into a triplet pattern:

    ♩ = [   ]

5. The beat in simple meters, a(n) (1) _____ (dotted *or* undotted) note, is normally divided into (2) _____ equal parts.
    The beat in compound meters, a(n) (3) _____ note, is normally divided into (4) _____ equal parts.

---

one

semitone higher

17

The first note is ___one___

___semitone___ ___higher___ than the second note.

(Students unfamiliar with the double sharp sign (**x**) should consult the note and key chart on page xi.)

---

one

semitone higher

18

The second note is ___one___

___semitone___ ___higher___ than the first note.

19

Write a note which lies one semi-tone higher than the given note. *(There is more than one correct answer.)*

Write here
↓

20

Write a note which lies one semitone lower than the given note. *(There is more than one correct answer.)*

---

one semitone

21

The distance between these notes is . *1 semitone.*

---

is

22

The same sort of relationship may be stated this way:
Example **x** is a semitone.
Example **y** . . *is* . . . . . .
(is *or* is not) a semitone.

---

is

23

This example . . *is* . . . . . . a semitone.

---

no

24

Do these notes form a semitone?
no

A *tie* indicates a single duration that has the combined duration of 2 note values. Ties are used in notating a sound that is sustained across a bar line and in certain other cases. The arrow in this example points to a

tie   57 _____.

$\frac{4}{4}$ 𝅗𝅥. 𝅘𝅥 𝅝 ‖

---

7   58 𝅗𝅥. 𝅘𝅥𝅮 = ___ *(how many?)* 𝅘𝅥𝅮's.

Write a pair of tied note values that is equal to

59 5 𝅘𝅥's: ☐

𝅝 𝅘𝅥 *or* 𝅗𝅥. 𝅗𝅥

Provide bar lines and beams for the pattern below. *(Note: The pattern need not begin with a complete measure.)*

60 $\frac{3}{4}$ 𝅘𝅥𝅮 𝅗𝅥 𝅘𝅥𝅮 𝅘𝅥𝅮 𝅗𝅥 𝅘𝅥𝅯 𝅘𝅥𝅯 𝅘𝅥𝅯 𝅘𝅥𝅯 𝅗𝅥 ⅞ ‖

𝅘𝅥𝅮 | 𝅗𝅥   𝅘𝅥𝅮 𝅘𝅥𝅮 | 𝅗𝅥   𝅘𝅥𝅯𝅘𝅥𝅯𝅘𝅥𝅯𝅘𝅥𝅯 | 𝅗𝅥 ⅞ ‖ $\frac{3}{4}$ ‖

Set 2 / DIATONIC AND CHROMATIC SEMITONES

1

In a *diatonic* semitone one note is written on a line, the other on a space. Examples **x** and (1) __y__ (**y** *or* **z**) are (2) __diatonic__ semitones.

(1) y
(2) diatonic

2

In a diatonic semitone one note is written on a (1) ___line___ , the other on a (2) ___space___ .

(1) line   (2) space
(either order is correct)

3

This example is a __diatonic__ semitone.

diatonic

4

In a *chromatic* semitone both notes are written on the *same* line or space. Example **x** is a (1) __chromatic__ semitone. Example **y** is a (2) __diatonic__ semitone.

(1) chromatic

(2) diatonic

5

In a chromatic semitone both notes are written on ___the___ ___same___ line or space.

the same

6

This is a __chromatic__ semitone.

chromatic

7

Which example is a diatonic semitone? __x__

x

8

Example **x** is a (1) ___chromatic semitone___ . Example **y** is a (2) ___diatonic semitone___ .

(1) chromatic semitone

(2) diatonic semitone

Rewrite the following rhythmic patterns using beams as appropriate:

52

Hint: **3/4** is a _____ (duple or triple) meter. Be sure to beam within beats.

triple

53

duple

Hint: **6/8** is a _____ (duple or triple) meter.

54

The beaming is incorrect.

What is wrong with the notation of this pattern?

. . . .

55 Correct the notation:

Complete the meter signature and provide bar lines and beams as appropriate for this pattern:

56

(1) diatonic semitone	9	Example **x** is a (1) _diatonic_ _semitone_ . Example **y** is a (2) _diatonic_ _semitone_ .
(2) diatonic semitone		

adjacent	10	On the piano keyboard two _adjacent_ keys form a semitone.

diatonic	11	A semitone in which one note is written on a line and the other on a space is a _diatonic_ semitone.

chromatic	12	A semitone in which both notes are written on the same line or space is a _chromatic_ semitone.

	13	Write the note which lies a diatonic semitone higher than the given note:

	14	Write the note lying a diatonic semitone lower than the given note:

	15	Add a second note, one chromatic semitone higher than the given note:

	16	Add a second note, one chromatic semitone lower than the given note:

chromatic semitone	17	Diatonic semitone will be abbreviated DST. Similarly, _chromatic_ _semitone_ will be abbreviated CST.

(1) diatonic semitone (2) CST	18	The abbreviation for (1) _diatonic_ _semitone_ is DST. The abbreviation for chromatic semitone is (2) _CST_ .

---

46 Provide the bar lines for this pattern:

$\frac{12}{8}$ (music notation)

(answer on left:) (music notation)

---

47 The two patterns notated below each have the equivalent of ___ ♩.'s. It is much easier to read pattern y because the notes within each beat are beamed together.

x

$\frac{9}{8}$ (music notation)

y

$\frac{9}{8}$ (music notation)

(answer on left:) 3

---

48 Although groups of 8ths, 16ths, and 32nds are commonly notated with flags in vocal music, in instrumental music groups of 8th, 16th, and 32nd notes *within a beat* are beamed together. Rewrite the pattern below using beams to connect 8th and 16th notes within beats:

$\frac{6}{8}$ (music notation)

$\frac{6}{8}$ (blank with double bar)

(answer on left:) (music notation)

---

49 Rewrite this pattern using beams to connect notes within beats. *Remember that in* $\frac{12}{16}$ *there are* ___ *(how many?) beats in a measure.*

$\frac{12}{16}$ (music notation)

$\frac{12}{16}$ (blank with double bar)

(answer on left:) 4

(music notation)

---

50 What is wrong with the notation of this pattern?

$\frac{9}{8}$ (music notation)

(answer on left:) The beaming is incorrect. *or* Notes are not beamed together within beats.

---

51 Notate the pattern from the previous frame correctly:

$\frac{9}{8}$ (blank with double bar)

(answer on left:) (music notation)

DST

19 In a ___*LST*___ (DST *or* CST) one note is on a line, the other on a space.

20 Add a second note, one DST higher than the given note:

21 Add a second note, one DST lower than the given note:

22 To each of these notes add a second note, one DST higher:

23 To each of these notes add a second note, one DST lower:

24 Arrange the above signs in their logical order, from lowest to highest:
___*bb b ♮ ♯ x*___

bb   b   ♮   ♯   x

CST

25 This example is a ___*CST*___.

CST

26 Changing the sign of a note to the next higher sign (for example, changing note **x** to note **y**) raises the pitch by one ___*CST*___.
(DST *or* CST)

♭

27 This note would be raised one CST by changing its sign to a ___*♭*___.

Follow the above instructions for each of the following simple and compound meters:

(1) ♪

(2) ♬

(3) ♬♬

$\frac{3}{8}$ beat = (1) ☐

division = (2) ☐

subdivision = (3) ☐

42

(4) ♪·

(5) ♬♬

(6) ♬♬♬

$\frac{6}{16}$ beat = (4) ☐

division = (5) ☐

subdivision = (6) ☐

(1) ♩·

(2) ♩ ♩ ♩

(3) ♬♬♬

43

(4) ♩

(5) ♪ ♪

(6) ♬♬

$\frac{9}{4}$ beat = (1) ☐

division = (2) ☐

subdivision = (3) ☐

$\frac{4}{4}$ beat = (4) ☐

division = (5) ☐

subdivision = (6) ☐

(1) 6

(2) 2

♩· ♪ ♪ ♪ | ♩· ♬♬ ♪ | ♩· ♩· ‖

44

A measure in $\frac{6}{4}$ will have the equivalent of (1) _____ ♩'s, or (2) _____ ♩·'s. Provide the bar lines for this pattern:

$\frac{6}{4}$ ♩· ♩ ♩ ♩ ♩· ♬♬ ♩ ♩ ♩· ♩· ‖

(1) 9

(2) 3

♩· ♬♬♬ ♬♬ | ♩ ⅄ ♬♬♬ ♩· | ♩· ⁊· ♩· ‖

45

A measure in $\frac{9}{8}$ will have the equivalent of (1) _____ ♪'s, or (2) _____ ♩·'s. Provide the bar lines for this pattern:

$\frac{9}{8}$ ♩· ♬♬♬ ♬♬ ♩ ⅄ ♬♬♬ ♩· ♩· ⁊· ♩· ‖

♮

28   Changing the sign of a note to the next lower sign lowers the pitch by one CST. Changing a ♯ to a ___♮___ lowers the pitch by one CST.

---

(1) lowers

(2) CST

29

Changing note x to note y

(1) _*lowers*_ (raises *or* lowers) the pitch by one (2) _CST_ .

♯

30

This note would be lowered one CST by changing the sign to a _♯_ .

31   Add a second note, one CST higher than the given note:

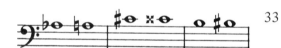

32   Add a second note, one CST lower than the given note:

33   To each of these notes add a second note, one CST higher:

---

34   To each of these notes add a second note, one CST lower:

---

(1) x

(2) y

(3) z

35

(1) Which example is a DST? _X_

(2) Which example is a CST? _Y_

(3) Which example is neither a DST nor a CST? _Z_

(1) compound

(2) duple

(3) 𝅗𝅥.

(4) simple

(5) triple

(6) ♪

(7) compound

(8) quadruple

(9) ♪.

For each of the following meters:
1. Classify as simple or compound.
2. Classify as duple, triple, or quadruple.
3. Notate the beat.

38

6/4 (1) _____ (2) _____ (3) ☐

3/8 (4) _____ (3) _____ (6) ☐

12/16 (7) _____ (8) _____ (9) ☐

---

three

39

The beat in compound meters is divided into _____ equal parts.

Although the *division* of the beat in compound meters is three equal parts, all further *subdivisions* are normally by 2, as illustrated in example **x**. Give the subdivision for example **y**:

40

	x		**y**
beat	= 𝅗𝅥.	beat	= 𝅗𝅥.
division	= ♩ ♩ ♩	division	= ♪ ♪ ♪
subdivision	= ♪ ♪ ♪ ♪ ♪ ♪	subdivision	= ☐

---

(1) 𝅗𝅥.

(2) ♪ ♪ ♪

(3) ♪ ♪ ♪ ♪ ♪ ♪

(4) 𝅗𝅥.

(5) ♩ ♩ ♩

(6) ♪ ♪ ♪ ♪ ♪ ♪

Notate the beat, the division of the beat, and the subdivision for each of these compound meters:

6/8 beat   = (1) ☐

division   = (2) ☐

41

subdivision = (3) ☐

12/4 beat   = (4) ☐

division   = (5) ☐

subdivision = (6) ☐

Write one of the following labels beneath each pair of notes: DST, CST, neither.

(1) neither
(2) CST
(3) DST
(4) neither

36

(1) *neither* (2) *CST* (3) *DST* (4) *neither*

Set 3 / THE WHOLE TONE

whole tone	1	Two semitones make a *whole tone*. The distance from key no. 1 to key no. 3 is two semitones or one ___whole___ ___tone___ .

| Two semitones | 2 | *Whole step* is a synonym for *whole tone*, but only the term *whole tone* will be used in this book. ___Two___ ___semitones___ make a whole tone. |

| (1) X (2) Z | 3 | Key **Y** is a semitone from key (1) _X_ (**X** or **Z**) and a whole tone from key (2) _Z_ (**X** or **Z**). |

| (1) whole tone (2) semitone | 4 | Key **Y** is a (1) *whole tone* from key **X** and a (2) *semitone* from key **Z**. |

| whole tone | 5 | Two keys separated by exactly one other key (for example, keys no. 2 and 4) make a *whole tone*. |

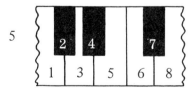

Give the note value of the beat for each of the following compound meters. In all cases the beat will be represented by a(n) (1) _____ (dotted *or* undotted) note.

(1) dotted

33

(2) ♩.   (3) ♩.

$\frac{12}{8}$ (2) ☐ $\frac{9}{4}$ (3) ☐

(4) ♪.   (5) ♩.

$\frac{6}{16}$ (4) ☐ $\frac{6}{8}$ (5) ☐

Classify each of these compound meters as duple, triple, or quadruple (according to the top number of the meter signature), and then give the note value of the beat (according to the bottom number of the meter signature):

(1) triple

$\frac{9}{16}$ (1) _____ (duple, triple, *or* quadruple)

(2) ♪.

    (2) ☐   *(note value of the beat)*

34

(3) duple   (4) ♩.

$\frac{6}{8}$ (3) _____ (4) ☐

(5) quadruple   (6) ♩.

$\frac{12}{4}$ (5) _____ (6) ☐

(7) triple   (8) ♩.

$\frac{9}{8}$ (7) _____ (8) ☐

---

(1) 2, 3, (and) 4

35

(2) 6, 9, (and) 12

Simple meters have top numbers of (1) ___, ___, and ___. Compound meters have top numbers of (2) ___, ___, and ___.

Classify each of these meters as simple or compound:

(1) simple   (2) compound

36 $\frac{3}{4}$ (1) _____ $\frac{12}{8}$ (2) _____

(3) simple   (4) compound

$\frac{4}{2}$ (3) _____ $\frac{6}{4}$ (4) _____

---

(1) simple

For each of the following meters:
1. Classify as simple or compound.
2. Classify as duple, triple, or quadruple.
3. Notate the beat.

(2) quadruple

37

(3) ♩

$\frac{4}{4}$ (1) _____ (2) _____ (3) ☐

(4) compound

(5) triple

$\frac{9}{8}$ (4) _____ (5) _____ (6) ☐

(6) ♩.

7	6	Key no. _7_ is a whole tone above key no. 5.

3	7	Key no. _3_ is a whole tone below key no. 5.

8 The distance between these notes .....*is*..... (is *or* is not) a whole tone.

is

9 The distance between these notes .....*is*..... a whole tone.

is

10 Are these notes a whole tone apart?
yes

yes

11 Do these notes form a whole tone?
No

no

12 In its broadest sense, the term *whole tone* includes cases **x**, **y**, and **z**. However, in elementary work it is convenient to use *whole tone* only for those cases where one note is on a line and the other note is on a space. Only case _y_ (**x**, **y**, *or* **z**) falls within this narrower definition. In this book whole tone means *diatonic* whole tone — one note on a line, the other on a space.

y

13 Write the note which lies a whole tone higher than the given note:

14 Write the note lying a whole tone higher than the given note:

15 Add a second note, one whole tone higher:

(1) triple

(2) quadruple

Meter signatures having a top number of 6 are duple, as is shown in example **x**. Meter signatures having a top number of 9 are (1) _____, as is shown in example **y**. Meter signatures having a top number of 12 are (2) _____, as is shown in example **z**.

.27

Classify the following compound meters as duple, triple, or quadruple:

(1) triple   (2) duple

(3) quadruple

28

9/8 (1) _____   **6/4** (2) _____

12/16 (3) _____

the number of divisions of the beat

29

The top number in a compound meter signature refers to . . . . in a measure.

(1) note value of the division of the beat

(2) 3

30

The bottom number of a compound meter signature gives the (1) . . . .

How many divisions equal the beat? (2) ___

𝅗𝅥.

31

Any compound meter signature with a bottom number of 8, such as **6/8**, **9/8**, or **12/8**, will have ♩. (=3 ♪'s) as the note value of the beat. Any compound meter signature with a bottom number of 4, such as **6/4**, **9/4**, or **12/4** will have ☐ (=3 ♩'s) as the note value of the beat.

♪.

32

Any compound meter signature with a bottom number of 16, such as **6/16**, **9/16**, or **12/16**, will have ☐ (= 3 ♬'s) as the note value of the beat.

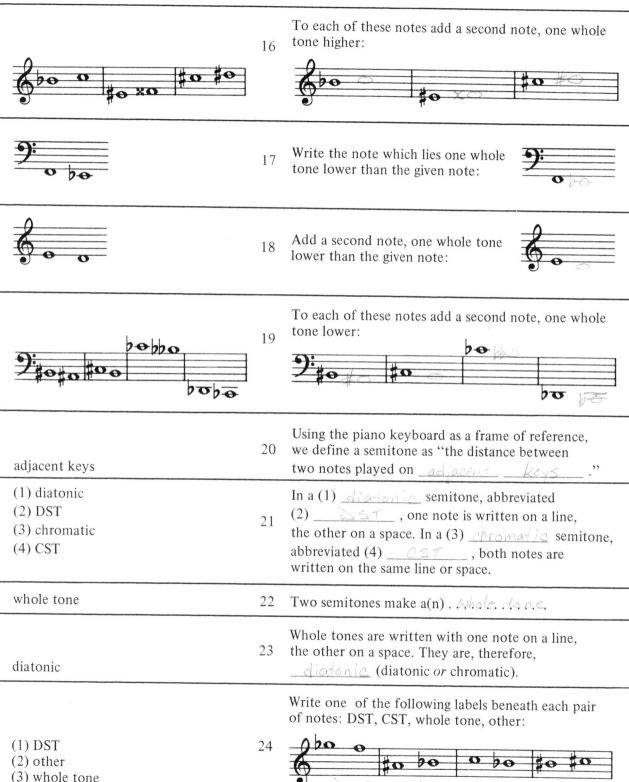

16 To each of these notes add a second note, one whole tone higher:

17 Write the note which lies one whole tone lower than the given note:

18 Add a second note, one whole tone lower than the given note:

19 To each of these notes add a second note, one whole tone lower:

adjacent keys

20 Using the piano keyboard as a frame of reference, we define a semitone as "the distance between two notes played on ___adjacent___ ___keys___ ."

(1) diatonic
(2) DST
(3) chromatic
(4) CST

21 In a (1) ___diatonic___ semitone, abbreviated (2) ___DST___ , one note is written on a line, the other on a space. In a (3) ___chromatic___ semitone, abbreviated (4) ___CST___ , both notes are written on the same line or space.

whole tone

22 Two semitones make a(n) . ___whole tone___

diatonic

23 Whole tones are written with one note on a line, the other on a space. They are, therefore, ___diatonic___ (diatonic *or* chromatic).

Write one of the following labels beneath each pair of notes: DST, CST, whole tone, other:

(1) DST
(2) other
(3) whole tone
(4) DST

24   (1) ___DST___ (2) ___other___ (3) ___whole tone___ (4) ___DST___

(1) dotted

(2) three

(3) ♪ + ♪ + ♪

21   The beat in compound meters is a(n) (1) _____ (dotted *or* undotted) note, which is divided into (2) _____ equal parts. Notate the division of this beat:

♩. = (3) ☐ + ☐ + ☐

♪.

22   Given the pattern below as the division of the beat, notate the beat:

♫ = ☐

---

(1) 𝅗𝅥.

(2) ♩.

23   Give the beat for which each of these patterns is the division:

♩ ♩ ♩ = (1) ☐

♫ = (2) ☐

♩.

24   In a measure of ⁶₈ the 8th notes are grouped in 2 groups of 3 as shown with the beaming below:

⁶₈ ♫ ♫

Each group of ♫ = ☐

---

(1) divisions
(2) division

25   In a compound meter, the meter signature gives the number of (1) _____ of the beat in a measure and the note value of the (2) _____.

6, 9, (or) 12

26   Usually, the top number of a compound meter signature is ____, ____, or ____.

Label each pair as in the preceding frame:

(1) CST
(2) CST
(3) other
(4) whole tone

25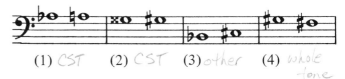

(1) CST   (2) CST   (3) other   (4) whole tone

Add a second note to the given notes, as indicated:

26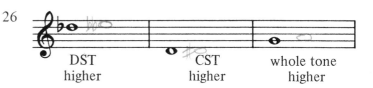

DST   CST   whole tone
higher   higher   higher

Add a second note to the given notes, as indicated:

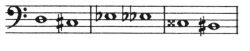

27

DST   CST   whole tone
lower   lower   lower

F♯	28 A DST above E♯ is F♯ .
E♭	29 A CST below E is E♭ .
A♯	30 A whole tone above G♯ is A♯ .
whole tone	31 C♭ and D♭ form a . whole tone . (DST *or* CST *or* whole tone)
DST	32 G and F♯ form a . . . . DST . . . . (DST *or* CST *or* whole tone)

(1) number (2) note value (*or* duration)	13	In simple meters the meter signature can be directly interpreted. The top number gives the (1) _____ of beats in a measure; the bottom number gives the (2) . . . . of the beat. The meter signatures for compound meters differ in both regards.
	14	The numbers in the meter signatures of simple meters refer directly to the beat; the numbers in the meter signatures of compound meters refer to the *division* of the beat. In compound meters the top number gives the number of *divisions* of the beat in a measure, and the bottom number gives the note value of the *division* of the beat.
2, 3, (and) 4	15	The common top numbers of simple meter signatures are ____, ____, and ____. The common top numbers of compound meter signatures are 6, 9, and 12.
compound	16	A meter having a top number of 6, 9, or 12 is a _____ meter.
compound	17	A meter signature with a top number of 6, for example, $\frac{6}{8}$, represents a _____ meter. The top number 6 indicates that each measure will contain the equivalent of 6 8th notes, however this *does not* mean that there are 6 beats in a measure.
9	18	The top number 9 of the meter signature $\frac{9}{4}$ indicates that each measure will contain the equivalent of ____ quarter notes.
division	19	The top number of the meter signature in a compound meter does not give the number of beats in a measure; instead, it gives the number of *divisions* of the beat in a measure. Likewise, the bottom number gives the note value of the _____.
division	20	The numbers in the meter signatures of simple meters refer directly to the beat: the numbers in the meter signatures of compound meters refer to the _____ of the beat.

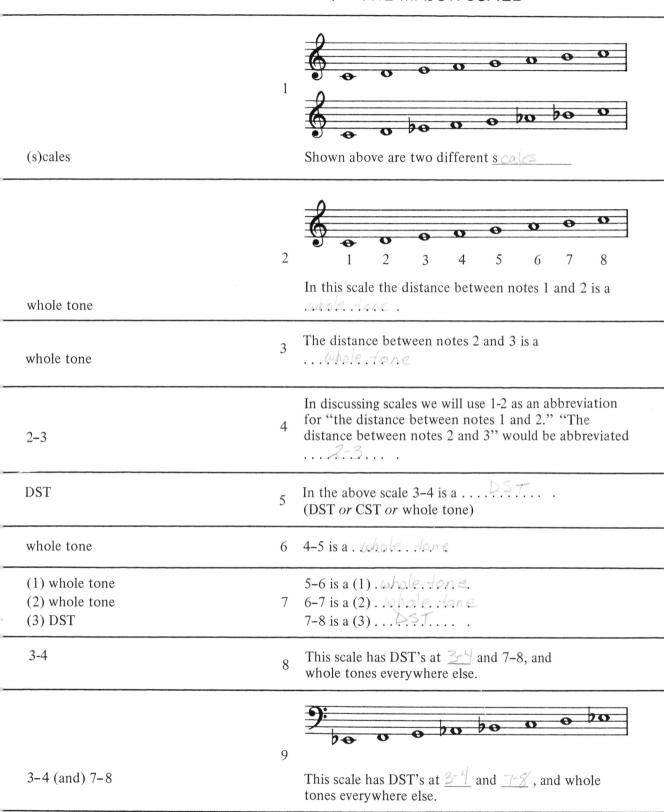

(s)cales

1

Shown above are two different s *cales*

2

In this scale the distance between notes 1 and 2 is a

whole tone

whole tone .

---

whole tone

3

The distance between notes 2 and 3 is a

... *whole tone*

2–3

4

In discussing scales we will use 1-2 as an abbreviation for "the distance between notes 1 and 2." "The distance between notes 2 and 3" would be abbreviated ... *2-3* ... .

DST

5

In the above scale 3–4 is a ... *DST* ... .
(DST *or* CST *or* whole tone)

---

whole tone

6

4–5 is a . *whole tone*

---

(1) **whole tone**

(2) **whole tone**

(3) **DST**

7

5–6 is a (1) . *whole tone* .

6–7 is a (2) . *whole tone*

7–8 is a (3) ... *DST* ... .

3-4

8

This scale has DST's at *3-4* and 7–8, and whole tones everywhere else.

9

This scale has DST's at *3-4* and *7-8* , and whole tones everywhere else.

3–4 (and) 7–8

The note values that most commonly represent the beat in compound meters are ♩. , ♩. , and ♪. . Notate the normal division of these notes (into three equal parts):

6

♩. = (1) ☐ + ☐ + ☐

♩. = (2) ☐ + ☐ + ☐

♪. = (3) ☐ + ☐ + ☐

(1) ♩ + ♩ + ♩

(2) ♪ + ♪ + ♪

(3) ♬ + ♬ + ♬

As with simple meters, beats in compound meters are generally grouped in 2's and 3's. A meter consisting of groups of 2 beats is (1) _____. A meter consisting of groups of 3 beats is (2) _____.

7

(1) duple
(2) triple

The metric accent in duple and triple meters is on the _____ beat of a measure.

8

first

The grouping of pattern **x** is duple. The grouping of of pattern **y** is _____. Mark with > the beats that have metric accent in both patterns:

9

x ♩. ♩. | ♩. ♩. ‖   **y** ♩. ♩. ♩. | ♩. ♩. ♩. ‖

triple

♩. ♩. | ♩. ♩. ‖ ♩. ♩. ♩. | ♩. ♩. ♩. ‖
>   >   >   >

Groups of 4 beats sometimes occur in compound meters as in this example. Mark the accents in the second measure:

10

♩. ♩. ♩. ♩. | ♩. ♩. ♩. ♩. ‖
>   >

♩. ♩. ♩. ♩. ‖
>   >

The beat in simple meters, a(n) (1) _____ (dotted *or* undotted) note, is normally divided into (2) _____ equal parts.

11

The beat in compound meters, a(n) (3) _____ note, is normally divided into (4) _____ equal parts.

(1) undotted

(2) two

(3) dotted
(4) three

The symbol for the meter of a piece of music is the _____ _____.

12

meter signature (*or* time signature)

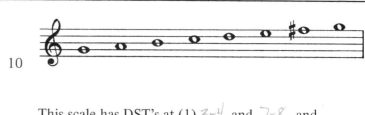

10

(1) 3–4 (and) 7–8
(2) whole tones

This scale has DST's at (1) <u>3-4</u> and <u>7-8</u> , and (2) <u>whole tones</u> everywhere else.

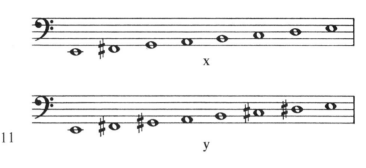

x

11

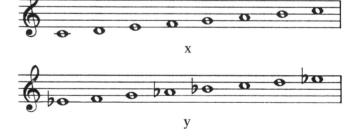

y

A scale with DST's at 3–4 and 7–8, and whole tones everywhere else, is a *major* scale.

(1) no

(1) Is scale x a major scale? <u>No</u>

(2) yes

(2) Is scale y a major scale? <u>Yes</u>

major

12

The <u>major</u> scale has DST's at 3–4 and 7–8, and whole tones everywhere else.

3–4 (and) 7–8

13

The DST's in the major scale are located at
<u>3-4</u> and <u>7-8</u> .

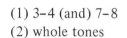

x

14

y

tonic

The note upon which a scale is built is called the *tonic*.
The tonic of scale x is C. E♭ is the <u>tonic</u> of scale y.

Provide bar lines for the following patterns:

67

68

69

Set 36 / COMPOUND METERS

	1	Meters are categorized in two ways: 1. As duple, triple, or quadruple, according to the grouping of the beats. 2. As *simple* or *compound*, according to whether the beat is represented by a dotted or an undotted note.
simple	2	When the beat is represented by an undotted note, the meter is _____; when the beat is represented by a dotted note, the meter is compound.
three	3	Dotted notes are normally divided into _____ equal parts.
(1) ♪ + ♪ + ♪ (2) ♪ + ♪ + ♪ (3) ♩ + ♩ + ♩	4	Divide these dotted notes into three equal parts: ♩. = (1) ☐ + ☐ + ☐ ♪. = (2) ☐ + ☐ + ☐ 𝅗𝅥. = (3) ☐ + ☐ + ☐
three	5	The normal division of a dotted note is into _____ equal parts.

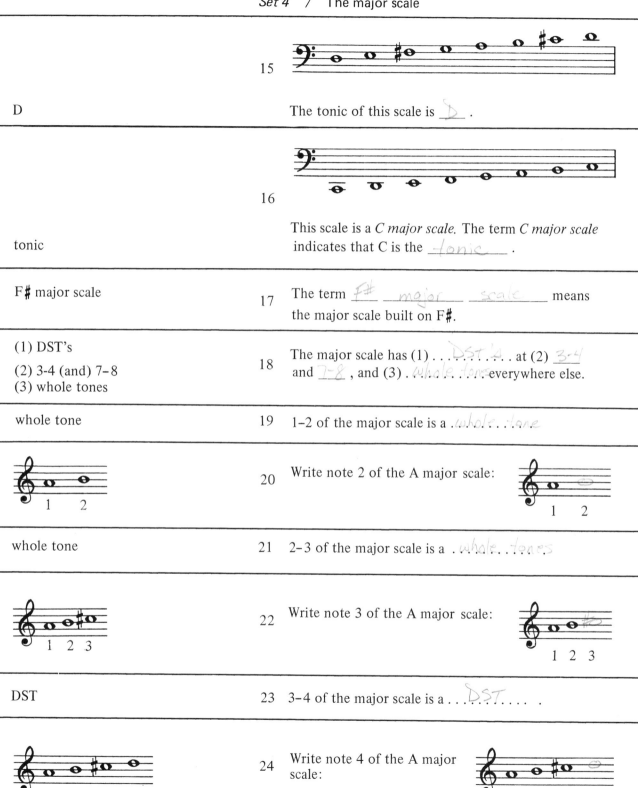

15

D   The tonic of this scale is ⟍D⟍ .

16

tonic   This scale is a *C major scale.* The term *C major scale* indicates that C is the _tonic_ .

F♯ major scale   17   The term _F♯_ _major_ _scale_ means the major scale built on F♯.

(1) DST's

(2) 3-4 (and) 7-8
(3) whole tones

18   The major scale has (1) .... DST's .... at (2) 3-4 and 7-8 , and (3) . whole tones everywhere else.

whole tone   19   1-2 of the major scale is a .whole. tone

20   Write note 2 of the A major scale:

whole tone   21   2-3 of the major scale is a . whole. tones

22   Write note 3 of the A major scale:

DST   23   3-4 of the major scale is a ..... DST ..... .

24   Write note 4 of the A major scale:

Sometimes music does not begin with a complete measure. The term for an incomplete measure at the beginning of a piece of music is *anacrusis*. An anacrusis is a *pick-up* leading to a strong beat. The pattern below does not begin with a complete measure; it begins on a weak beat with a pick-up. In other words, it has an

60

anacrusis

_____.

When a piece begins with an anacrusis, its final measure will be incomplete, as well. The sum of the beats in the anacrusis and the final measure will equal the number of beats in a complete measure, which in this example is

61

3

___.

Insert bar lines and a meter signature for this example. *(Hint: There is an anacrusis.)*

62

Insert bar lines and a meter signature for this example:

63

In simple meters, the beat is normally divided into _____ equal parts.

64

two

When a note that is normally divided into two equal parts is divided into three equal parts, the three equal parts are called _____.

65

triplets

Divide these note values into triplets:

66

(1) whole tone
(2) whole tone

25 4–5 of the major scale is a (1) whole tone.
5–6 is a (2) whole tone.

26 Continue the A major scale through 6:

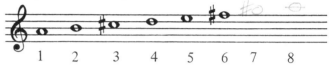

(1) whole tone
(2) DST

27 6–7 of the major scale is a (1) whole tone
7–8 of the major scale is a (2) . . . . . . DST . . . .

28 Complete the A major scale:

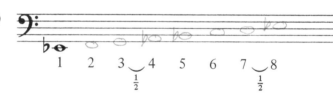

Write the E♭ major scale. (The "½'s" show DST locations.)

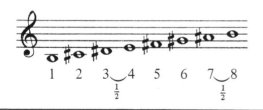

29

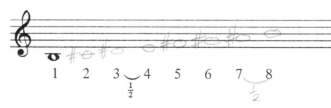

The location of one DST is marked "½." Mark the location of the other one and construct the B major scale:

30

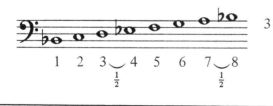

Mark the locations of the DST's and construct the B♭ major scale:

31

You are given the meter for this pattern. Provide
the bar lines. *(Remember, each measure must equal
4 ♩'s.)*

53

Provide the bar lines for the following rhythmic
patterns:

54

55

56

Note the placement of the meter signature on the
staff in the example below. Insert the remainder of
the bar lines:

57

Insert bar lines and complete the meter signature for
the following example:

58

Insert bar lines and a meter signature for this example.
*(Remember that bar lines generally come before ac-
cented notes.)*

59

Construct the G major scale. *(Write the note numbers and mark the DST locations first, if you wish.)*

32

Write the G♭ major scale:

33

Write the major scale *down* from the tonic D. Mark the DST locations first.

34

Write the descending A♭ major scale. *(Write the note numbers and mark the DST locations first, if you wish.)*

35

Occasionally it is necessary to work from a note other than the tonic. Using F as note 3 of a major scale, complete the scale in both directions. Mark the DST locations first:

36

Using C♯ as note 5, complete the major scale in both

37

is not

C♯ . . . .*is. .not.*. . (is *or* is not) the tonic of this scale.

47 In $\frac{4}{4}$ meter it is obviously not always the case that quarter notes, and only quarter notes, appear on every beat. However, within each measure there is

the equivalent of ___ *(how many?)* 𝅘𝅥 's.

4

The quarter note represents the beat in the example below. Using the example in frame 46 as a guide, notate the beats under the example, being careful to align the beats with the appropriate attack points.

(3) $\frac{3}{4}$

48 (3) [□] 𝄴 beats pattern ‖

(1) beats

(1) [music notation]

Each measure equals (2) ___ *(how many?)* 𝅘𝅥 's. Fill in the top number of the meter signature.

(2) 3

Notate the beats under the rhythmic patterns and fill in the top number of the meter signature for the following:

49

(2) $\frac{2}{2}$

(2) [□ over 2] [music notation] ‖

(1) beats

(1) [music notation]

---

(2) $\frac{4}{8}$

50

(2) [□ over 8] [music notation] ‖

(1) beats

(1) [music notation]

---

(2) $\frac{2}{4}$

51

(2) [□ over 4] [music notation] ‖

(1) beats

(1) [music notation]

---

(2) $\frac{3}{2}$

52

(2) [□ over 2] [music notation] ‖

(1) beats

(1) [music notation]

38

tonic

F♯ is the ...*tonic*... of this scale.

39

Naming the notes of a scale or chord is called *spelling.* For example, the D major scale is spelled: D E F♯ G A B C♯ D.
Spell the F major scale:

F G A B♭ C D E F

F *G A B♭ C D E♭* F

40

Facility in spelling major scales will prove valuable in later work. Spell *aloud* each of the following major scales, checking your answer after each scale. Repeat frames 40–56 until speed and assurance are felt. If spelling aloud is difficult for you, practice spelling the scales by writing them on a separate sheet of paper. When you can do this easily, go back to spelling aloud. You may find it helpful to think of the scale notes on a familiar instrument as you spell.

E F♯ G♯ A B C♯ D♯ E

E *F♯ G♯ A B C♯ D♯ E*

B♭ C D E♭ F G A B♭	41	B♭ *C D E♭ F G A B♭*
G♭ A♭ B♭ C♭ D♭ E♭ F G♭	42	G♭ *A♭ B♭ C♭ D♭ E♭ F G♭*
A B C♯ D E F♯ G♯ A	43	A *B C♯ D E F♯ G♯ A*
C♯ D♯ E♯ F♯ G♯ A♯ B♯ C♯	44	C♯ *D♯ E♯ F♯ G♯ A♯ B♯ C♯*
E♭ F G A♭ B♭ C D E♭	45	E♭ *F G A♭ B♭ C D E♭*
D♭ E♭ F G♭ A♭ B♭ C D♭	46	D♭ *E♭ F G♭ A♭ B♭ C D♭*
G A B C D E F♯ G	47	G *A B C D E F♯ G*
B C♯ D♯ E F♯ G♯ A♯ B	48	B *C♯ D♯ E F♯ G♯ A♯ B*
F♭ G♭ A♭ B♭♭ C♭ D♭ E♭ F♭	49	F♭ *G♭ A♭ B♭♭ C♭ D♭ E♭ F♭*
A♭ B♭ C D♭ E♭ F G A♭	50	A♭ *B♭ C D♭ E♭ F G A♭*
D E F♯ G A B C♯ D	51	D *E F♯ G A B C♯ D*

Notate the beat, division, and subdivision for the following meters:

(1) 𝅗𝅥

(2) ♩ ♩

(3) ♫♫

(4) ♪

(5) ♬

(6) ♬♬

43

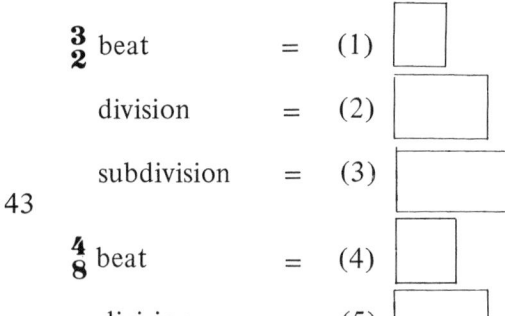

$\frac{3}{2}$ beat   =   (1) ☐

    division   =   (2) ☐

    subdivision   =   (3) ☐

$\frac{4}{8}$ beat   =   (4) ☐

    division   =   (5) ☐

    subdivision   =   (6) ☐

32nd

44

Further subdivisions of the beat, though not common, do occur, and follow the same principle of division by 2, as illustrated below:

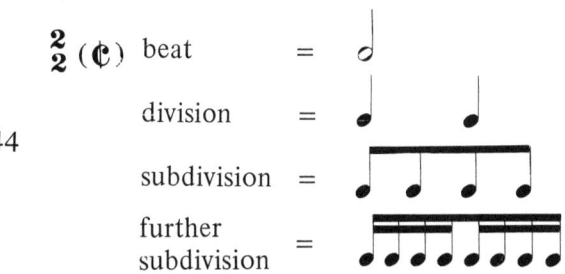

$\frac{2}{2}$ (¢) beat   =   𝅗𝅥

    division   =   ♩   ♩

    subdivision   =   ♫♫

    further
    subdivision   =   ♬♬♬♬

The beat in this example could be subdivided even further into 16 _____ notes.

---

(1) 2

(2) 16

45

In simple meters, the beat is normally divided into (1) ___ equal parts and subdivided into 4, 8, (2) ___ , or more equal parts.

---

do not

46

Musical notation gives the point of attack and the duration of each sound. As is evident in the example below, points of attack and beats . . . . (do *or* do not) always coincide.

$\frac{4}{4}$ 𝅗𝅥 ♩ ♩ | ♫♫𝅗𝅥 ‖

beats ♩ ♩ ♩ ♩   ♩ ♩ ♩ ♩

C D E F G A B C	52	C D E F G A B C
F♯ G♯ A♯ B C♯ D♯ E♯ F♯	53	F♯ G♯ A♯ B C♯ D♯ E♯ F♯
C♭ D♭ E♭ F♭ G♭ A♭ B♭ C♭	54	C♭ D♭ E♭ F♭ G♭ A♭ B♭ C♭
F G A B♭ C D E F	55	F G A B♭ C D E F
G♯ A♯ B♯ C♯ D♯ E♯ F✕ G♯	56	G♯ A♯ B♯ C♯ D♯ E♯ F✕ G♯

TEST COVERING PART 1

The questions below will test your mastery of the material in Part 1. Complete the entire test, then check your answers with the correct ones on page 135. For each question that you miss, the corresponding material may be reviewed in the set whose number is given with the correct answer.

1. DST is an abbreviation for *diatonic . semitone*

2. In a *chromatic* semitone, both notes are written on the same line or space.

3. Two semitones make a . .*whole* . *tone*

4. Write one of the following labels beneath each pair of notes: DST, CST, whole tone

5. After each note write a second note as indicated. The first item is completed as a sample.

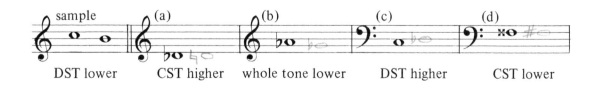

Divide these note values into two equal parts. This is called the *division* of a note value.

(1) ♪ + ♪

(2) ♩ + ♩

39   ♩ = (1) ☐ + ☐

𝅗𝅥 = (2) ☐ + ☐

In example **y** and the following frame, notate the beat and the division of the beat for each meter, as is illustrated in example **x**. Use beams where appropriate.

40

        x   **y**

(1) 𝅗𝅥

(2) ♩ ♩

$\frac{3}{4}$ beat = ♩

division = ♪ ♪

$\frac{2}{2}$ (¢) beat = (1) ☐

division = (2) ☐

- - - - - - - - - - - - - - - - - - - -

(1) ♩

(2) ♫

$\frac{4}{4}$ (C) beat = (1) ☐

division = (2) ☐

41

(3) 𝅗𝅥

(4) ♩ ♩

$\frac{3}{2}$ beat = (3) ☐

division = (4) ☐

Further division by 2 of the division of a beat is called *subdivision*, as is illustrated in example **x**. Notate the beat, division, and subdivision for the meter in example **y**:

        x   **y**

(1) ♩

42 $\frac{3}{8}$ beat = ♪

$\frac{2}{4}$ beat = (1) ☐

(2) ♫

division = ♫

division = (2) ☐

(3) ♬

subdivision = ♬

subdivision = (3) ☐

6. B C♯ D♯ E F♯ G♯ A♯ B spells the *B† scale* . (Be specific.)

7. Write the indicated scales:

(a) F major

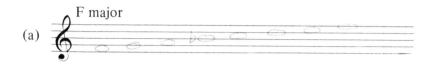

(b) E major

(c) D♭ major

8. Using B♮ as note 6 of a major scale, complete the scale in both directions.

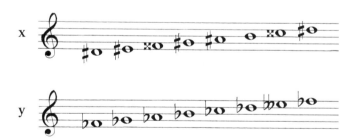

6

9. Which of the following scales, if any, are major scales?

x

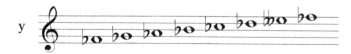

y

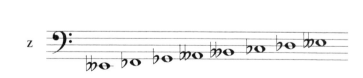

z

z

Classify each meter as duple, triple, or quadruple (from the top number), and then give the note value of the beat (from the bottom number):

32 $\frac{2}{4}$ (1) _____ (2) ☐

(1) duple   (2) ♩

$\frac{4}{2}$ (3) _____ (4) ☐

(3) quadruple   (4) 𝅗𝅥

---

(1) quadruple

33 The symbol **C** is often used to represent a $\frac{4}{4}$ meter. Both $\frac{4}{4}$ and **C** indicate a (1) _____ (duple, triple,

(2) ♩

or quadruple) meter having (2) ☐ as the note value of the beat.

---

(1) duple

34 Often the symbol **₵** is used to represent a $\frac{2}{2}$ meter. Both **₵** and $\frac{2}{2}$ refer to a (1) _____ (duple, triple, *or*

(2) 𝅗𝅥

quadruple) meter having (2) ☐ as the note value of the beat.

$\frac{3}{16}$ ♬♪ | ♬♪ ‖

35 Sometimes note values other than ♩ , 𝅗𝅥 , and ♪ represent the beat, as in this example. This is a

(1) triple

(1) _____ (duple, triple , *or* quadruple)

(2) ♪

meter. The note value of the beat is (2) ☐

---

36 Theoretically, any note value can represent the beat, though beats in simple meters are most often repre-

♩, 𝅗𝅥, ♪
(any order)

sented by the note values: ☐ , ☐ , ☐ .

---

37 Not all simple meters are duple, triple, and quadruple. Meters such as $\frac{5}{8}$, a *quintuple* meter, and $\frac{7}{8}$, a *septuple* meter, are commonly found in 20th-century music.

(1) quint(uple)

$\frac{5}{4}$ is a (1) _____uple meter. The note value that

(2) ♩

represents the beat is (2) ☐

---

two

38 An undotted note, such as, ♩ , 𝅗𝅥 , and ♪ , is normally divided into _____ equal parts.

interval	1	The relationship between two pitches is called an *interval.* Between any two notes there is a pitch relationship or an ___*interval*___.
relationship *(Was your answer distance? The next few frames show why relationship is preferred.)*	2	An interval is the ___*relationship*___ between two pitches.
close together	3	Intervals vary in size. Two pitches that are far apart form a large interval. A small interval is formed by two pitches that are ___*close together*___
larger *(or greater)*	4	The greater the distance between two pitches, the ___*larger*___ the interval.
(1) smaller (2) larger	5	Interval **y** is slightly (1) ___*smaller*___ (larger *or* smaller) than interval **x**, and interval **z** is slightly (2) ___*larger*___ than interval **x**.
(1) smaller (2) larger *(either order)*	6	Interval **y** is smaller than interval **x** and sounds harsh compared to interval **x**. Interval **z** is larger than interval **x** and *also* sounds harsh compared to it. This shows that the harsher of two intervals is sometimes the (1) ___*smaller*___ interval and sometimes the (2) ___*larger*___ .
relationship between two pitches	7	As shown above, the sound of an interval is not simply a matter of size. For this and other reasons it is not quite right to say that an interval is the *distance* between two pitches. It is better to say that an interval is the ___*relationship*___ ___*between*___ ___*two*___ ___*pitches*___ .

2	24	All meter signatures having a top number of 2 represent duple meters; they indicate ____ beats per measure.
(1) triple (2) 3	25	All meter signatures having a top number of 3 represent (1) _____ meters; they indicate (2) ____ beats per measure.
(1) quadruple (2) 4	26	All meter signatures having a top number of 4 represent (1) _____ meters; they indicate (2) ____ beats per measure.
(1) triple (2) duple (3) triple (4) quadruple	27	Classify these meters as either duple, triple, or quadruple: (1) $\frac{3}{8}$ _____ (2) $\frac{2}{2}$ _____ (3) $\frac{3}{4}$ _____ (4) $\frac{4}{4}$ _____
beats	28	The top number of a meter signature refers to the number of _____ in each measure.
(1) half (2) 8th (eighth)	29	The bottom number of a meter signature gives the *note value* of the beat. **4** stands for quarter note. **2** stands for (1) _____ note. **8** stands for (2) _____ note.
(1) ♩ (2) 𝅗𝅥 (3) ♪ (4) ♩	30	For each of these meters, give the note value of the beat (♩ , 𝅗𝅥 , or ♪): (1) $\frac{3}{4}$ ☐ (2) $\frac{2}{2}$ ☐ (3) $\frac{2}{8}$ ☐ (4) $\frac{4}{4}$ ☐
(1) triple (2) 𝅗𝅥 (3) quadruple (4) ♪	31	Classify each meter as duple, triple, or quadruple (from the top number), and then give the note value of the beat (from the bottom number): $\frac{3}{2}$ (1) _____ (duple, triple, *or* quadruple) (2) ☐ *(note value of the beat)* $\frac{4}{8}$ (3) _____ (4) ☐

x   y

(1) melodic
(2) harmonic

8 Two pitches sounded together form a harmonic interval. Two pitches sounded consecutively form a melodic interval. Interval **x** is a (1) _melodic_ interval. Interval **y** is a (2) _harmonic_ interval. (For the sake of consistency, all intervals in this part of the book are written as harmonic intervals.)

general

9 Every interval has a *general name*. Ordinal numbers (2nd, 3rd, 4th, etc.) are used as general names. 5th is the _general_ name of an interval.

2nd   3rd   4th   5th   6th 7th   x   y

(1) 3rd
(2) 4th

10 The general name of an interval is found by counting *inclusively* the lines and spaces from one note to the other. Shown above are some intervals and their general names. The general name of interval **x** is (1) _3rd_ . Interval **y** is a (2) _4th_ .

(1) 6th
(2) 2nd
(3) 5th
(4) 9th

11 Give the general names of these intervals:

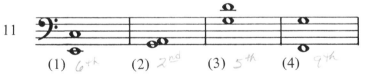

(1) _6th_   (2) _2nd_   (3) _5th_   (4) _9th_

(1) prime
(2) octave
(3) 7th
(4) prime

12 Instead of the number "1st" the word *prime* is used as a general name. Instead of the number "8th" the word *octave* is used. Give the general names of these intervals:

(1) _prime_ (2) _octave_ (3) _7th_   (4) _prime_

---

duple

17

The grouping of the ♩'s in this example is _____ (duple *or* triple). Mark the beats that have metric accent with $>$ under the note heads:

---

triple

18

The grouping of the ♩'s in this example is _____. Mark the beats that have metric accent:

19

Often 2 groups of 2 beats are combined to form a group of 4, a *quadruple* meter. A meter having groupings of 4 is a _____ meter.

quadruple

20

In a quadruple meter the first and third beats have metric accents, though the primary emphasis is on the first beat, as is indicated in example x. Mark the accents in example y:

x   y

---

meter

21

The *meter signature* (also called time signature) is the symbol which indicates the regular, repeating pattern of accented and unaccented beats, or _____, in a piece of music.

---

meter signature
(*or* time signature)

22

The symbol for the meter is the _____
_____.

2

23

A meter signature consists of two vertically aligned numbers, as shown below. (Note that the numbers *are not* written as a fraction, separated by a line.) In simple meters the top number gives the number of beats in each measure. In this example, ___ beats in each measure are indicated.

$$\frac{2}{4}$$

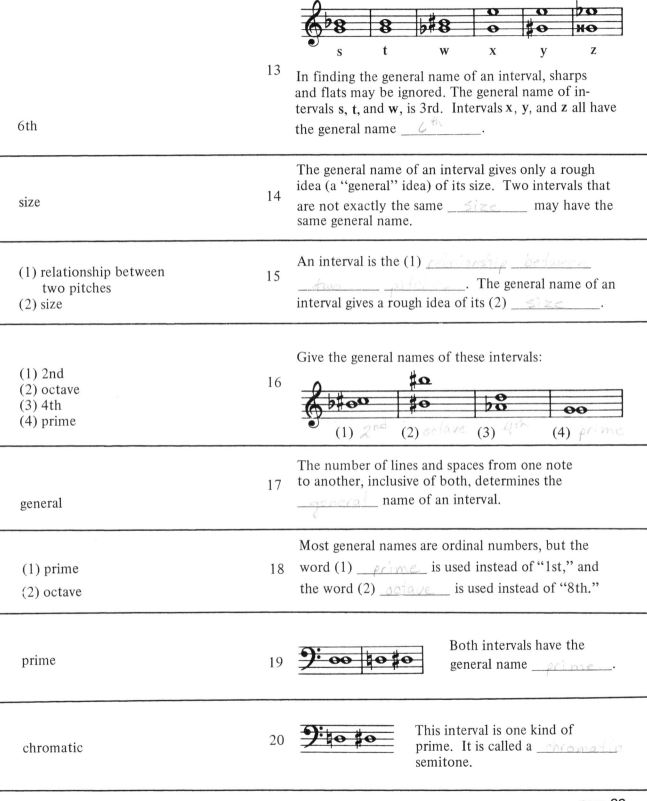

13 In finding the general name of an interval, sharps and flats may be ignored. The general name of intervals **s**, **t**, and **w**, is 3rd. Intervals **x**, **y**, and **z** all have the general name ___6th___.

6th

14 The general name of an interval gives only a rough idea (a "general" idea) of its size. Two intervals that are not exactly the same ___size___ may have the same general name.

size

15 An interval is the (1) ___relationship between two pitches___. The general name of an interval gives a rough idea of its (2) ___size___.

(1) relationship between two pitches
(2) size

16 Give the general names of these intervals:

(1) ___2nd___ (2) ___octave___ (3) ___4th___ (4) ___prime___

(1) 2nd
(2) octave
(3) 4th
(4) prime

17 The number of lines and spaces from one note to another, inclusive of both, determines the ___general___ name of an interval.

general

18 Most general names are ordinal numbers, but the word (1) ___prime___ is used instead of "1st," and the word (2) ___octave___ is used instead of "8th."

(1) prime
(2) octave

19 Both intervals have the general name ___prime___.

prime

20 This interval is one kind of prime. It is called a ___chromatic___ semitone.

chromatic

beat	9	The continuous, underlying rhythmic pulse of a piece is its _____. Although, theoretically, any note value can represent the beat in music, the most commonly used note values in simple meters are: ♩ , ♩. , and ♪ .
triple	10	Beats in music are most often grouped in 2's and 3's. A meter that consists of groups of 2 beats is termed *duple*. Similarly, a meter that consists of groups of 3 beats is called _____.
2	11	A duple meter consists of groups of ___ *(how many?)* beats, the first of which is accented.
3	12	A triple meter consists of groups of ___ beats, the first of which is accented.

13 — Our system for notating rhythm has evolved historically from the practice of inserting a bar line (a vertical line) before an accented note, as in example **x**. Insert a bar line before the accented note in example **y**:

14 — Although there are certainly exceptions, especially in 20th-century music, the standard practice is to notate rhythmic patterns in *measures* of equal duration separated by bar lines. The arrows in this example point to a _____ .

measure

15 — Within each measure the first beat receives a *metric accent*, as is indicated in example **x**. Mark with > the metric accents in example **y**:

16 — Accents of duration, pitch, and dynamics tend to coincide with the metric accent on the _____ beat of each measure.

first

2nd	21	Both intervals have the general name __2nd__ .
diatonic	22	This interval is one kind of 2nd. It is called a __diatonic__ semitone.
whole tone	23	This interval is another kind of 2nd. It is called a __whole tone__ .
(1) 2nd (2) prime (3) 2nd	24	A DST is one kind of (1) __2nd__ . *(gen. name)* A CST is one kind of (2) __prime__ . *(gen. name)* A whole tone is one kind of (3) __2nd__ . *(gen. name)*
		x y
is not	25	Raising (or lowering) both notes of an interval *equally* does not change the size of the interval. If both notes of interval **x** are raised one CST, we have interval **y**. The size of the interval ...__is not__. (is *or* is not) changed.
the same (*or* equal in *or* of equal)	26	Lowering both notes of interval x one CST makes interval y. Intervals x and y are __the same__ size. x y
		Fill in the upper note of interval **y**, making interval **y** the same size as interval **x**. *(Hint: What must be done to the lower note of **x** to change it to the lower note of **y**?)*

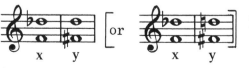

*(Each note of **x** is raised one CST to make **y**.)*

27

Circle the number of the accented pitch in this example:

3

1 2 3 4 5 6

④

Another kind of accent is *dynamic* accent. When one note stands out by having a different dynamic level, that note is accented, as is note 2 in example x. Circle the number of the accented note in example y:

4

1 2 3   1 2 3 4

③

For each note that is accented, indicate the type of accent (duration, pitch, dynamic) by writing the number of the note and the appropriate term.

3 duration
5 pitch
8 dynamic
11 duration

5

1 2 3   4 5 6 7 8 9 10 11

An important aspect of music is the pulse or *beat*. When we listen to music, we often find ourselves tapping a foot or moving our bodies. We feel a continuous, underlying regular pulse. This is the _____.

6

beat

Beats in music are most often organized in a regular repeating pattern of accented and unaccented beats. The term for this pattern is *meter*. A regular, repeating pattern of accented and unaccented beats is called

7

_____.

meter

Basically there are two general categories of meters differing in the complexity of the pattern of the accented beats: *simple* meters and *compound* meters. We will deal with simple meters in the remainder of this set and with compound meters in Set 36.

8

	28	Fill in the lower note of interval y, making interval y the same size as interval x:
upper	29	Raising or lowering only *one* note of an interval *does* change the size of the interval. An interval may be expanded by raising the ___upper___ (upper *or* lower) note.
lowering	30	An interval may be expanded by ___lowering___ (raising *or* lowering) the lower note.
(1) expands (2) contracts	31	Raising the upper note one CST (1) ___expands___ (expands *or* contracts) the interval one CST. Raising the lower note one CST (2) ___contracts___ the interval one CST.
(1) expand (2) one CST	32	Placing a sharp before F would (1) ___expand___ the interval (2) .1.C.ST... (how much?)
D	33	Placing a flat before ___D___ would expand the interval one CST.
	34	Expand this interval one CST by changing the sign of the upper note. (The "sign" of the upper note as it stands is an understood ♮.)
	35	Expand this interval one CST by changing the sign of the lower note:
larger	36	Interval **x** is one CST ___larger___ (larger *or* smaller) than interval **y**.
larger	37	Interval **x** is one CST ___larger___ than interval **y**.

Complete the following:

(1) 1

 = (1) ___ *(how many?)* ♩

(2) 2

21 ♩♩♩ = (2) ___ ♩'s.

(3) 2

♫♫ = (3) ___ ♪'s.

Write the three-note triplet rhythm that has the same duration as one 8th note:

22

[ ]

Set 35 / ACCENT, SIMPLE METERS

In music some sounds are more prominent than others. These sounds are said to be accented. A note may be accented as a result of its *duration* as is note 3 in example x. What note is accented as a result of its duration in example y? ___

2

1

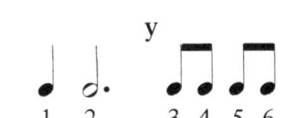

x
♩♩ ♩   ♫♩
1 2 3   4 5

y
♩ ♩.   ♫♫
1 2   3 4 5 6

A note may also be accented as a result of its *pitch*. A comparatively high or low pitch, or a pitch emphasized by a preceding large leap is heard to be accented. Circle the number of the accented pitch in this example:

2

1   2   3   4   5

③

---

smaller	38	Interval **x** is one CST _smaller_ than interval **y**.
smaller	39	Interval **x** is one CST _smaller_ than interval **y**.
	40	Contract this interval one CST by changing the sign of the upper note:
	41	Write the upper note of interval **x** so that interval **x** is one CST larger than interval **y**:
	42	Write the lower note of interval **x** so that interval **x** is one CST smaller than interval **y**:
the same size as	43	Interval **x** is .._same_.. (one CST larger than *or* one CST smaller than *or* the same size as) interval **y**.
one CST larger than	44	Interval **x** is ..._CST larger_ interval **y**.

45

(1) one CST larger than
(2) one CST larger than
(3) two CST's larger than

Interval **x** is (1) _CST larger_ . interval **y**.
Interval **z** is (2) _CST larger_ . interval **x**.
Therefore interval **z** is (3) _2 CST A_ .. interval **y**.

15

Sometimes notes or rests are doubly dotted. A second dot increases a note or rest value by one-half the value of the preceding dot. Therefore,

$$♩.. = ♩ + ♪ + ♪$$

$$♩.. = ♩ + (1)\boxed{} + \boxed{}$$

$$𝄽.. = (2)\boxed{} + \boxed{} + \boxed{}$$

(1) ♩ + ♪

(2) 𝄾 + 𝄾 + 𝄾

16

A dotted note is normally divided into three equal parts; an undotted note is normally divided into _____ equal parts.

two

17

When a note that is normally divided into two equal parts is divided into three equal parts, the three equal parts are called *triplets*. Label the indicated pattern:

$$♩ = ♪♪ = ♪♪♪ ← _____$$
$$\llcorner 3 \lrcorner$$

triplet(s)

18

The note value used in notating a triplet pattern is the same as the note value used to indicate the normal division of a note into two equal parts. Because the triplet is not the normal division, the figure 3 with a bracket must accompany the pattern as is indicated in example **x**. Complete the triplet notation in example **y**:

x $♩ = ♩ ♩ = ♩♩♩$
$\llcorner 3 \lrcorner$

y $♩ = ♪♪ = ♪♪♪$

(triplet pattern answer for 17/18)

19

$$♪ = ♪♪ = \boxed{} \quad \text{(triplet pattern)}$$

(Don't forget to include $\llcorner 3 \lrcorner$ *).*

20

Divide the following note values into triplet patterns:

$$♩ = (1) \boxed{}$$

$$♪ = (2) \boxed{}$$

$$𝅝 = (3) \boxed{}$$

(1) ♪♪♪ $\llcorner 3 \lrcorner$

(2) ♪♪♪ $\llcorner 3 \lrcorner$

(3) ♩ ♩ ♩ $\llcorner 3 \lrcorner$

two CST's smaller than	46	Interval x is *.2.C.S.T.s.* *smaller* interval y.
one CST larger than	47	Interval x is *.1.C.S.T. larger* interval y.
two CST's larger than	48	Interval x is *.2.C.S.T.s* *larger* interval y.
general	49	Prime, 2nd, 3rd, etc., and octave, are ___*general*___ names.

Set 6 / 2nds, 3rds, 6ths, and 7ths (1)

(1) specific (2) general	1	All intervals have double names. The double names consist of a *specific* name followed by a *general* name. In the double name *major 3rd,* the word *major* is the (1) ___*specific*___ name, and *3rd* is the (2) ___*general*___ name.
(1) specific (2) general (3) double	2	Another example of a double name is *minor 6th. Major* and *minor* are (1) ___*specific*___ names. *3rd* and *6th* are (2) ___*general*___ names. *Major 3rd* and *minor 6th* are (3) ___*double*___ names.
(1) double (2) specific (3) general	3	Every interval has a (1)___*double*___ name, consisting of a (2) ___*specific*___ name followed by a (3) ___*general*___ name.
(1) rough *(or* general) (2) exact	4	Double names refer to exact interval sizes. The name *7th,* by itself, gives only a (1) ___*general*___ idea of interval size, but *major 7th* refers to an (2) ___*exact*___ interval size.

Dotted notes are often used in combination with un-dotted notes in patterns such as the following:

9 𝅘𝅥𝅭 **x** 𝅘𝅥 𝅘𝅥𝅮𝅭 **y** 𝅘𝅥𝅯 (also written 𝅘𝅥𝅭 𝅘𝅥𝅯)

In examples **x** and **y** the value of the dotted note is
(1) 3
(2) 4

(1) ___ times the value of the undotted note. Al-together, pattern **x** = (2) ___ *(how many?)* 𝅘𝅥 's.

Add the appropriate note value to the following:

10 𝅘𝅥𝅭 + ·(1) ☐ = 𝅘𝅥 𝅘𝅥 𝅘𝅥 𝅘𝅥

(1) 𝅘𝅥

(2) 𝅘𝅥𝅮

(3) 𝅗𝅥

𝅘𝅥𝅮𝅭 + ·(2) ☐ = 𝅘𝅥

𝅘𝅥𝅭 + 𝅘𝅥𝅮 = (3) ☐

Enter the correct note value in each box:

11 𝅘𝅥 = 𝅘𝅥𝅮 + (1) ☐

(1) 𝅘𝅥𝅮

(2) 𝅘𝅥𝅭

(3) 𝅘𝅥𝅮

𝅗𝅥 = 𝅘𝅥𝅮 + (2) ☐

𝅘𝅥𝅮 + 𝅘𝅥𝅯 = (3) ☐

The 8th note in pattern **x** can be divided into two 16th notes as in pattern **y**. Each pattern equals

12 ___ *(how many?)* 𝅘𝅥 's.

𝅘𝅥𝅭 **x** 𝅘𝅥𝅮   𝅘𝅥𝅭 **y** 𝅘𝅥𝅯𝅘𝅥𝅯

2

13 𝅘𝅥𝅭 𝅘𝅥𝅮𝅘𝅥𝅭 𝅘𝅥𝅯𝅘𝅥𝅯𝅝 = ___ *(how many?)* 𝅗𝅥 's.

5

A dot always increases a note or rest value by

one-half

14 . . . . *(how much?)* of the duration of the symbol which it follows.

The first step in finding the specific name of
an interval is to construct a major scale on
the lower note of the interval, as shown below
for interval **x**. Complete this step for
interval **y**.

5

interval x   scale

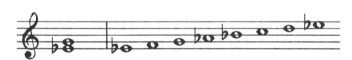

interval y   scale

Construct a major scale on the lower note of the
following interval:

6
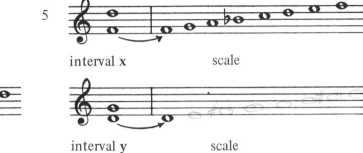

interval   scale

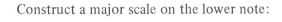

7 Is the upper note of the interval present in the
major scale built on the lower note? *yes*

yes *(The upper note of the interval, G,
is 3 in the Eb major scale.)*

Construct a major scale on the lower note:

8

is not *(The interval has F♯ ;
the scale has F♮.)*

The upper note of the interval . . *is not* . . . (is *or* is
not) present in the major scale built on the lower note.

Supply the appropriate note values for the following:

(1) ♪

3 ♪. = ♪ + (1) ☐

(2) ♪ + ♪

♪. = (2) ☐ + ☐

(3) ♩.

(3) ☐ = ♩ + ♪

Supply the appropriate rest values for the following:

(1) ▬ + 𝄽

4 ▬· = (1) ☐ + ☐

(2) 𝄽 + 𝄾

𝄽· = (2) ☐ + ☐

(3) 𝄾·

(3) ☐ = 𝄾 + 𝄾

♩

A dotted note may be divided into three equal parts.

5 For example, ♩. = ♩ + ♩ = ♩ + ♩ + ☐

- -

♪

6 ♩. = ♪ + ♪ + ☐

An undotted note is normally divided into two equal parts. For example:

(1) ♩

♩ = ♩ + (1) ☐

7 A dotted note, on the other hand, is normally divided into three equal parts. For example:

(2) ♩ + ♩ + ♩

♩. = (2) ☐ + ☐ + ☐

Supply the appropriate note values for the following:

(1) ♩ + ♩ + ♩

𝅝· = (1) ☐ + ☐ + ☐

(2) ♪ + ♪ + ♪

8 ♪. = (2) ☐ + ☐ + ☐

(3) ♩.

(3) ☐ = ♩ + ♩ + ♩

(4) ♪ + ♪ + ♪

♩. = (4) ☐ + ☐ + ☐

Construct a major scale on the lower note:

9

Does the upper note of the interval match a note in the scale? _No_

no

Construct a major scale on the lower note:

10

Does the upper note of the interval match a note in the scale? _No_

no

Only the relevant portion of the scale on the lower note need be constructed. In frame 10

11

the first _5_ *(how many?)* notes of the scale would have been enough to show a "non-match."

5

Write just enough of the major scale on the lower note to show whether the upper note matches a note in the scale:

12

(no match)

In considering specific names of intervals not larger than the octave, two groups of intervals are recognized. One group includes 2nds, 3rds, 6ths, and 7ths. The other group therefore in-

13

cludes primes, _4th_ , _5ths_ , and _octaves_ .

4ths, 5ths, (and) octaves

Enter the correct *rest* symbol in each box:

(1) 𝄽

37 (1) 𝅗𝅥 = 𝅘𝅥 + ☐

(2) 𝄾

(2) 𝄾 = 𝅘𝅥𝅮 + ☐

(3) ▬

(3) ▬ = 𝅗𝅥 + ☐

5

38 𝅘𝅥 𝄾 𝄾 ▬ 𝅘𝅥 = ___ *(how many?)* 𝅘𝅥 's.

6

39 𝄾 𝄾 𝅘𝅥𝅮 𝅘𝅥 𝄾 𝅘𝅥𝅮𝅘𝅥𝅮 = ___ *(how many?)* 𝅘𝅥𝅮 's.

6

40 ▬ 𝅘𝅥 𝅘𝅥𝅮𝅘𝅥𝅮 𝅗𝅥 𝄽 𝄽 𝅘𝅥 𝄽 = ___ *(how many?)* 𝅗𝅥 's.

Enter the correct *note* value in each box:

41 (1) ▬ = 𝄾 + 𝅘𝅥𝅮 + ☐

(1) 𝅘𝅥

(2) 𝅘𝅥𝅮

(2) 𝅘𝅥 = 𝄾 + ☐ + 𝅘𝅥𝅮

Set 34 / DURATION SYMBOLS (2)

When a note value or rest is followed by a dot, its value is increased by one-half. For example, a dotted half note is equal to the combined durations of a half note and a quarter note, as indicated below:

$$𝅗𝅥. = 𝅗𝅥 + 𝅘𝅥$$

1 Complete the following:

$$𝅗𝅥. = 𝅘𝅥 + (1) ☐$$

(1) 𝅘𝅥𝅮

(2) 𝅗𝅥

$$𝅝. = 𝅝 + (2) ☐$$

---

one-half

2 A dot increases the value of the note or rest it follows by . . . . *(how much?).*

major

14   In the case of 2nds, 3rds, 6ths, and 7ths, if (and only if) the upper note of the interval matches a note in the major scale built on the lower note, the specific name is *major*. The above interval has the specific name __Major__ .

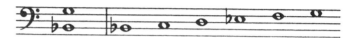

(1) upper

(2) lower
(3) major

15

The (1) __upper__ note of the interval matches a note in the major scale built on the

(2)__lower__ note. Therefore, the specific name is (3) __major__ .

From this point on you should try to *spell* (silently or aloud) the major scales needed for interval work. Spell the scales on paper or write out the notes (on a separate sheet of music paper) only when you feel it necessary.

(1) does (The major
    scale on the lower
    note goes G A B C D *E*.)

(2) is

16

The upper note (1) ..does.. (does *or* does not) match a note in the major scale built on the lower note. Therefore the specific name (2) ..is..... (is *or* is not) major.

---

(1) does not (The major
    scale on the lower note
    goes Db Eb F Gb Ab *Bb*.)
(2) is not

17

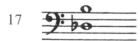

The upper note (1) ..doesn't.. match a note in the major scale built on the lower note. The specific name (2) ..is. not. major.

---

is

18

The specific name ...is..... major.

♪ is the symbol for an 8th rest. Practice drawing the 8th rest below:

33

♪ is the symbol for a 16th rest. Just as additional flags are used to indicate progressively smaller note values, additional hooks are used to indicate rests of smaller value. Each additional hook decreases the rest value by half. Complete this chart:

(1) 32nd

(2) 64th

34   ♪   ♪   16th

(1) _____

(2) _____

(1) 3
(2) 3

A 32nd note has (1) ____ flags.
A 32nd rest has (2) ____ hooks.

Draw each:

35

(3) ♪   (4) ♪

(3) ☐ (note)   (4) ☐ (rest)

Complete the following chart of note and rest-durational symbols:

	note	rest
whole	𝅝	▬
half	(1) ☐	(2) ☐
quarter	(3) ☐	(4) ☐
8th	(5) ☐	(6) ☐
16th	(7) ☐	(8) ☐
32nd	(9) ☐	(10) ☐

(1) 𝅗𝅥   (2) ▬

(3) ♩   (4) 𝄽

(5) ♪   (6) ♪

(7) ♪   (8) ♪

(9) ♪   (10) ♪

36

is not	19	The specific name ..*is.not*.. major.
yes	20	Is the specific name major? *yes*
3rds, 6ths , (and) 7ths	21	The group of intervals under consideration includes 2nds, ___*3rds*___, ___*6ths*___ , and ___*7ths*___.
no	22	Is this interval a major 6th? *No*
yes	23	Is this interval a major 2nd? *yes*
major	24	This interval is a ___*major*___ 3rd.
major 7th	25	This interval is a ___*major*___ ___*7th*___.

The symbol for a half rest is ◼ , placed on the staff:

3rd

26 Be careful not to confuse the half rest with the whole rest. The whole rest hangs below the 4th line of the staff; the half rest sits above the _____ line. Draw a half rest:

half

27 _____ is a _____ rest.

whole

28 _____ is a _____ rest.

29 The symbol for a quarter rest is 𝄽
Practice drawing the quarter rest below:

Draw the rest-durational symbol equivalent to the given note value:

(1)

𝅝 = (1) _____

(2)

30 𝅗𝅥 = (2) _____

(3)

♩ = (3) _____

2

31 ◼ = ___ *(how many?)* 𝄽 's .

4

32 ◼ = ___ 𝄽 's.

(1) major 6th
(2) one CST
    smaller

1

Interval **x** is a (1) _majar_ _6th_.
Interval **y** is (2) _one_ _CST_
smaller than interval **x**.

An interval one CST smaller than a major interval
is *minor*. Interval **x** is a (1) _major_ 3rd.
Interval **y** is a (2) _minor_ 3rd.

(1) major
(2) minor

2

one CST smaller

3

An interval _1_ _CST_ _smaller_
than a major interval is minor.

(1) minor
(2) major

4

x is a (1) _minor_ 2nd.
y is a (2) _major_ 2nd.

major 7th

5

This interval is a _major_ _7th_.

minor 7th
(A major 7th would be

since the D major scale has a C♯.)

6

Name the interval: _minar_ _7th_.

Sometimes notes having more than two flags are used. Each additional flag decreases the note value by half.

(1) 16th

20   𝅘𝅥𝅮 is a (1) _____ note.

𝅘𝅥𝅯 is a 32nd note.

(2) 64th

𝅘𝅥𝅰 is a (2) _____ note.

Draw the following notes:

(1) 𝅗𝅥

Half   (1) ☐

(2) 𝅘𝅥𝅮

21   8th   (2) ☐

(3) 𝅘𝅥𝅯

32nd   (3) ☐

(4) 𝅘𝅥

Quarter   (4) ☐

---

(1) 4

22   𝅝 = (1) ___ *(how many?)* 𝅘𝅥 's.

(2) 32

𝅝 = (2) ___ 𝅘𝅥𝅯 's.

---

(1) 4

23   𝅗𝅥 = (1) ___ *(how many?)* 𝅘𝅥𝅮 's.

(2) 1

𝅘𝅥𝅯𝅘𝅥𝅯𝅘𝅥𝅯𝅘𝅥𝅯 = (2) ___ 𝅘𝅥

Silences or *rests* in music also have duration. Rests have the same value as notes of the same name. For

24   example, the duration of a whole rest is the same as

whole

that of a _____ note.

The symbol for a whole rest is ▬ , and its placement on the staff is:

25

Draw a whole rest like the one above:

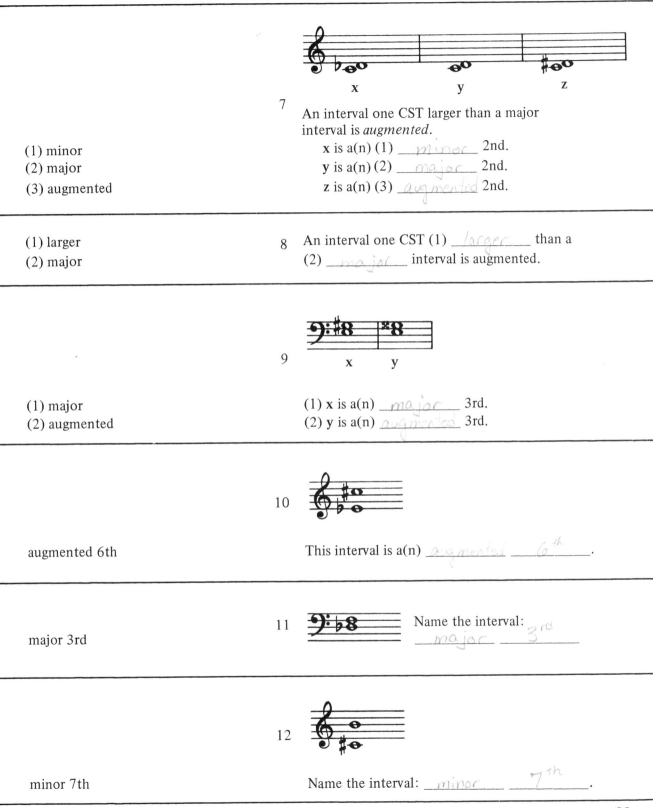

7 An interval one CST larger than a major interval is *augmented*.

(1) minor
(2) major
(3) augmented

 x is a(n) (1) _minor_ 2nd.
 y is a(n) (2) _major_ 2nd.
 z is a(n) (3) _augmented_ 2nd.

---

(1) larger
(2) major

8 An interval one CST (1) _larger_ than a (2) _major_ interval is augmented.

9

(1) major
(2) augmented

 (1) x is a(n) _major_ 3rd.
 (2) y is a(n) _augmented_ 3rd.

10

augmented 6th

This interval is a(n) _augmented_ _6th_.

---

11 Name the interval: _major_ _3rd_

major 3rd

---

12 Name the interval: _minor_ _7th_.

minor 7th

The diagram below gives the most commonly used note-durational symbols and shows the division of each note into two equal parts. Fill in the missing note names:

𝅝   whole note

♩   ♩   half notes

16   ♩ ♩ ♩ ♩   (1) _____ notes

♪ ♪ ♪ ♪ ♪ ♪ ♪ ♪   8th notes

(1) quarter

(2) 16th (*or* sixteenth)   𝅘𝅥𝅰𝅘𝅥𝅰𝅘𝅥𝅰𝅘𝅥𝅰𝅘𝅥𝅰𝅘𝅥𝅰𝅘𝅥𝅰𝅘𝅥𝅰   (2) _____ notes

Study this diagram carefully.

Draw these note symbols (without referring to the diagram in the previous frame, if possible):

(1) 𝅝

17 (1) ☐   whole note

(2) ♩

(2) ☐   half note

Draw these note symbols:

(1) ♩

(1) ☐   quarter note

18 (2) ☐   8th note

(2) ♪

(3) ☐   16th note

(3)  𝅘𝅥𝅰

---

(1) quarter

(2) 16th (sixteenth)

(3) half

19

♩ is a (1) _____ note.

𝅘𝅥𝅰 is a (2) _____ note.

♩ is a (3) _____ note.

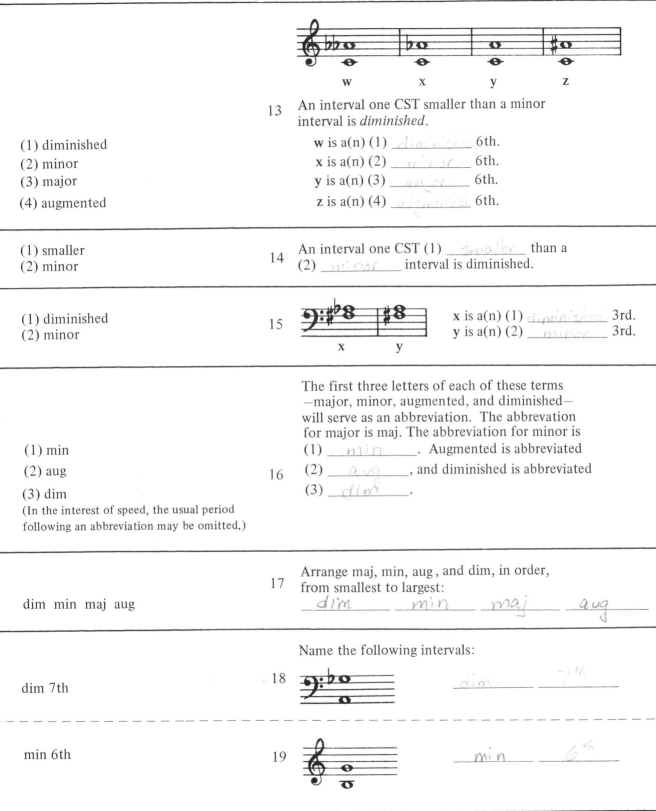

13 An interval one CST smaller than a minor interval is *diminished*.

(1) diminished   **w** is a(n) (1) _diminished_ 6th.

(2) minor   **x** is a(n) (2) _minor_ 6th.

(3) major   **y** is a(n) (3) _major_ 6th.

(4) augmented   **z** is a(n) (4) _augmented_ 6th.

---

(1) smaller

(2) minor

14 An interval one CST (1) _smaller_ than a (2) _minor_ interval is diminished.

---

(1) diminished

(2) minor

15 **x** is a(n) (1) _diminished_ 3rd.

y is a(n) (2) _minor_ 3rd.

The first three letters of each of these terms —major, minor, augmented, and diminished— will serve as an abbreviation. The abbreviation for major is maj. The abbreviation for minor is (1) _min_. Augmented is abbreviated (2) _aug_, and diminished is abbreviated (3) _dim_.

(1) min

(2) aug

(3) dim

(In the interest of speed, the usual period following an abbreviation may be omitted.)

16

---

17 Arrange maj, min, aug, and dim, in order, from smallest to largest:

dim min maj aug

dim _min_ _maj_ _aug_

Name the following intervals:

18 _dim_ _7th_

dim 7th

---

19 _min_ _6th_

min 6th

(1) (q)uarter (2) (e)ighth (3) (s)ixteenth	9 Whole, half, (1) q_____, (2) e_____, and (3) s_____ are names for durational symbols.
heads	10 Musical note symbols have distinct parts. All note symbols have an oval part called the note *head*. o and ● are note _____.
(1) stem (2) note head	11 Most note symbols have a *stem* attached to the note head. Label the parts of the note symbol: (1)········· (2)·········
(1) note head (2) stem	12 Label the parts of this note symbol: (1)········· (2)·········
(1) flag (2) stem (3) note head	13 Some notes have a *flag* (or flags) attached to the stem. Label the parts of this note: (1)········· (2)········· (3)·········
flags	14 Label the indicated part of this note: ·········
beam(s)	15 Instead of flags, *beams* are sometimes used to join notes together, as in example **x**. Label the indicated part in example **y**: ·········

Name the following intervals:

aug 2nd	20		_____ aug _____ 2nd	

maj 7th	21		_____ maj _____ 7th

min 2nd	22		_____ dim _____ 2nd

dim 3rd	23		_____ dim _____ 3rd.

---

(1) one CST smaller

(2) one CST larger
(3) smaller than a min 3rd

A min 3rd is (1) ... *1 CST sm.* than a maj 3rd.
(Be precise.)
24 An aug 3rd is (2) *1 CST larg.* than a maj 3rd.
A dim 3rd is one CST (3) *smaller ... min 3*

---

two CST's smaller

25 A dim 6th is *2 CST's smaller* than a maj 6th.

---

two CST's larger

26 An aug 2nd is *2 CST's larger* than a min 2nd.

Set 8 / CONSTRUCTION OF INTERVALS

Write the D major scale:

B

1

The note lying a maj 6th above D is _B_ .

1   *Rhythm* refers to the patterns of duration and accent of musical sounds moving through time.

duration

2   All musical sounds have a point of *attack* and a *duration.* The duration of a sound is sometimes referred to as the note (or time) *value.* The terms value and _____ both refer to the amount of time a musical sound lasts.

two

3   Durations are expressed in terms of a unit duration called a whole note. A whole divides into _____ *(how many?)* halves.

two

4   A half divides into _____ quarters.

two

5   A quarter divides into _____ eighths.

two sixteenths

6   An eighth divides into _____ _____.

four

7   There are _____ quarters in a whole.

four

8   There are _____ eighths in a half.

(1) E (2) F♯ (3) C♯	2	What note lies a maj 2nd above D? (1) _E_ A maj 3rd above D is (2) _F♯_. A maj 7th above D is (3) _C♯_.
major scale	3	To find major intervals above a given note, we refer to the _major_ _scale_ built on the note.
	4	Write the note which lies a maj 2nd above the given note:
	5	Construct a maj 2nd above the given note:
	6	In naming and constructing intervals, always try to spell (silently or aloud) the needed scales. Write a scale (on scratch paper) only when necessary. Construct a maj 3rd above the given note:
	7	Construct a maj 7th above the given note:
(1) contracted (2) CST	8	A maj 3rd (1) _contracted_ (expanded *or* contracted) one (2) _CST_ makes a min 3rd.
	9	Interval **x** shows a maj 6th above E. Construct interval **y** a min 6th above E:
	10	Construct a min 3rd above the given note. *(Hint: First find the maj 3rd above.)*

In each of the questions below, harmonize the given soprano, using chords and spacing for the first chord as indicated:

5.

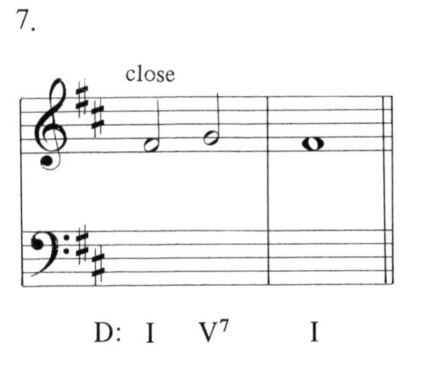

B♭: I V I

6.

open

c♯: I V I V I

7.

close

D: I V⁷ I

8.

open

d: I V⁷ I
incomplete

9.

f♯: I V⁸⁻⁷ I

10.

open

G♭: I V⁷ I V⁷ I
complete

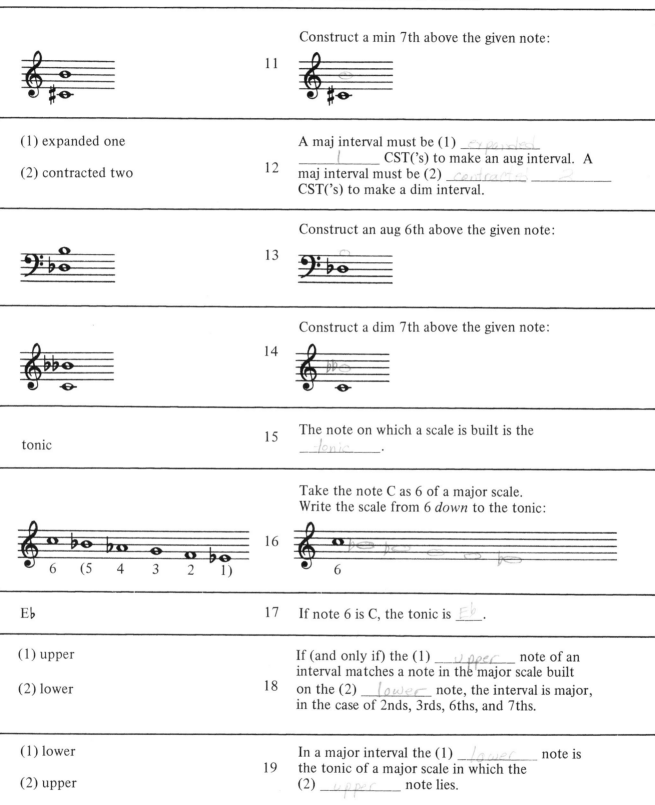

Construct a min 7th above the given note:

11

(1) expanded one

(2) contracted two

12 A maj interval must be (1) _expanded_ 1 CST('s) to make an aug interval. A maj interval must be (2) _contracted_ 2 CST('s) to make a dim interval.

Construct an aug 6th above the given note:

13

Construct a dim 7th above the given note:

14

tonic

15 The note on which a scale is built is the _tonic_.

Take the note C as 6 of a major scale. Write the scale from 6 *down* to the tonic:

16

6   (5   4   3   2   1)

6

Eb

17 If note 6 is C, the tonic is _Eb_.

(1) upper

(2) lower

18 If (and only if) the (1) _upper_ note of an interval matches a note in the major scale built on the (2) _lower_ note, the interval is major, in the case of 2nds, 3rds, 6ths, and 7ths.

(1) lower

(2) upper

19 In a major interval the (1) _lower_ note is the tonic of a major scale in which the (2) _upper_ note lies.

The questions below will test your mastery of the material in Part 6. Complete the entire test, then check your answers with the correct ones on page 139. For each question that you miss, the corresponding material may be reviewed in the set whose number is given with the correct answer.

1. V^7 is a _____-_____ *(structural type)* seventh chord.

2. In the incomplete V^7 chord the _____ *(chord member)* is doubled.

3. Indicate, in terms of scale degree numbers, the tendency tones in V^7 and their resolutions:

    ____ resolves to ____

    ____ resolves to ____

4. Each of the following chord pairs contains one or two of the errors listed below. Beneath each chord pair write one or two of the letters *a* through *f* designating the error(s). Consider each chord pair as a separate chord connection. The first item is completed as a sample.

    List of Errors

    (a) voice out of range
    (b) incorrect doubling
    (c) incorrect spacing
    (d) a too-large leap in alto or tenor
    (e) parallel or consecutive octaves, primes, or perfect 5ths
    (f) tendency tone treated incorrectly

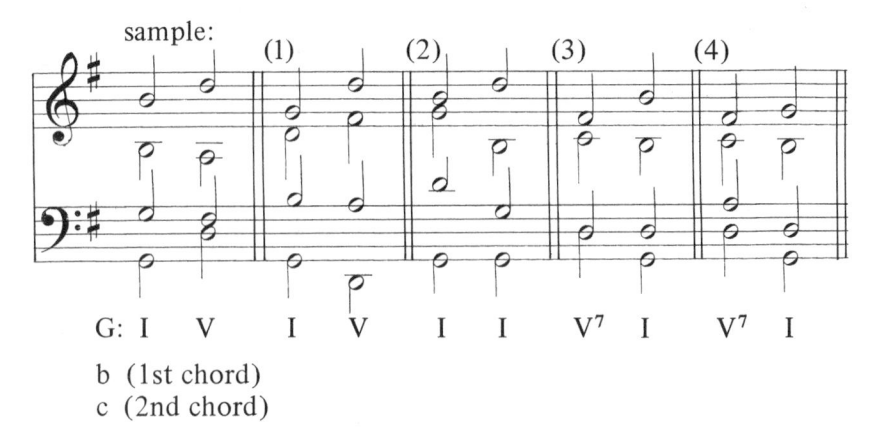

b (1st chord)
c (2nd chord)

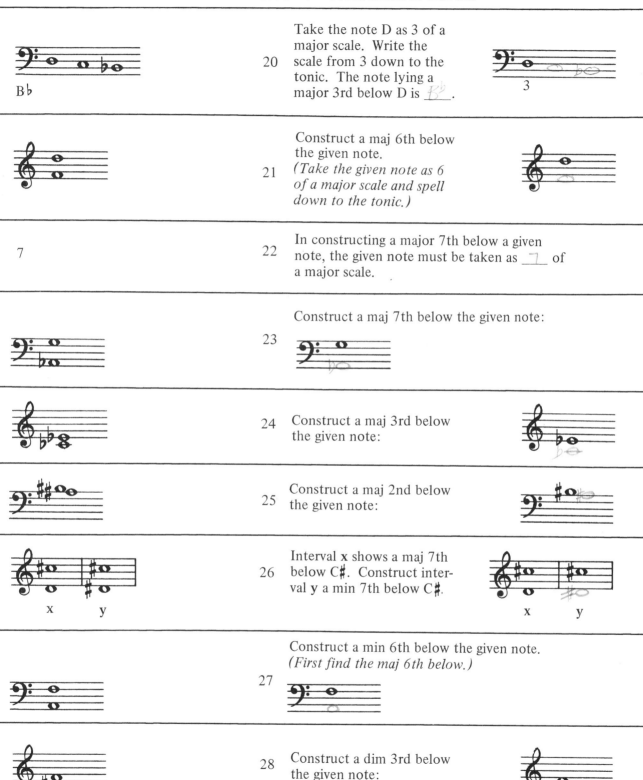

20 Take the note D as 3 of a major scale. Write the scale from 3 down to the tonic. The note lying a major 3rd below D is _Bb_ .

21 Construct a maj 6th below the given note. *(Take the given note as 6 of a major scale and spell down to the tonic.)*

22 In constructing a major 7th below a given note, the given note must be taken as _7_ of a major scale.

23 Construct a maj 7th below the given note:

24 Construct a maj 3rd below the given note:

25 Construct a maj 2nd below the given note:

26 Interval **x** shows a maj 7th below C#. Construct interval **y** a min 7th below C#.

27 Construct a min 6th below the given note. *(First find the maj 6th below.)*

28 Construct a dim 3rd below the given note:

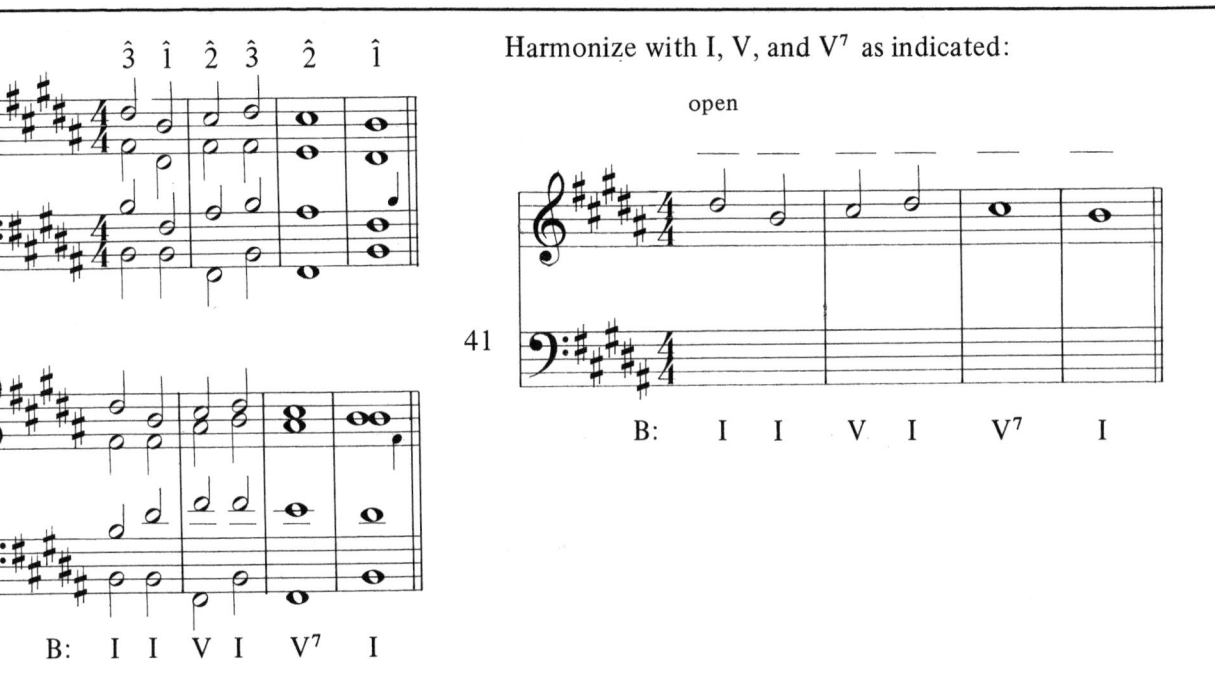

Harmonize with I, V, and V⁷ as indicated:

B: I   I   V   I   V⁷   I

	29	Construct an aug 2nd below the given note:

	30	Construct a maj 6th *above* the given note:

	31	Construct a dim 7th below the given note:

Set 9 / PRIMES, 4ths, 5ths, and OCTAVES

relationship between two pitches	1	An interval is the _relationship__between_ __two__ _pitches_ .
(1) double (2) general (3) specific *((2) and (3) in either order)*	2	Every interval has a (1) _double_ name, consisting of a (2) _general_ name and a (3) _specific_ name.
(1) prime (2) octave *(either order)*	3	Except for the names (1) _octave_ and (2) _prime_, general names are ordinal numbers.
primes, 4ths, 5ths, (and) octaves	4	The specific names *major* and *minor* are used for 2nds, 3rds, 6ths, and 7ths, *only*. They are not used for _primes_ , _4ths_ , _5ths_, and _octaves_ .
major	5	In the case of 2nds, 3rds, 6ths, and 7ths, if the upper note of the interval matches a note in the major scale built on the lower note, the specific name is _major_.

Harmonize with I V⁷ I:

close

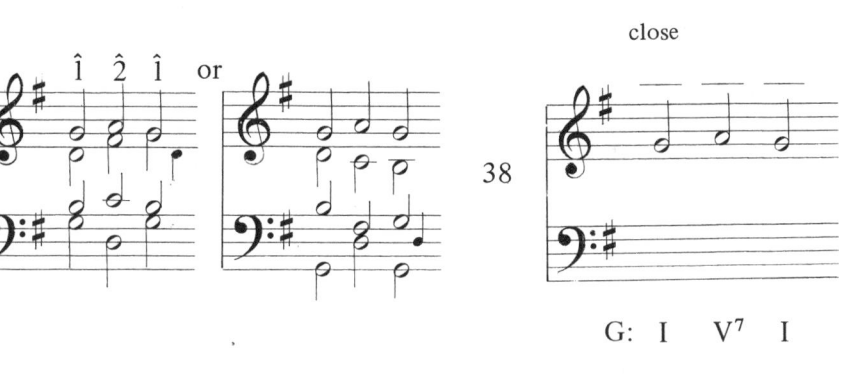

38

G: I   V⁷   I

Harmonize the following melodies with I, V, and V⁷
as indicated. (Follow the procedure outlined in previous frames.)

close

39

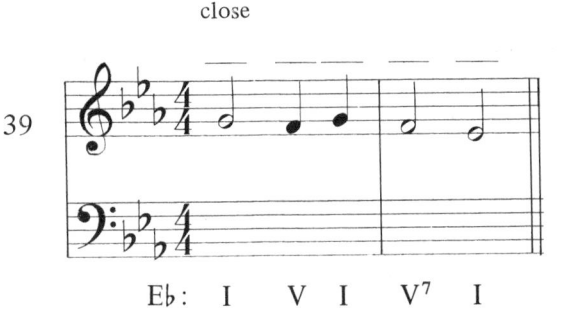

E♭: I   V   I   V⁷   I

open

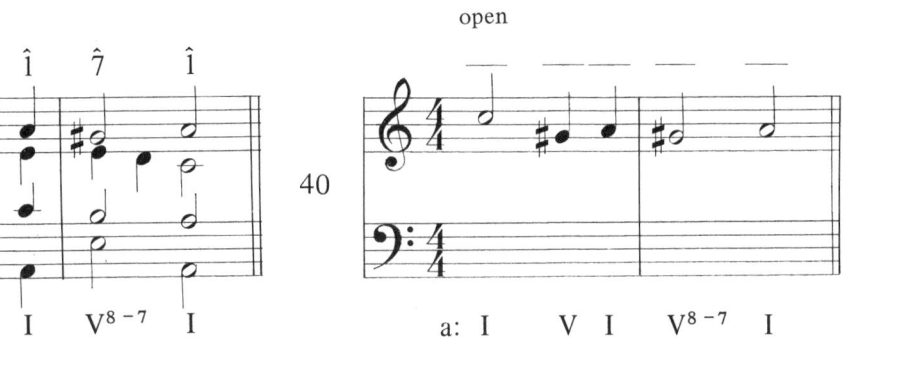

40

a: I   V   I   V$^{8-7}$ I

perfect

6   In the case of primes, 4ths, 5ths, and octaves, if (and only if) the upper note matches a note in the major scale built on the lower note, the specific name is *perfect*. The given interval has the specific name ___perfect___.

7

perfect

The upper note of the interval matches a note in the major scale built on the lower note. Therefore, the specific name is ___perfect___ ;

(1) is not

(2) is not

8

This interval (1) ...*is not*... (is *or* is not) perfect because the upper note (2) ...*is not*... (is *or* is not) in the major scale built on the lower note.

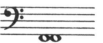

9

(1) will

(2) perfect

When two notes are identical, there is no upper or lower note, but, obviously, a scale constructed on either note (1) ...*will*.... (will *or* will not) contain the other note. Therefore, the interval is a (2) ___perfect___ prime.

is not

10

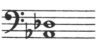

This interval ...*is not*.... (is *or* is not) a perfect prime.

(1) does

(2) is

11

The upper note (1) ...*does*.... (does *or* does not) match a note in the major scale built on the lower note. *(Spell the relevant portion of the scale.)* Therefore, the specific name (2) ...*is*....... perfect.

Harmonize the following soprano patterns with I V⁷ I.
Proceed in this order:
1. Label soprano scale degrees.
2. Complete the first chord using the indicated spacing.
3. Write the bass line.
4. Connect I V⁷ in the smoothest way. (Use either a common tone-stepwise or an all stepwise connection, if possible.)
5. Resolve V⁷ I.

35

open

c#: I   V⁷   I

36

open

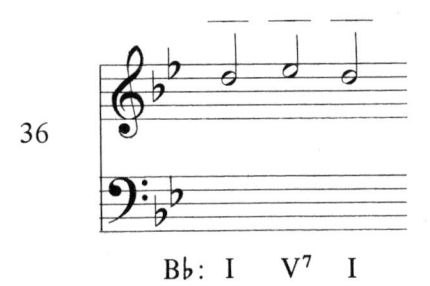

Bb: I   V⁷   I

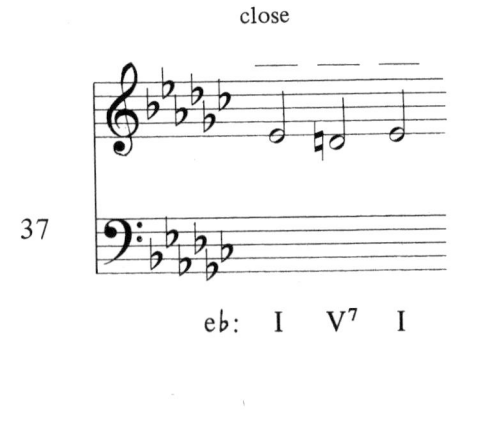

close

37

or

eb: I   V⁷   I

perfect octave

12

Interval **x** is a perfect prime.
Interval **y** is a __perfect__ __octave__.

---

(1) does not

13

(2) is not

The upper note of the interval (1) __does not__ match a note in the major scale built on the lower note. Therefore, the specific name (2) __is not__ perfect.

---

perf 4th

14

Perfect is abbreviated perf. This interval is a __perf__ __4th.__ *(Use the abbreviation.)*

---

(1) primes, 4ths, 5ths, and octaves

(2) 2nds, 3rds, 6ths, (and) 7ths

15

The group of intervals under consideration includes
(1) __primes__ , __4ths__ , __5ths__ , and __octaves__ . It does not include
(2) __2nds__ , __3rds__ , __6ths__ , and __7ths__ .

---

(1) perf 5th
(2) one CST larger

16

Interval **x** is a(n) (1) __perf__ __5th__ .
Interval **y** is (2) __1__ __CST__ __larger__ than interval **x**.

---

(1) perfect
(2) augmented

17

An interval one CST larger than a perfect interval is *augmented.*
x is a(n) (1) __perf__ 4th.
y is a(n) (2) __aug.__ 4th.

---

(1) y

(2) There is a large leap in the alto and more than an octave between AT.

Which of the two solutions to the problem below is correct? (1) ____ What is wrong with the incorrect solution? (2) . . . .

32

A: I V⁷ I V⁷

Complete these connections. *(First think of the notes to be written. Then move to them following the rules in frame 31.)*

33

d: I V⁷

34

E: I V⁷

one CST larger

18

An interval _____/_____ ___CST___ ___larger___
than a perfect interval is augmented.

19

(1) aug octave

(2) perf octave

Interval **x** is a(n) (1) __aug.__ __oct.__ .
Interval **y** is a(n) (2) __perf__ __oct.__ .

(1) aug

(2) chromatic semitone
(*or* CST)

20

This interval is a(n)
(1) __aug.__ prime.
Another name for the
interval is (2) ...CST.... .

21

aug 5th

This interval is a(n) __aug.__ __5th__ .

22

perf 5th

Name the interval : __perf.__ __5th__ .

23

(1) diminished
(2) perfect
(3) augmented

An interval one CST smaller than a perfect
interval is *diminished*.
 x is a(n) (1) __dim.__ 5th.
 y is a(n) (2) __perf__ 5th.
 z is a(n) (3) __aug.__ 5th.

one CST smaller

24

An interval _____/_____ ___CST___ ___smaller___
than a perfect interval is diminished.

or

Follow the instructions in the previous frame:

28

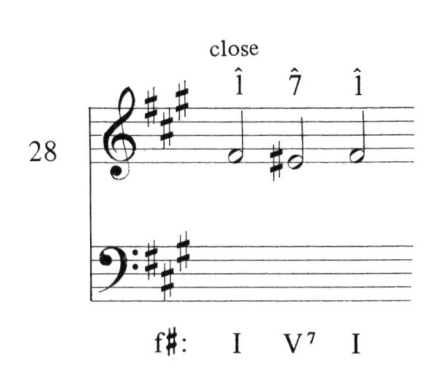

f♯:   I   V⁷   I

---

common tone-stepwise   (or)
all stepwise

29

The smoothest connections of I V⁷ are either
· · · · · · · · · · or · · · · · · · · · ·

---

third

30

Sometimes a given soprano for I V⁷ permits neither a common tone-stepwise nor an all stepwise connection. This is the case with soprano pattern 1̂ 2̂ , as is illustrated in the examples below. Both connections are faulty because the V⁷ has no _____ *(chord member)*.

B♭: I   V⁷   I   V⁷

---

(1) AT

(2) ranges
(3) SA (or) AT

31

When one of the smoothest connections between I and V⁷ is not possible, you must use a different procedure to complete the chord connections. Base your voice leading on the following rules:

1. Avoid leaps of a 5th or more in the (1) · · · · · · · · *(voices)*.
2. Keep voices within their respective (2) _____.
3. Use spacing in the V⁷ resulting in no more than an octave between (3) · · · · · · · · · *(voices)* or · · · · · · · *(voices)*.

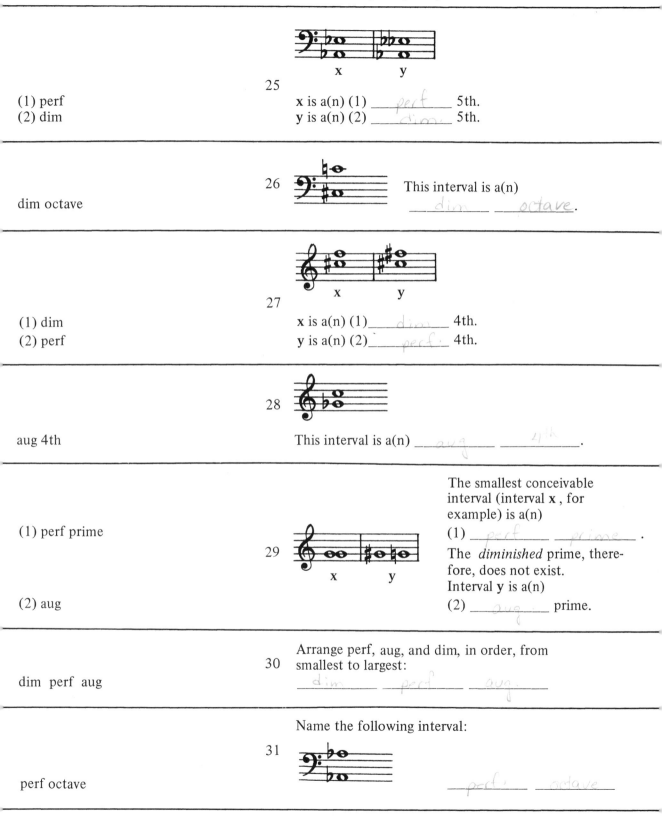

25

(1) perf
(2) dim

x is a(n) (1) _perf_ 5th.
y is a(n) (2) _dim_ 5th.

26

dim octave

This interval is a(n) _dim_ _octave_.

27

(1) dim
(2) perf

x is a(n) (1) _dim_ 4th.
y is a(n) (2) _perf_ 4th.

28

aug 4th

This interval is a(n) _aug_ _4th_.

29

(1) perf prime

(2) aug

The smallest conceivable interval (interval **x**, for example) is a(n)
(1) _perf_ _prime_ .
The *diminished* prime, therefore, does not exist.
Interval **y** is a(n)
(2) _aug_ prime.

30

dim perf aug

Arrange perf, aug, and dim, in order, from smallest to largest:
dim _perf_ _aug_

31

perf octave

Name the following interval:

perf _octave_

Follow the instructions in the previous frame:

25

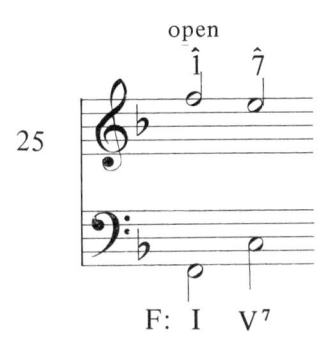

F: I V⁷

26

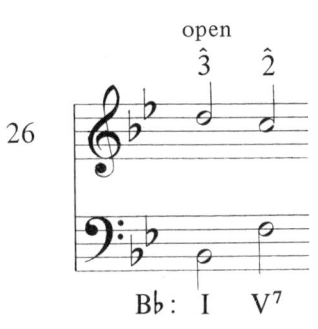

B♭: I V⁷

Complete the following I V⁷ I connections. Follow this procedure:
1. Write the first chord using the indicated spacing.
2. Write the bass line.
3. Connect I V⁷.
4. Resolve V⁷ I.

27

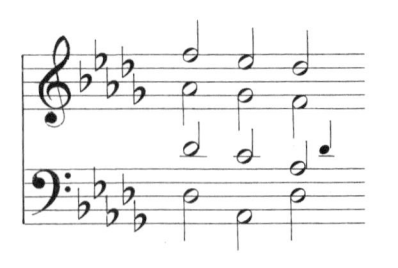

D♭: I V⁷ I

dim 4th	32	Name the following interval: _____ dim _____ 4th _____
aug prime (and) CST	33	This interval has two names. Give both: _____ aug _____ prime _____ and _____ CST _____ .
aug 4th	34	Name the following intervals: _____ aug _____ 4th _____
aug 5th	35	_____ aug. _____ 5th _____
one CST larger	36	An aug 4th is ___ 1 ___ ___ CST ___ larger than a perf 4th.
one CST smaller	37	A dim octave is ___ 1 ___ ___ CST ___ smaller than a perf octave.
two CST's larger	38	An aug 5th is ___ 2 ___ CST's larger than a dim 5th.
(1) G (2) A (3) D	39	Write the D major scale: The note lying a perf 4th above D is (1) _G_ . A perf 5th above D is (2) _A_ , and, obviously, a perf prime or perf octave from D is (3) _D_ .
(1) perfect (2) major scale	40	To construct major or (1) _perf_ intervals above a given note, refer to the (2) _major_ _scale_ built on the given note.

(1) F♮ E
(2) C♯ E

What notes are needed in the AT for an incomplete V⁷?
(1) ___ ___ What notes are needed for a complete V⁷?
(2) ___ ___ Complete the connection. *(If both a common tone-stepwise and an all stepwise connection are possible, write either.)*

23

b: I   V⁷

Almost all of the soprano patterns possible for I V⁷ will allow either a common tone-stepwise connection (to an incomplete V⁷) or an all stepwise connection (to a complete V⁷), and sometimes both types of connection will be possible.

Use this procedure in completing the following:
1. Complete the first chord using the indicated spacing.
2. Determine what notes are needed in the AT of the second chord for a complete V⁷, and, if applicable, for an incomplete V⁷.
3. Complete the connection in the smoothest way, using either common tone-stepwise or all stepwise movement. If there are two correct solutions, write either.

24

c: I   V⁷

Construct a perf 5th above the given note:

41

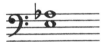

Construct a perf octave above the given note:

42

Interval x shows a perf 5th above B♭. Construct interval y a dim 5th above B♭, and interval z an aug 5th above B♭:

43

Construct a dim 4th above the given note.
(First find the corresponding perf interval.)

44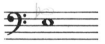

Construct an aug 4th above the given note:

45

Construct a perf 4th below the given note.
(Follow the same procedure as for maj intervals: take the given note as 4 of a major scale.)

46

Construct a dim 5th below the given note.
(First find the perf 5th below the given note.)

47

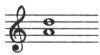

(C♯ E G)

Complete this connection. *(The notes to be added are:* ___ ___ ___ .*)*

19

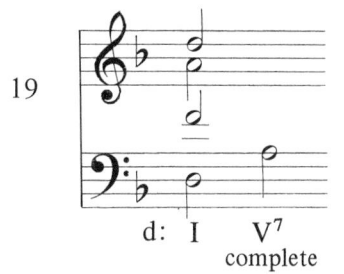

d: I   V⁷
    complete

---

common tone-stepwise
(or) all stepwise

20

The smoothest connections of I V⁷ are either . . . .
or . . . .

(1) fifth
(2) complete

2̂ is the (1) _____ *(chord member)* of V⁷. If 2̂ is the given soprano of V⁷, the V⁷ must be (2) _____ *(complete or incomplete)*. Complete this connection in the smoothest way.

21

3̂   2̂

E♭: I   V⁷

---

(1) D F♯
(2) F♯ A

(3) incomplete

What notes are needed in the AT below for an incomplete V⁷? (1) ___ ___ What notes are needed in the AT for a complete V⁷? (2) ___ ___ Which will allow for the smoothest connection, an incomplete or complete V⁷? (3) . . . . Complete the connection:

22

3̂   4̂

g: I   V⁷

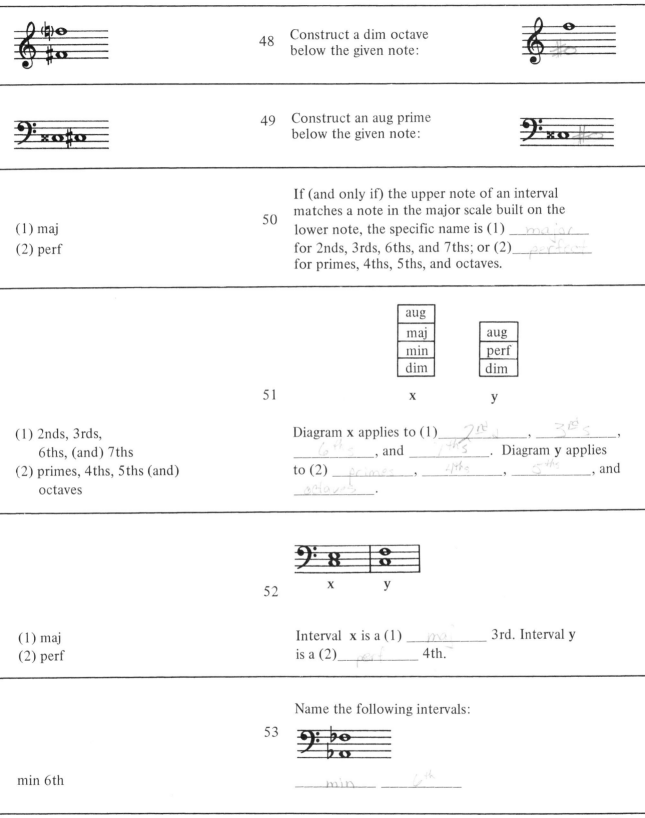

48   Construct a dim octave below the given note:

49   Construct an aug prime below the given note:

(1) maj
(2) perf

50   If (and only if) the upper note of an interval matches a note in the major scale built on the lower note, the specific name is (1) _____major_____ for 2nds, 3rds, 6ths, and 7ths; or (2)___perfect___ for primes, 4ths, 5ths, and octaves.

aug	
maj	aug
min	perf
dim	dim
x	y

51

(1) 2nds, 3rds,
    6ths, (and) 7ths
(2) primes, 4ths, 5ths (and)
    octaves

Diagram x applies to (1)____2nd____, ____3rds____, ____6ths____, and ____7ths____. Diagram y applies to (2) ___primes___, ____4ths____, ____5ths____, and ___octaves___.

52   x   y

(1) maj
(2) perf

Interval x is a (1) ____maj____ 3rd. Interval y is a (2)___perf___ 4th.

Name the following intervals:

53

min 6th

_____min_____ ____6th____

Complete this connection. *(First think of the notes to be written.)*

16

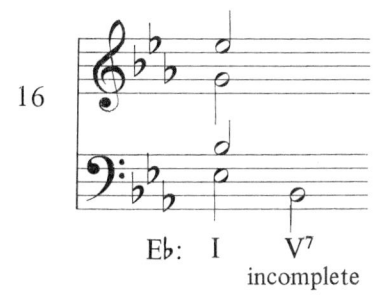

E♭: I   V⁷
incomplete

---

(1) stepwise   (2) perfect

(3) diminished

(4) is not
(Only parallel perfect 5ths are faulty.)

The connection of I V⁷ in the example below is all

(1) _____. The AT move from a (2) _____

(specific name) 5th to a (3) _____ 5th. This

(4) · · · · · · · · · (is *or* is not) faulty movement.

17

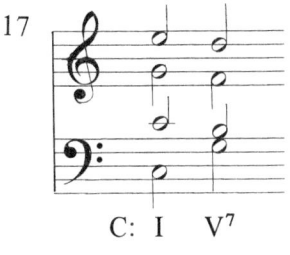

C: I   V⁷

---

(1) stepwise

(2) G♯ B D

The smoothest connection of I to complete V⁷ is

all (1) _____. What notes are to be written in

the SAT of the complete V⁷ below? (2) ___ ___ ___

Complete the connection, using all stepwise movement.

(Recall that in the all stepwise connection, all three voices move <u>down</u> by step.)

18

A: I   V
complete

Name the following intervals:

dim 5th

54
dim _5th_

----

maj 7th

55 _maj_ _7th_

----

perf octave

56
perf _octave_

Set 10 / DOUBLY DIMINISHED AND AUGMENTED INTERVALS

t	w	x	y	z

1   An interval one CST larger than an augmented interval is *doubly augmented*.

(1) dim   t   is a(n) (1) . . . _dim_ . . . . 6th.
(2) min   w is a(n) (2) . . . . _min_ . . . 6th.
(3) maj   x is a(n) (3) . . . . _maj_ . . . 6th.
(4) aug   y is a(n) (4) . . . . . _aug_ . . . 6th.
(5) doubly aug   z is a(n) (5) . _doubly aug_ . . 6th.

2   x   y

(1) doubly aug   x is a(n) (1) _doubly aug_ . 4th.
(2) aug   y is a(n) (2) . . . _aug_ . . . . 4th.

(1) 7 2 4		The SAT of complete V⁷ contain scale degrees
(2) 5 7 4 (3) incomplete	11	(1)___ ___ ___ . The SAT of incomplete V⁷ contain
		scale degrees (2) ___ ___ ___ . I and (3) _____
(4) complete		V⁷ have a common tone in the SAT, whereas I and
		(4) _____ V⁷ do not.

		The smoothest connections of I V⁷ are marked by
	12	either common tone-stepwise movement, resulting in
(1) incomplete		a(n) (1) _____ V⁷, or all stepwise movement, re-
(2) complete		sulting in a(n) (2) _____ V⁷.

D F♯ C

What notes are to be written in the SAT of the incomplete V⁷ in the example below? ___ ___ ___
(Give the notes in any order.)
Complete the connection. Write the common tone in
the same voice. Move the other voices stepwise.

13

G: I   V⁷
incomplete

	14	The smoothest connection of I to incomplete V⁷ is
common tone-stepwise		. . . .

---

(1) C E♮ B♭
(2) common tone-stepwise

The notes to be written in the SAT of the incomplete
V⁷ below are: (1) ___ ___ ___. The connection will
be (2) . . . . Complete the connection.

15

f: I   V⁷
incomplete

t   w   x   v   z

3

An interval one CST smaller than a diminished interval is *doubly diminished*.

(1) doubly dim

(2) dim

(3) perf

(4) aug

(5) doubly aug

t is a(n) (1) ...doubly dim... 5th.

w is a(n) (2) ...dim... 5th.

x is a(n) (3) ...perf... 5th.

y is a(n) (4) ...aug... 5th.

z is a(n) (5) ...doubly aug. 5th.

4

x   y

(1) dim

(2) doubly dim

x is a(n) (1) ...dim... 7th.

y is a(n) (2) ..doubly dim. 7th.

two CST's
larger

5

A doubly aug 6th is ___2___ ___CST___
___larger___ than a maj 6th.

two CST's
smaller

6

A doubly dim 4th is ___2___ ___CST___
___smaller___ than a perf 4th.

doubly aug 3rd

7

 Name the interval doubly.... 3rd

Construct a doubly dim 4th above the given note:

8

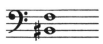

Construct a doubly dim 5th below the given note:

9

Complete the connections:

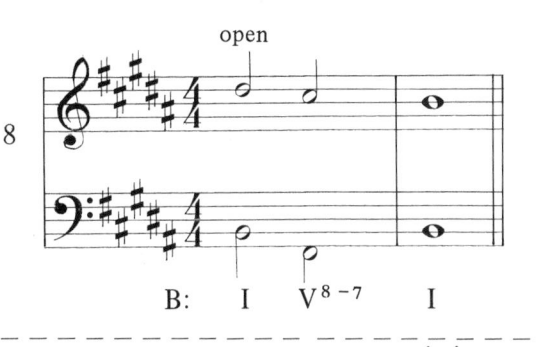

B: I   V⁸⁻⁷   I

(Hint: Does I V with soprano 1̂ 2̂ allow a common tone-stepwise connection? ___)

(no)

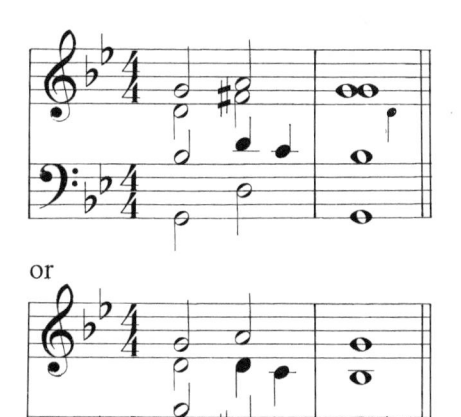

or

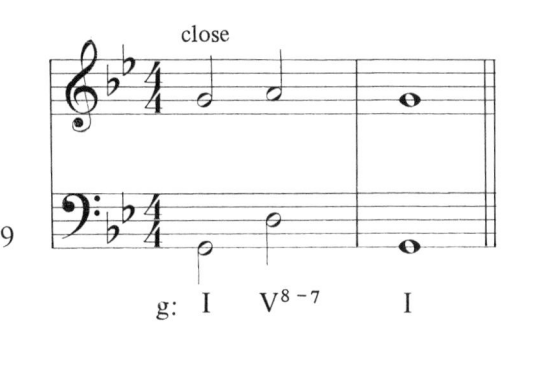

g: I   V⁸⁻⁷   I

(1) x   (2) y

Sometimes an opening tonic moves directly to V⁷. An opening tonic may move to an incomplete V⁷ as in case (1) ___ or to a complete V⁷ as in case (2) ___ . The connection in case **x** is *common tone-stepwise*. In case **y** the movement is *all stepwise*. (All upper voices move down by step.)

10

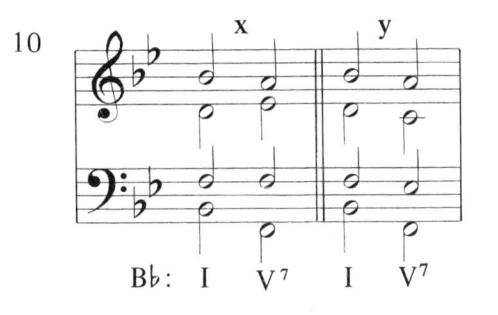

B♭: I   V⁷   I   V⁷

Construct an aug 6th below the given note:

10

---

is not

11 If both notes of an interval are raised (or lowered) one CST, the size of the interval ..*is not*.. (is *or* is not) changed.

---

transposed

12

x   y

If both notes of an interval are raised (or lowered) equally, the interval is *transposed*. Raising both notes of interval **x** one CST results in interval **y**. Interval **x** has been ___*transposed*___ up one CST.

13 Rewrite the given interval, transposed up one CST:

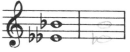

14 Transpose the given interval down one CST:

---

transposed

15

x   y

Interval **x**, ___*transposed*___ down one CST, becomes interval **y**.

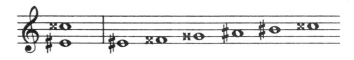

maj 6th

16 In some cases the major scale built on the lower note of an interval will have ✗'s or ♭♭'s. To find the name of the above interval, an E♯ major scale is constructed, showing the interval to be a(n) ..*maj 6th*.. .

Convert the V to a V⁷, changing the value of the appropriate note to a quarter note. Then resolve V⁷ to I, following the resolution procedures you have learned. *(Remember that the 7th, $\hat{4}$, is part of a descending passing motion from $\hat{5}$ to $\hat{3}$.)*

4

f♯: V⁸⁻⁷   I

5

B♭: V⁸⁻⁷   I

6

complete

Although a closing tonic may be either a complete or an incomplete chord, an opening tonic should be a(n) _____ chord.

Think of each of the following I V⁸⁻⁷ I progressions as a chain of individual connections. First connect I V; then add a passing 7th to V; then resolve V⁷ to I. Complete the connections, using the indicated spacing for the first chord:

7

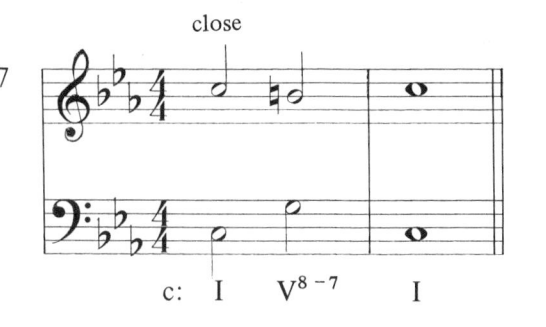

close

c: I   V⁸⁻⁷   I

When the lower note of an interval supports a major scale with **x**'s or ♭♭'s, it is simpler to measure a transposition of the interval than the interval itself. Show how the given interval might be transposed for more convenient measurement:

17

18

maj 6th

This interval is a(n) *maj. 6th*

(Mentally transpose the interval up one CST.)

Name the following intervals:

19

dim 7th

dim. 7th

20

aug 4th

aug. 4th

21

aug 6th

aug. 6th

22

dim 3rd

dim. 3rd

23

min 6th

min. 6th

(Transpose down two CST's.)

(1) V⁷   (2) $\hat{4}$

In this example, a passing 7th converts a V chord into a (1).........(symbol) chord. The 7th, (2) ____ (scale degree), provides a stepwise, passing connection between $\hat{5}$ and $\hat{3}$.

D: V   I

7th

A V chord is converted into a V⁷ through the movement of $\hat{5}$ (in S, A, or T) to $\hat{4}$, as shown in example **x**. Stated another way, the octave above the bass moves to a _____ above the bass. Convert the V in example **y** to a V⁷ using this procedure. (Change the value of the appropriate note to a quarter note.)

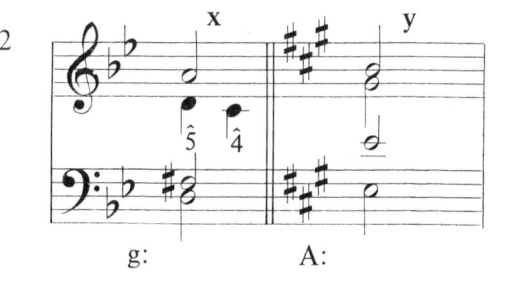

g: A:

7th

A: V⁸⁻⁷   I

As shown in example **x** below, the addition of a passing 7th to a V chord is symbolized V⁸⁻⁷. The "8-7" part of the symbol represents the movement from an octave above the bass to a _____ above the bass. Complete the chord symbol in example **y**.

g: V⁸⁻⁷   I   A: V   I

Name the following interval:

24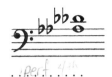

perf 4th

Sometimes transposition avoids unwieldy scales in *construction* of intervals, too. Construct a maj 6th above the given note, B♯, in this way: First construct a maj 6th above B, then transpose up one CST.

25

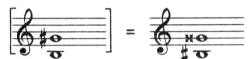

Construct a dim 5th below the given note:

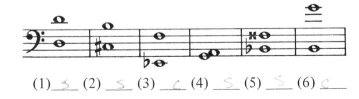

26

(To avoid complications, construct from B♭, then transpose.)

Set 11 / COMPOUND INTERVALS, CONSONANCE AND DISSONANCE, ENHARMONIC EQUIVALENTS, INVERSION

Intervals with general names not larger than "octave" are *simple* intervals. Intervals with general names larger than "octave" are *compound* intervals. Label each of these intervals simple or compound (s or c):

1

(1) simple   (2) simple
(3) compound (4) simple
(5) simple   (6) compound

(1) _s_ (2) _s_ (3) _c_ (4) _s_ (5) _s_ (6) _c_

Resolve the following V⁷ :

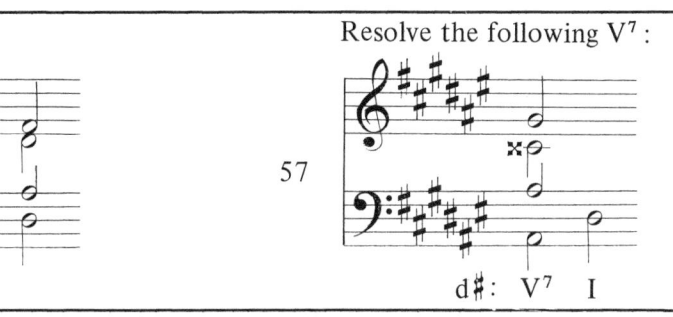

57

d♯: V⁷   I

Using the given SB's, complete the following progressions. *(If there is more than one correct solution for a problem, write any one.)*

or

58

E♭: V⁷   I
complete

or

59

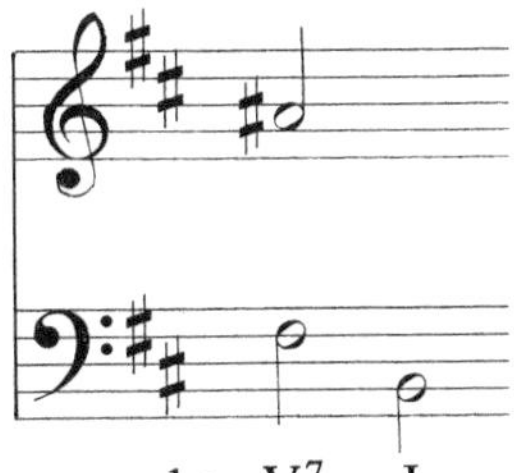

b: V⁷   I
incomplete

or

60

A: V⁷   I

$\hat{7}$ $\hat{1}$

$\hat{2}$ $\hat{1}$

$\hat{4}$ $\hat{3}$

61

Possible soprano scale degree patterns for V⁷ I are:

$\hat{7}$ ____

$\hat{2}$ ____

$\hat{4}$ ____

$\hat{5}$ $\hat{5}$ in the soprano is a possiblility, but it rarely occurs.

2 The general name of a compound interval is found in the usual way, by counting the lines and spaces from one note to the other, inclusively. The general name of the given interval

10th

is ____10th____ .

3 Give the general names:

(1) 9th
(2) 11th
(3) 12th

(1) __9th__ (2) __11th__ (3) __12th__

To find the specific name of a compound interval, reduce it to a simple interval by subtracting one or more octaves. Subtracting an octave from interval **x** results in interval **y**. Write the interval which results when an octave is subtracted from interval **z**:

4

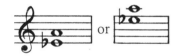

or

    x   y   z

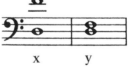

5   x   y

A compound interval has the same specific name as the corresponding simple interval. Interval **x** has the same specific name as

min

interval **y**. The specific name is __minor__ .

6

aug

This interval has the specific name ____aug____ .

In V⁷ I resolutions:

(1) 1̂

(2) 3

(3) 1̂

(4) common

(5) 1̂

(6) down (a) 3rd

52   5̂ in the bass always goes to (1) ____. In the upper voices, 4̂ always goes to (2) ____; 2̂ always goes to (3) ____. 5̂, if present in an upper voice, remains a (4) _____ tone. The only variable is 7̂, which may resolve to (5) ____, as it must if it is in the soprano, or which may move (6) _____ a _____ if it is in the alto or tenor.

(1) 7̂

(2) soprano

53   There is only one case of V⁷ that cannot resolve to a complete I chord, and that is a complete V⁷ with (1) ____ *(scale degree)* in the (2) _____ *(voice)*.

Resolve the following V⁷'s arriving at a complete I chord whenever possible. *(Suggestion: In each case the first step is to determine whether the V⁷ is complete or incomplete.)*

54

c♯:   V⁷   I

55

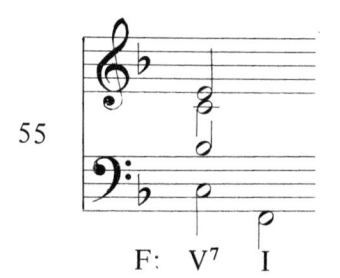

F: V⁷   I

56

g: V⁷   I

7

The specific name of this interval is___dim___.

dim

Sometimes more than one octave must be subtracted from the interval in order to reduce it
to a simple interval. Subtract two octaves
from the given interval:

8

or   or

min

The specific name is _____.

Name the following intervals:

9

maj 10th

..maj.10th...

10

aug 13th

...aug..13th..

A 9th reduced by an octave becomes a 2nd.

11   A 10th reduced by an octave becomes a

3rd

___3rd___.

The simple interval corresponding to an 11th

12   is a 4th. The simple interval corresponding

5th

to a 12th is a___5th___.

6th

13   A ___6th___ corresponds to a 13th.

For every compound general name there is a

14

simple

corresponding ___simple___ general name.

Resolve the incomplete V⁷:

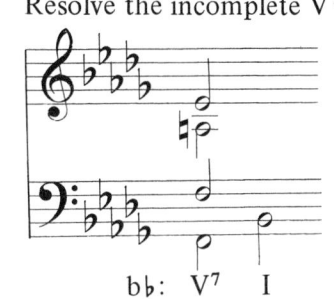

49

bb: V⁷   I

---

(1) $\hat{1}$

(2) $\hat{3}$

(3) $\hat{5}$

(4) $\hat{5}$

(5) $\hat{7}$

(6) $\hat{2}$

(7) $\hat{4}$

50

Scale degree designations for the members of I are:

root (1) ____

third (2) ____

fifth (3) ____

Scale degree designations for the members of V⁷ are:

root (4) ____

third (5) ____

fifth (6) ____

seventh (7) ____

In summary, there are 3 types of V⁷ resolution:

1. Complete V⁷ to incomplete I

upper voices $\begin{bmatrix} \hat{4} \to \hat{3} \\ \hat{2} \to \hat{1} \\ \hat{7} \to \hat{1} \end{bmatrix}$

bass $\quad \hat{5} \to \hat{1}$

$\qquad$ **V⁷   I**

2. Complete V⁷ to complete I

upper voices $\begin{bmatrix} \hat{4} \to \hat{3} \\ \hat{2} \to \hat{1} \\ \hat{7}* \to \hat{5} \end{bmatrix}$

51

bass $\quad \hat{5} \to \hat{1}$

$\qquad$ **V⁷   I**

* $\hat{7}$ must be in A or T

3. Incomplete V⁷ to complete I

upper voices $\begin{bmatrix} \hat{4} \to \hat{3} \\ \hat{7} \to \hat{1} \\ \hat{5} \smile \hat{5} \end{bmatrix}$

bass $\quad \hat{5} \to \hat{1}$

$\qquad$ **V⁷   I**

7th

15   Compound intervals are sometimes called by the same general name as their corresponding simple intervals. 14ths and larger intervals are usually so called. A 14th is usually called a(n) ___7th___ .

5th

16   10ths, 11ths, 12ths, and 13ths are occasionally called by their corresponding simple names. The given interval might be called a ___5th___ instead of a 12th.

x   y   z

17

(1) z
(2) y
(3) x

9ths usually are *not* called 2nds. Shown are three groups of compound intervals. Which group is usually called by simple general names? (1) _z_ . Which group is occasionally so called? (2) _y_ . Which group is not usually so called? (3) _x_ .

18

(1) dim 12th
(2) dim 5th

This interval is, strictly speaking, a(n) (1) ..dim..12th.., but might also be called a(n) (2) ..dim..5th.. .

19

maj 7th

This interval is usually called a(n) ....maj.7th.... .

20

aug 9th

This interval is usually called a(n) ....aug.9th... .

There is another way to obtain a complete I chord:
The *incomplete* V⁷ leads naturally to a complete I.
The third and seventh are resolved according to their
tendencies. The root of V⁷ is doubled and becomes
a common tone, which is kept in the same voice in
the S, A, or T.
Write the doubled root in the alto of the given V⁷:

46

Gb: V⁷   I

fifth

Now write the alto of I. The doubled root of V⁷,
a common tone, becomes the _____ of I.

Resolve each of the following incomplete V⁷'s, resulting in a complete I chord. *(Suggestion: First
resolve the tendency tones. Then write the common
tone in the same voice.)*

47

e: V⁷   I

48

A: V⁷   I

Construct a perf 11th above the given note.
(Construct the corresponding simple interval; then add an octave.)

21

Construct a minor 10th below the given note:

22

	23	A major 10th above F is *A* .
A		

	24	A perfect 12th below G♯ is *C♯* .
C♯		

	25	A major 3rd above B is *D♯* .
D♯		

	26	A diminished 7th below A♭ is *B* .
B		

	27	G lies a . . *perf 5th* . . (*what simple interval?*) above C.
perf 5th		

	28	E♭ lies a . . *min 7th* . . (*what simple interval?*) below D♭.
min 7th		

	29	A *consonant* interval is one which sounds stable. The opposite of consonant is *dissonant.* A dissonant interval sounds *unstable* .
unstable		

In traditional harmony the consonant intervals are:

all perfect intervals
major and minor 3rds and 6ths

30

s   t   w   x   y   z

	Intervals s, (1) *w* , and *z* are (2) *consonant* intervals.
(1) w (and) z (2) consonant	

In case **x** and case **y** connect the complete V⁷ to I, resolving the leading tone according to its tendency (resulting in an incomplete I). In case **z** connect the complete V⁷ to I, using the exceptional movement of the leading tone (resulting in a complete I).

43

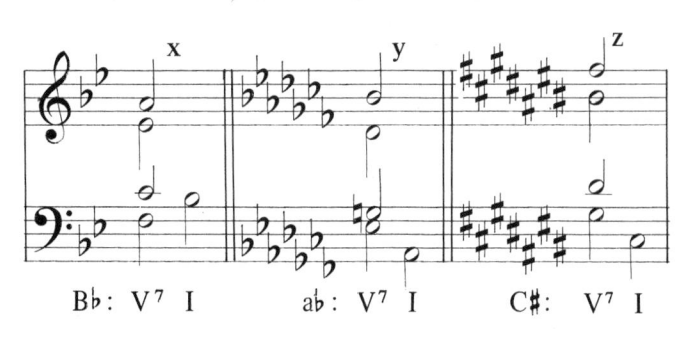

Bb: V⁷ I   ab: V⁷ I   C#: V⁷ I

---

(1) **x**

(2) **y**

(3) **z**

(4) complete

In case (1) ____ the leading tone must resolve up by step. In case (2) ____ the leading tone is free to move down a 3rd but does not. In case (3) ____ the leading tone moves down a 3rd in order to obtain a(n) (4) _____ I chord.

44

Bb: V⁷ I   ab: V⁷ I   C#: V⁷ I

---

(1) incomplete   (2) fifth

(3) root

45

In the (1) _____ V⁷ the (2) _____ is omitted and the (3) _____ is doubled.

Intervals other than those listed in frame 30 are dissonant. Thus:

31

    all aug and dim intervals
    all 2nds and 7ths

dissonant

are _dissonant_ intervals.

One irregularity: The perfect 4th is consonant only when accompanied by a note a 3rd lower than its bottom note.

32

(1) consonant

(2) dissonant

    x   y

In case **x** the perf 4th G – C is (1) _consonant_ . In case **y** the perf 4th G – C is (2) _dissonant_.

---

stable

33

A consonant interval sounds _stable_ .

---

  w   x   y   z

34

Two intervals written differently but played identically on the keyboard are *enharmonic equivalents.* Interval **w** is the enharmonic equivalent of interval ____.

z

---

enharmonic equivalents

35

These two intervals are _enharmonic intervals_ .

---

  w x y z

36

A simple interval is *inverted* when its lower note is raised an octave, or when its upper note is lowered an octave. Interval _y_ is an inversion of interval **w**.

y

---

or

37

Invert:

(There are two possible correct answers.)

In the connection of complete V⁷ to I, a complete
I chord may be obtained by allowing the leading tone
to move *down a 3rd*, in violation of its upward tendency.
In case x the leading tone moves (1) . . . ., resulting in a I chord with tripled (2) _____. In case
y the leading tone moves (3) . . . ., resulting in
a(n) (4) _____ (complete *or* incomplete) I chord.

(1) up by step
(2) root
(3) down a 3rd
(4) complete

39

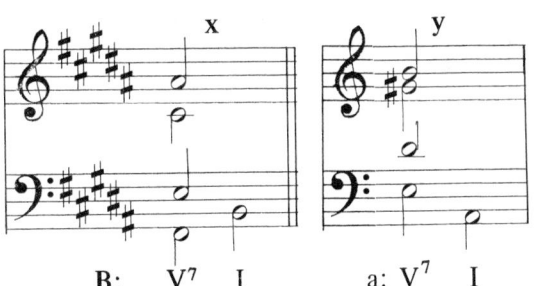

Movement of the leading tone down a 3rd is permissible
only when the leading tone is in the alto or tenor,
where its failure to resolve "correctly" is scarcely
noticeable. In which case(s) below is the exceptional
movement of the leading tone down a 3rd permissible?

. . . . Where it is permissible, move the
leading tone down a 3rd; otherwise, resolve it according to its tendency. Then complete each connection
by resolving the seventh and moving the fifth correctly.

y

40

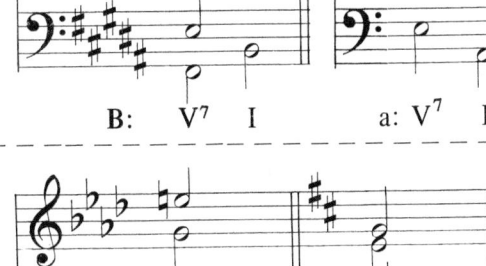

41

complete

42

A leading tone in the alto or tenor may move down
a 3rd in order to obtain a(n) _____ (complete *or*
incomplete) I chord.

4th

38 When the general name of an interval is subtracted from 9, the result is the general name of the inversion. Thus a 3rd becomes a 6th when inverted. A 5th becomes a _____4th_____ when inverted.

major	←——————→	minor
augmented	←——————→	diminished
perfect	←——————→	perfect

maj 2nd

39 The above diagrams show the effect of inversion on specific interval names. Major intervals become minor and vice versa. Augmented intervals become diminished and vice versa. Perfect intervals remain perfect. A minor 7th becomes a(n) __maj__ __2nd__ when inverted.

dim 5th

40 The inversion of an aug 4th is a(n) ___dim___ ___5th___.

inversion

41

x   y

Interval **y** is an __inversion__ of interval **x**.

TEST COVERING PART 2

The questions below will test your mastery of the material in Part 2. Complete the entire test, then check your answers with the correct ones on page 136. For each question that you miss, the corresponding material may be reviewed in the set whose number is given with the correct answer.

1. An interval is _____.

2. Every interval has a (1) __double__ name, consisting of a (2) __specific__ name followed by a (3) __general__ name.

3. Most general names are ordinal numbers. The two exceptions are __octaves__ and __primes__.

4. Intervals with general names not greater than *octave* are (1) __simple__ intervals. Intervals with general names greater than *octave* are (2) __compound__ intervals.

Connect the given V⁷ to I. *(Suggested procedure: Resolve the tendency tones first. Then move the fifth in the proper manner. The result should be a I chord with tripled root and one third.)*

35

C: V⁷   I

---

(1) fifth
(2) root

36

Connecting the complete V⁷ to I as in the previous example, leads to a I chord with the (1) _____ *(chord member)* omitted and the (2) _____ tripled.

The complete V⁷ with all tendency tones resolved will always move to an incomplete I (with tripled root and omitted fifth). In the following examples connect the complete V⁷ (given) to I:

37

g♯: V⁷   I

38

f♯: V⁷   I

5. The general name (1) ___*14th*___ and larger general names are usually reduced to simple general names. The general name (2) ___*9th*___ is usually *not* reduced. General names falling between those two limits are occasionally reduced.

6. Give the word for which each abbreviation stands:
   maj (1) ___*major*___   dim (4)___*diminished*___
   min (2) ___*minor*___   perf (5) ___*perfect*___
   aug (3) ___*augmented*___

7. List these terms – min, aug, maj, dim – in order from smallest to largest:
   (1) ___*dim*___ ___*min*___ ___*maj*___ ___*aug*___   List these terms – perf, dim, aug – in
   the same way: (2) ___*dim*___ ___*perf*___ ___*aug*___

8. For the purpose of applying specific names, intervals not larger than the octave are divided into two groups. One group includes (1) . . . . *2, 3, 6, 7* . . . and the other includes (2) . *1, 4, 5, 8, prime*

9. If (and only if) the upper note of the interval falls into the major scale built on the lower note, the specific name is (1) ___*maj*___ in the case of 2nds, 3rds, 6ths, and 7ths; and (2) ___*perf*___ in the case of primes, 4ths, 5ths, and octaves.

10. The specific name of a compound interval is the same as the specific name of the corresponding ___*simple*___ interval.

11. When the major scale built on the lower note of an interval includes **x**'s or **♭♭**'s, it is convenient to ___*transpose*___ the interval in order to determine its name.

12. Write an enharmonic equivalent of this interval:

13.

       t   w   x   y   z
   Which intervals are consonant? (1) . *y, z* . . . . . The other intervals are (2) ___*dissonant*___.

14. The inversion of a major 6th is a(n) ___*min*___ ___*3rd*___ .

When complete V^7 goes to I, the fifth of V^7 must move *down by step* to avoid faulty parallels or faulty doubling, Only in case (1) ____ (**x, y,** *or* **z**) is the fifth handled correctly. In case (2) ____ the fifth and root make faulty parallels. In case (3) ____ the motion of the fifth results in faulty doubling in the I chord.

(1) y
(2) x
(3) z

30

In V^7 I, the fifth of V^7, though it has no special tendency, must move (1) _____ by _____. In other words, $\hat{2}$ moves to (2) ____.

(1) down (by) step
(2) $\hat{1}$

31

The tendency tones in V^7 are the (1) _____ *(chord member)*, also called the leading tone, and the (2) _____ *(chord member)*.

(1) third

(2) seventh

32

An exception will presently be noted, but, as a rule, the third and seventh of V^7 must resolve according to their tendencies. The third moves (1) _____ by _____ . The seventh moves (2) _____ by _____ .

(1) up (by) step
(2) down (by) step

33

Tendency tones are truly resolved only when the note of resolution is in the same voice as the tendency tone. The example shown is incorrect: The (1) _____ of V^7 is not truly resolved because it occurs in the (2) _____ *(voice)* , while its note of resolution appears in the (3) _____ *(voice)*.

(1) seventh

(2) alto
(3) tenor

34

15. Name the following intervals:

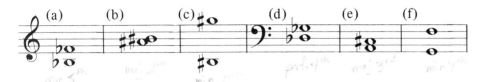

Note: The clef sign at the beginning of a staff applies to the entire staff, unless it is replaced by a different clef sign.

16. Construct intervals as indicated:

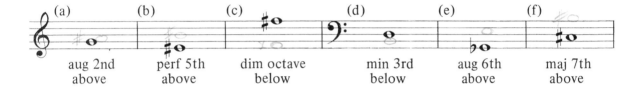

(a)	(b)	(c)	(d)	(e)	(f)
aug 2nd above	perf 5th above	dim octave below	min 3rd below	aug 6th above	maj 7th above

In each case, find the third ($\hat{7}$) and seventh ($\hat{4}$) and write their notes of resolution:

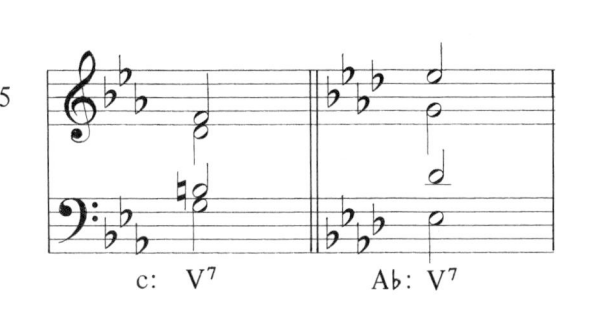

25

c: V⁷   Ab: V⁷

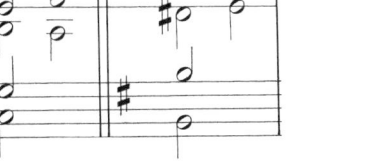

26

F: V⁷   e: V⁷

---

complete

27

No chord member is doubled in the _____ V⁷, which contains one root, one third, one fifth, and one seventh.

C♯ (to) F♯

28

The root and fifth of V⁷ are not tendency tones, but their behavior is controlled by other considerations. When complete V⁷ goes to I, the root of V⁷ (present only in the bass) obviously must move to the next bass note—the root of I. This is shown here in the bass motion from ___ to ___. *(note names)*

F♯: V⁷   I

---

(1) fifth

(2) root

29

The (1) _____ of V⁷ is present only in the complete V⁷. It is omitted in the incomplete V⁷, which contains a doubled (2) _____.

PART 3 KEY SIGNATURES
THE MINOR SCALES

Set 12 / THE SERIES OF 5ths

	1	Construct a perfect 5th above each of the following notes:	

	2	Construct a perfect 5th below each of the following notes:	

E	3	A perfect 5th above A is _E_ .
D♭	4	A perfect 5th above Gb is _D♭_ .
B♭	5	A perfect 5th below F is _B♭_ .
F♯	6	A perfect 5th below C♯ is _F♯_ .

---

(2) A major

C G D ?

A

7 Shown above is a series of perfect 5ths beginning on C. G is a perfect 5th higher than C; D is a perfect 5th higher than G. What is the next higher member of the series? _A_

(C G D A) E B F♯ (C♯)

8 Fill in the three missing members of this series:

C G D A _E_ _B_ _F♯_ C♯

? B♭ F C

E♭

9 Above is another series of perfect 5ths. It proceeds *down* from C. F is a perfect 5th lower than C. B♭ is a perfect 5th lower than F. What is the next member of the series? _E♭_

(C♭) G♭ D♭ A♭ (E♭ B♭ F C)

10 Fill in the three missing members of this series:

C♭ _G♭_ _D♭_ _A♭_ E♭ B♭ F C

C♭ G♭ D♭ A♭ E♭ B♭ F C G D A E B F♯ C♯

perf 5th

11 This series is a combination of the series above C and the series below C. Each member of the series is a _Perf_ _5th_ higher than the next lower member.

The seventh of V^7, $\hat{4}$, tends to move *down by step* to $\hat{3}$. In chord **x** the seventh is C. It resolves to B. In chord **y** the seventh is ___. Write its note of resolution:

E

20

G: V^7 I   b: V^7

---

(1) 4
(2) down (by) step
(3) 3

21

The seventh of V^7, scale degree (1) ___, tends to resolve (2) _____ by _____ to scale degree (3) ___.

In each case find the seventh and write its note of resolution:

22

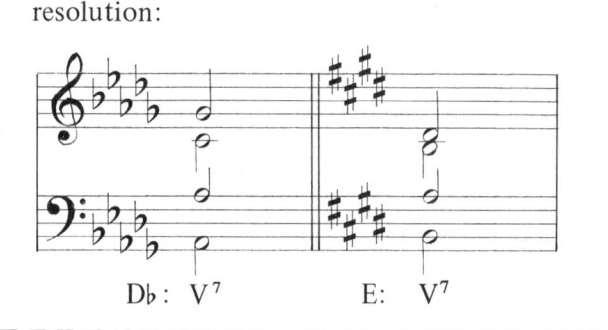

Db: V^7 E: V^7

23

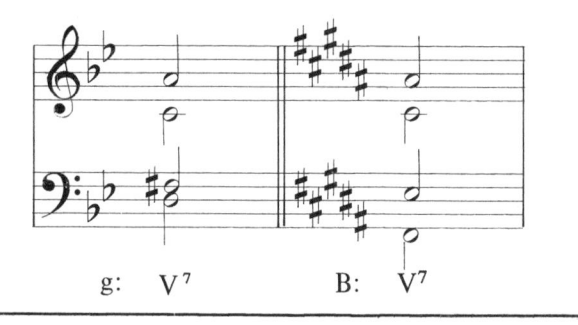

g: V^7 B: V^7

---

(1) up (by) step
(2) $\hat{1}$
(3) down (by) step
(4) $\hat{3}$

24

The third of V^7, $\hat{7}$, tends to resolve (1) _____ by _____ to (2) ___ (*scale degree*). The seventh of V^7, $\hat{4}$, tends to resolve (3) _____ by _____ to (4) ___ (*scale degree*).

Cb Gb Db (Ab) Eb Bb F

(C) G D A (E) B F♯ C♯

12

Fill in the missing members of this series of perfect 5ths:

__Cb__ __Gb__ __Db__ Ab __Eb__ __Bb__ __F__

C __G__ __D__ __A__ E __B__ __F♯__ __C♯__

x   y

(1) D major

13

Scale x is the (1) __D maj__ scale.

Scale y is the (2) __A maj__ scale.

(1) 5

(2) perf 5th

14

In frame 13 the arrow shows that scale y is built on note (1) __5th__ *(what number ?)* of scale x. The interval between the two tonics is a (2) __perf 5th__.

(1) ♮

(2) ♯

15

Examination shows that the D major scale contains the same notes as the A major scale with one exception: The D major scale contains G (1) __♮__ (b, ♮, or ♯), while the A major scale contains G (2) __♯__.

(1) A(♮)

(2) A♯

16

These two scales have tonics a perfect 5th apart. Again there is one point of difference in the scales' content: The E major scale contains (1) __A♮__ *(name of note)* while the B major scale contains (2) __A♯__.

17

When the tonics of two scales lie a perfect 5th apart, the higher scale will have one more sharp than the lower scale. The example above shows that the

(1) C♯ major

(2) F♯ major

(1) __C♯ maj__ scale has one more sharp than the (2) __F♯ maj__ scale.

7 (and) 4

14   A tone with a special melodic tendency is called a *tendency tone.* Scale degrees ___ and ___ in V⁷ are tendency tones.

(1) $\hat{7}$

(2) $\hat{4}$

15   Be careful not to confuse $\hat{7}$ with the seventh of V⁷. The third of V⁷ is (1) ___ *(scale degree).* The seventh of V⁷ is (2) ___ *(scale degree).*

F♯

16   The third of V⁷, $\hat{7}$, tends to move *up by step* to $\hat{1}$. In chord **x**, $\hat{7}$ is E. It resolves to F. In chord **y**, $\hat{7}$ is ___ *(note name).* Write its note of resolution. *(Do not write the whole chord.)*

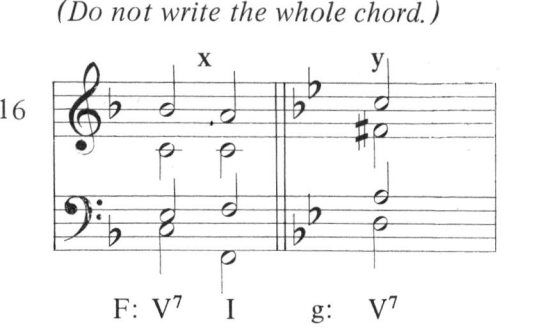

F: V⁷   I   g: V⁷

(1) 7

(2) up (by) step

(3) 1

17   The third of V⁷, scale degree (1) ___ , tends to resolve (2) _____ by _____ to scale degree (3) ___ .

(1) $\hat{7}$

(2) leading tone

18   The third of V⁷ is (1) ___ *(scale degree),* also called the (2) _____ _____ .

In each case, find the leading tone and write its note of resolution:

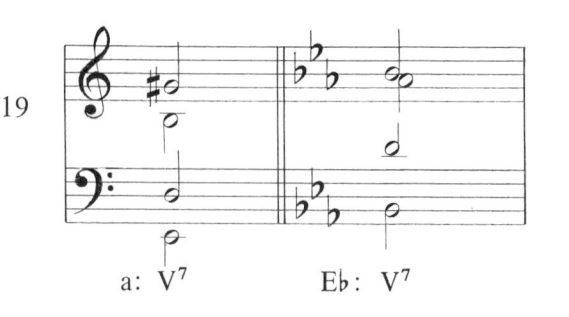

19

a: V⁷   E♭: V⁷

18

7

In counting the number of signs in a scale the same note name is not counted twice. In the C♯ major scale, C♯ is counted only once. The C♯ major scale has __7__ sharps.

19

one

The F♯ major scale has ___1___ more sharp(s) than the B major scale.

one more

20

When the tonics of two scales lie a perfect 5th apart, the higher scale will have ___1___ ___more___ sharp(s) than the lower scale.

perf 5th

21

C G D A E B F♯ C♯

Each member of this series is a ___perf___ ___5th___ higher than the next lower member.

one more
sharp

22

Suppose that the notes in the above series represent the tonics of scales. Each note is a perfect 5th higher than the note to its left and represents a scale having ___1___ ___more___ ___♯___ than the note to its left.

one more
sharp

23

(Refer to the series in frame 21 for the next two frames.)

The E major scale has ___1___ ___more___ ___♯___ than the A major scale.

two more
sharps

24

The E major scale has ___2___ ___more___ ___♯s___ than the D major scale.

more	7	The min 7th and dim 5th occur in V⁷, but not in V. These two intervals lend to V⁷ a quality of unrest. In other words, V⁷ sounds _____ (more *or* less) active than V.
dissonance	8	In addition to "unrest" and "activeness," other qualities sometimes attributed to V⁷ are "tension" and "instability." The technical term for intervals and chords judged to possess such qualities, is dissonance. For example, V⁷ is a _____.
(1) min 7th (2) dim 5th *(either order)*	9	The dissonant intervals in the V⁷ chord are the (1) _____ _____ and the (2) _____ _____.
(1) minor triad (2) consonances (*or* consonant)	10	The opposite of dissonance is consonance. All 7th chords, the diminished triad, and the augmented triad, are dissonances. Of the chord structures studied, only the major triad and the (1) _____ _____ are (2) _____.
(1) dissonance (2) consonance	11	When dissonance is followed by consonance, tension is relaxed. Technically speaking, resolution takes place. (1) _____ is resolved by motion to a (2) _____.
(1) dissonance (2) resolves (3) consonance	12	The regular resolution of V⁷ is to I. V⁷, a (1) _____, regularly (2) _____ to I, a (3) _____.
(1) B♯ (and) F♯ (2) 7 (and) 4	13	The dissonant intervals min 7th and dim 5th set up in the V⁷ a harmonic tendency toward I. They also set up special melodic tendencies in two of the chord members, the *third* and *seventh*. In the example the notes with special melodic tendencies are (1) ____ and ____ (*note names*). These notes are scale degrees (2) ____ and ____, respectively.

c♯: V⁷

(1) perf 5th
(2) one more

25 The tonics of these two scales lie a (1) *perf 5th* apart. The *lower* scale has (2) _one_ _more_ flat(s) than the *upper* scale.

(1) perf 5th
(2) one more
(The note Bb is counted only once in the Bb scale.)

26 The tonics in these scales are a(n) (1) *perf 5th* apart. The lower scale has (2) _one_ _more_ flat(s) than the upper scale.

(1) lower

(2) higher

27 When the tonics of two major scales in flats lie a perfect 5th apart, the (1) _lower_ (higher *or* lower) scale will have one more flat than the (2) _higher_ scale.

one more flat

28 Cb Gb Db Ab Eb Bb F C
Suppose that these notes represent the tonics of scales. Each note is a perfect 5th lower than the note to its right and represents a scale having _one_ _more_ _b_ than the note to its right.

one more
flat

29 *(Refer to the above series for the next two frames.)*
The Db major scale has _one_ _more_ _b_ than the Ab major scale.

three more
flats

30 The Gb major scale has _3_ _more_ _b_ than the Eb major scale.

(1) sharp
(2) flat

31 These relationships are easily remembered by associating *sharp* with *high,* and *flat* with *low.* Thus, if the tonics of two scales lie a perfect 5th apart, the higher scale has one more (1) _#_ , or the lower scale has one more (2) _b_ .

V⁷

The entry of C converts the V chord into a . . . . *(symbol)* chord.

2

G: V   I

---

z

When, in a V I connection, a leap of a 3rd is filled in by stepwise motion forming a 7th above the bass, the 7th is referred to as a *passing 7th*. Though it creates a momentary V⁷, the passing 7th is mainly a melodic, rather than harmonic, fact. Which of these examples contains a passing 7th? . . . . *(Hint: The passing 7th must pass [fill in a 3rd] and it must be a 7th above the bass.)*

3

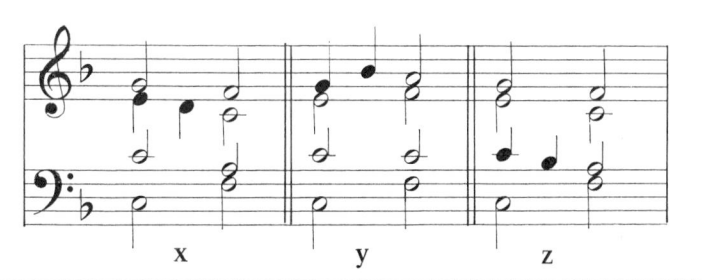

x   y   z

---

(1) melodic   (2) passing

4

Historically, the earliest uses of V⁷ are those arising from the passing 7th. This is typical of the way in which harmonic facts (such as V⁷) have their origin in (1) _____ facts (such as the (2) _____ 7th).

---

(1) I V I
(2) tonic

5

I V⁷ I is another version of the fundamental harmonic progression, (1) . . . . As with V, the function of V⁷ is to lead to a closing (2) _____ .

---

(1) min 7th
(2) dim 5th

6

The interval formed by the root and seventh of V⁷ is a(n) (1) _____ _____ . The interval formed by the third and seventh of V⁷ is a(n) (2) _____ _____ . *(See example if necessary.)*

a: V⁷

Since the C major scale has no sharps or flats, the G major scale has one sharp and the F major scale has one flat. Fill in the blanks in the following chart:

7 6 5 (4) 3 2 (1 no 1)

2 3 (4) 5 6 7

32

Cb	Gb	Db	Ab	Eb	Bb	F	C	G	D	A	E	B	F#	C#
7	*6*	*5*	4	*3*	*2*	1	no 1	*2*	*3*	4	*5*	*6*	*7*	

                flats   ♯'s   sharps
                             or
                             ♭'s

Cb Gb Db Ab Eb Bb F (C)

G D A E B F# C#

33

Fill in the blanks:

Cb	*Gb*	*Db*	*Ab*	*Eb*	*Bb*	*F*	C	*G*	*D*	*A*	*E*	*B*	*F#*	*C#*
7	6	5	4	3	2	1	no 1	1	2	3	4	5	6	7

                flats   ♯'s   sharps
                             or
                             ♭s

Set 13 / MAJOR KEY SIGNATURES

key

1

A piece in the k*ey* of F major ordinarily uses the F major scale.

Db major scale

2

A piece in the key of Db major ordinarily uses the *Db major scale*.

3

signature

Signs at the beginning of a piece (3 flats in this example) are called a key *signature*.

signs (or sharps)

4

Write the A major scale above. The key signature of A major (shown) has the same *sharps* as an A major scale.

signs

5

The scale and key signature of a given major key have the same *signs*.

Write V⁷'s as indicated:

D: complete V⁷

48

F♯: incomplete V⁷

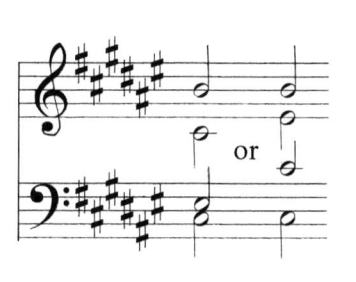

49

Set 31 / V⁷, RESOLUTION TO I

C

The V I connections in cases **x** and **y** are identical, except that in case **y** the tenor motion of a 3rd from D to B is filled in by ____ *(note name)*.

1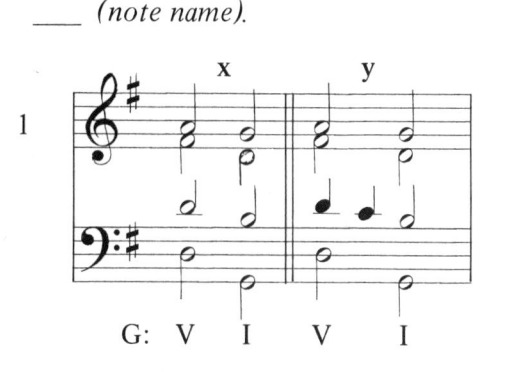

G: V   I   V   I

	6	C♭ G♭ D♭ A♭ E♭ B♭ F C G D A E B F♯ C♯ 7 6 5 4 3 2 1 no 1 2 3 4 5 6 7 flats ♯'s sharps or ♭'s This chart shows not only the signs for each major scale, but also the signs for each

(major key) signature

. maj. key. sig. (handwritten)

(Refer to the above chart for frames 7, 8, 9, and 10.)

no sharps
(or) flats

7 The key signature of C major is _no_ ___♯'s___
or ___♭'s___ .

---

4 sharps

8 The key signature of E major is __4__ __♯'s__ .

---

(1) flat   (2) sharp

(3) flat

(4) sharp

9 Keys having one or more sharps in the signature are called "sharp keys." Keys having one or more flats in the signature are called "flat keys." D♭ major is a (1) ___♭___ key. F♯ major is a (2) ___♯___ key. F major is a (3) ___♭___ key. A major is a (4) ___♯___ key.

F

10 The only "flat" major key without "flat" in its name (as in B♭, E♭, etc.) is __F__ major.

---

(1) sharp
(2) flat
(3) flat
(4) sharp

11 Tell whether each key is a "sharp" key or a "flat" key:
C♯ major is a (1) ___♯___ key.
A♭ major is a (2) ___♭___ key.
F major is a (3) ___♭___ key.
D major is a (4) ___♯___ key.

---

(1) F

(2) sharp

12 With the exception of C major and (1) __F__ major, all major keys without "flat" or "sharp" in their names are (2) ___♯___ keys.

---

(1) 2

(2) 2 sharps

13 Since D major is a *sharp* key its signature can be found by going *up* the series of fifths from C. D lies (1) __2__ *(how many?)* perfect fifths above C. Therefore, the signature of D major is (2) __2__ __♯'s__ .

Label the spacing of each chord as correct or incorrect. If the spacing is incorrect, explain why.

43

Correct

. . . .

Incorrect. There is more than an octave between AT.

44

. . . .

Incorrect. There is more than an octave between AT.

45

. . . .

Using the given SB's, write V⁷'s as indicated. (For some problems there will be more than one correct answer.)

B♭: complete V⁷

46

only one correct answer

g♯: incomplete V⁷

47

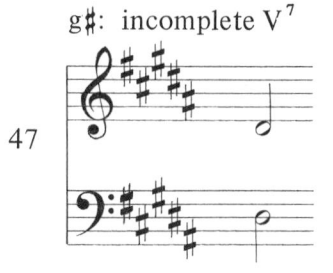

(1) flat		Eb major is a (1) _____ key. Therefore
(2) down		its signature is found by going (2) _down_
	14	the series of 5ths from C. The signature of
(3) 3 flats		Eb major is (3)_____ .

		Give the signatures of the following keys:
5 sharps	15	B major _____ .
1 flat	16	F major _____
1 sharp	17	G major _____ .
6 flats	18	Gb major _____ .
2 flats	19	Bb major _____ .

	20	Major key signatures can also be found by scale
(1) 6		construction. The F# major scale, containing (1) _6_
		sharps, shows that the signature of F# major is
(2) 6		(2) _6_ sharps.

		Write the Cb major scale:
	21	
		This shows that the signature of Cb major
7 flats		is _____ .

		Find the signatures of the following keys, using
		either the series of 5ths or scale construction:
	22	
(1) 3 sharps		(1) A major: _____
(2) 7 sharps		(2) C# major: _____

		To find the major key when the signature is known,
		count up (for sharps) or down (for flats) from C in
	23	the series of 5ths. What major key has a signature
E *(4 perf 5th above C)*		of 4 sharps? _E_

third, fifth, (and) seventh	38	In the complete V⁷ all four members are present, and the root is in the bass. Which chord members are therefore in the SAT? _____, _____, and _____.

(1) fifth (2) root	39	In the incomplete V⁷ the (1) _____ is omitted and the (2) _____ doubled.

root, third, (and) seventh	40	Which members of the incomplete V⁷ are in the SAT? _____, _____, and _____.

(1) incomplete V⁷ (2) complete V⁷ (3) incomplete V⁷ (4) complete V⁷	41	Label each of the following chords incomplete V⁷ or complete V⁷:  (1) . . . . (2) . . . . (3) . . . . . . (4) . . . .

SA	42	The notes in a complete or incomplete V⁷ chord for four voices may be written close together or with gaps. The general spacing rules that are used for V⁷ and other 7th chords and for triads in inversion (to be covered in the second volume of this series) are: 1. Voices must stay within their respective ranges. 2. There may be no more than an octave between SA and no more than an octave between AT. The spacing below is incorrect because there is more than an octave between . . . . *(voices).* 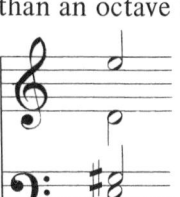

Db	24	What major key has a signature of 5 flats? _Db_
B	25	5 sharps is the signature of _B_ major.
4 flats	26	What is the signature of Ab major? _4 b's_
D	27	What major key has a signature of 2 sharps? _D_

Set 14 / THE NOTATION OF KEY SIGNATURES

1

x

The signs in a key signature are always written in the same order. The key signature of E major is written as in _x_ (x *or* y).

G D A E B F# C#

G#

2 These are the key signatures of 1 through 7 sharps, and the major key corresponding to each signature. In all the signatures the first sharp is F#. In those having two or more sharps, the second sharp is C#. In those having three or more sharps, the third sharp is _G#_.

F#

3 The first sharp is _F#_.

C#

4 In the sharp signatures, each sharp lies a 5th higher (or a 4th lower) than the preceding sharp. Since the first sharp is F#, the second sharp is _C#_.

C major (and) C minor

33

V⁷ is, of course, built on $\hat{5}$. This V⁷ chord is built on G. G is $\hat{5}$, and this chord is V⁷, in the keys of

____ _____ and ____ _____.

E major (and) E minor.

34

This chord is V⁷ in ____ _____ and ____ _____
(In what keys is B $\hat{5}$?)

A major (and) A minor

35

Construct a major-minor 7th chord on the root E. This chord is V⁷ in ____ _____ and ____ _____.

C♯ major (and) C♯ minor

36

This note is the third of a major-minor 7th chord. Write the complete chord in root position:

This chord is V⁷ in ____ _____ and ____ _____

37

In four-part writing the fifth of V⁷ is sometimes omitted, in which case the root is doubled. This results in an *incomplete V⁷*, the arrangement with all four members present being the *complete V⁷*. Label each of the following chords *complete V⁷, incomplete V⁷,* or *triad:*

(1) incomplete V⁷
(2) triad
(3) incomplete V⁷
(4) complete V⁷

(1) . . . . (2) . . . . (3) . . . . . . (4) . . . .

5 The order of sharps in the key signatures is a series of ascending 5ths. Complete this table:

(F♯ C♯) G♯ D♯ A♯ E♯ B♯

1st♯	2nd♯	3rd♯	4th♯	5th♯	6th♯	7th♯
F♯	C♯	*G♯*	*D♯*	*A♯*	*E♯*	*B♯*

---

(1) C

(2) G

(3) F♯

6 The key with no sharps or flats is (1) _C_ major.

The key with one sharp is (2) _G_ major.

The first sharp is (3) _F♯_.

7

x   y   z

In "signature" **x** the order of sharps is correct (F♯, C♯, G♯). The signature looks strange because the first sharp should be written an octave higher, as in signature **y**. In signature **z** the last sharp

an octave lower

should be written .. *an octave lower*

---

x   y

8 Signature **x** has a regular down-up pattern, but requires ledger lines. Signature **y** has a slightly irregular pattern, but avoids ledger lines. Which is correct? _y_

y

---

9 Copy signature **y** in the space provided above.

Copy the signature and add three more sharps making a total of 7 sharps:

10

C♯

11 7 sharps is the signature of _C♯_ major.

V	21	There are exactly two diatonic *triads* that have the same structure in both major and minor keys. One is VII. The other is ___.
major	22	V is a _____ triad in both major and minor keys.
major-minor	23	V⁷ has the same structure in both major and minor keys. All dominant 7th chords are _____-_____ *(structural type)* 7th chords.
(1) major-minor (*or* dominant) (2) F A C E♭	24	All V⁷'s are (1) . . . . 7th chords. To spell V⁷ in a given key, find $\hat{5}$ and spell a major-minor 7th chord. Spell B♭: V⁷ ___ ___ ___ ___.
A C♯ E G	25	Spell the following: d: V⁷ ___ ___ ___ ___
D♭ F A♭ C♭	26	G♭: V⁷ ___ ___ ___ ___
B D♯ F♯ A	27	e: V⁷ ___ ___ ___ ___
G♯ B♯ D♯ F♯	28	C♯: V⁷ ___ ___ ___ ___

Write the indicated V⁷'s with key signature:

29

D♭ : V⁷

30

g: V⁷

31

f♯ : V⁷

D major (and) D minor	32	The note G is $\hat{5}$ in the keys of C major and C minor. The note A is the dominant in the keys of ___ _____ and ___ _____ .

12 Write the signature of F♯ major:

F   B♭   E♭   A♭   D♭   G♭   C♭

(1) E♭

(2) A♭

13 These are the key signatures of 1 through 7 flats with the corresponding major key for each. Examination shows that the first flat is B♭, the second flat is (1) _E♭_ and the third flat is (2) _A♭_ .

D♭

14 In the flat signatures, each flat lies a 5th lower (or a 4th higher) than the preceding flat. The third flat is A♭. The fourth flat is _D♭_ .

15 The order of flats in the key signatures is a series of *descending* fifths. Complete this table:

B♭ E♭ (A♭ D♭) G♭ C♭ F♭

1st♭	2nd♭	3rd♭	4th♭	5th♭	6th♭	7th♭
B♭	E♭	A♭	D♭	G♭	C♭	F♭

(1) F

(2) B♭

16 The key with one flat is (1) _F_ major. The first flat is (2) _B♭_ .

17 Copy the given signature in the extra space:

are

In the flat signatures, flats ...*are*.... (are *or* are not) placed on the staff in a regular up-down pattern.

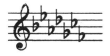

18 Write the signature of C♭ major:

(1) diatonic 7th chords (2) B♭ major	14	Diatonic 7th chords, like diatonic triads, may be constructed on all scale degrees. Shown are the seven (1) _____ _____ _____ in the key of (2) ___ _____ .

(1) harmonic minor (2) D minor	15	In the minor keys, diatonic 7th chords, like diatonic triads, are derived from the (1) . . . . scale. Shown are diatonic 7th chords in the key of (2) ___ _____ .

	16	Symbols for the diatonic 7th chords in root position are made by adding the Arabic numeral 7 to the appropriate Roman numeral, as for chord **x**. Write the appropriate symbol for chord **y**:

V⁷

A: V⁷   F: ___

V⁷	17	The 7th chord constructed on the dominant has the symbol . . . . It is also referred to as the dominant 7th chord.
dominant 7th	18	V⁷ symbolizes the . . . . chord.

f♯: (1)___

(1) V⁷ (2) major-minor	19	Write the appropriate chord symbol. The structural type of this 7th chord is (2) _____-_____ .

(1) $\hat{7}$ (2) $\hat{2}$ (3) $\hat{4}$	20	Be careful not to confuse $\hat{7}$ and the seventh of a chord. The root of V⁷ is $\hat{5}$. The third of V⁷ is (1) ___ *(scale degree)*. The fifth of V⁷ is (2) ___ . The seventh of V⁷ is (3) ___ .

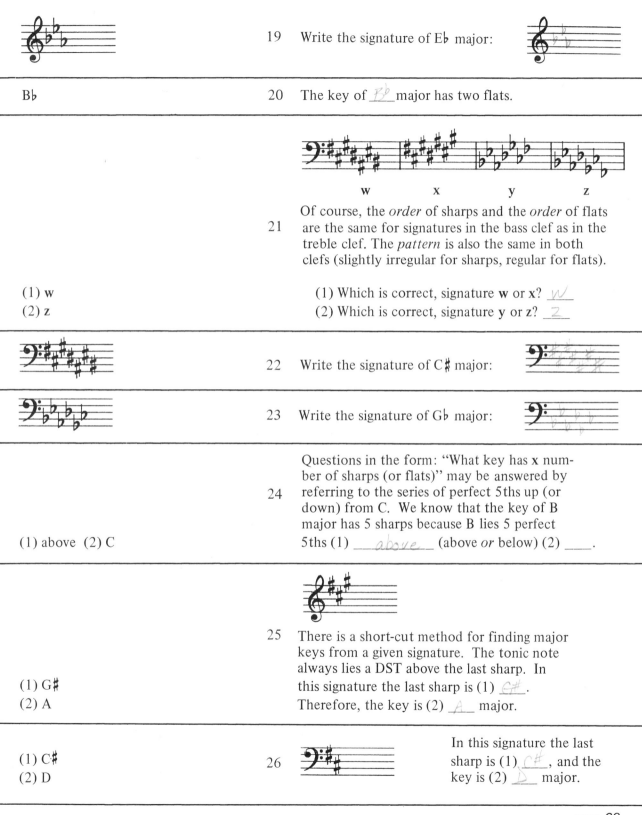

19   Write the signature of E♭ major:

B♭

20   The key of _B♭_ major has two flats.

w   x   y   z

21   Of course, the *order* of sharps and the *order* of flats are the same for signatures in the bass clef as in the treble clef. The *pattern* is also the same in both clefs (slightly irregular for sharps, regular for flats).

(1) w
(2) z

(1) Which is correct, signature **w** or **x**? _w_
(2) Which is correct, signature **y** or **z**? _z_

22   Write the signature of C♯ major:

23   Write the signature of G♭ major:

24   Questions in the form: "What key has **x** number of sharps (or flats)" may be answered by referring to the series of perfect 5ths up (or down) from C. We know that the key of B major has 5 sharps because B lies 5 perfect 5ths (1) _above_ (above *or* below) (2) ____.

(1) above (2) C

25   There is a short-cut method for finding major keys from a given signature. The tonic note always lies a DST above the last sharp. In this signature the last sharp is (1) _G♯_. Therefore, the key is (2) _A_ major.

(1) G♯
(2) A

(1) C♯
(2) D

26   In this signature the last sharp is (1) _C♯_, and the key is (2) _D_ major.

---

(1) minor

(2) minor

9

Chord **x** consists of a major triad capped by a minor 7th. Chord **y** consists of a (1) _____ triad capped by a (2) _____ 7th.

major
triad — minor 7th

x

y

10

minor-minor

Just as there are different structural types of triads, there are different structural types of 7th chords. There are two parts to the name used in describing the structural type of a 7th chord. The first part of the name refers to the type of triad formed by the 7th chord's root, third, and fifth; and the second part refers to the kind of 7th formed by the root and seventh of the chord. Chord **x** in the previous frame is a major-minor 7th chord. Chord **y** is a _____-_____ 7th chord.

---

major-minor

11

The major-minor 7th chord is the most important structural type of 7th chord. The chord shown in this frame is a _____-_____ 7th chord. (Other structural types of 7th chords will be covered in the second volume of this series.)

---

(1) triad

(2) root, third, (and) fifth

(3) 7th (*or* interval)

(4) root (and) seventh

12

In the term *major-minor 7th chord, major* refers to the type of (1) _____ formed by the (2) _____, _____, and _____ .

Minor refers to the kind of (3) _____ formed by the (4) _____ and _____ .

---

diatonic 7th chords

13

Triads derived from a particular scale are diatonic triads. Similarly, 7th chords derived from a particular scale are _____ _____ _____ .

F♯	27	This is the signature of F♯ major.

A different short-cut is used for the flat signatures. The tonic is the same as the next-to-the-last flat. The next-to-the-last flat of signature **x** is E♭. Therefore, the key is E♭ major. The next-to-the-last flat of signature **y** is (1) A♭. Therefore, the key is (2) A♭ major.

(1) A♭
(2) A♭

28

x   y

---

(1) higher (*or* upper)
(2) lower
(3) lower
(4) higher (*or* upper)

F

29 — For a signature of only one flat the short-cut does not work, but is hardly necessary. One flat is the signature of F major.

30 — If the tonics of two scales are a perfect 5th apart, the (1) higher scale has one more sharp than the (2) lower scale, or the (3) lower scale has one more flat than the (4) higher.

---

(1) scale (2) key signature
  (either order)

31

The (1) scale and the (2) key signature of a given major key have the same signs.

---

(1) F♯
(2) B♭

32

The first sharp is (1) F♯.
The first flat is (2) B♭.

---

(1) ascending (*or* upward)
(2) descending (*or* downward)

33

The order of sharps in a key signature is a series of (1) ascending 5ths. The order of flats is a series of (2) descending 5ths.

E

34

Name the major key corresponding to the following signature:

E

---

(1) 3rd

(2) 5th   (3) 7th

4   A triad in root position has notes which lie a 3rd and a 5th above the root. A four-note chord in root position has notes which lie a (1) ___third___, a (2) ___fifth___, and a (3) ___seventh___ above the root.

---

(1) triad

(2) 7th chord

5   Four-note chords built in 3rds, as a class, are named for the interval that distinguishes them from triads. They are called *7th chords*.

Chord **x** is a (1) . . .*triad*. . . .

Chord **y** is a (2) . . . .*7th chord*.

---

(1) 7th chord

(2) E♭

6   This is a (1) .*7ᵗʰ chord*. . whose root is (2) __E♭__ *(pitch)*.

---

(1) fifth   (2) seventh

7   7th chord members, like triad members, are named by their intervals above the root. In the 7th chord shown, G is the root, B♭ is the third, D is the (1) ___5ᵗʰ___, and F is the (2) ___7ᵗʰ___.

---

seventh

8   Chord **y** consists of triad **x** plus an added note. The added note is the ___7ᵗʰ___ *(which chord member?)* of chord **y**.

Name the major key corresponding to the
following signatures:

Eb

35 *E♭*

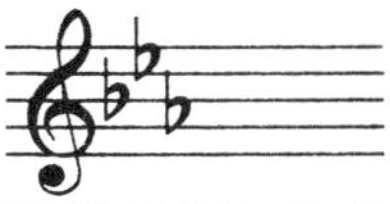

Bb

36 *B♭*

F♯

37 *F♯*

Db

38 *D♭*

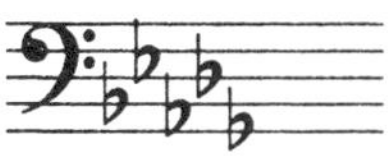

Write the key signatures:

39 A major:

40 C♭ major:

41 A♭ major:

42 B major:

43 G major:

Harmonize this melody using I and V.
(Follow the procedure given in previous frames.)

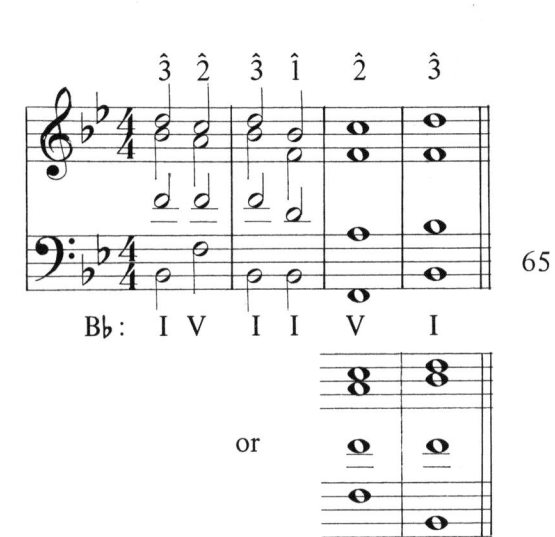

B♭: I V I I V I

or

65

close

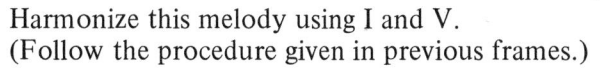

B♭: _ _ _ _

Set 30 / V⁷, CONSTRUCTION

triad	1 A three-note chord built in 3rds is a ___triad___.

---

three

2 Chord **x**, a triad, contains two 3rds (F–A and A–C). Chord **y**, a four-note chord, contains __3__ 3rds.

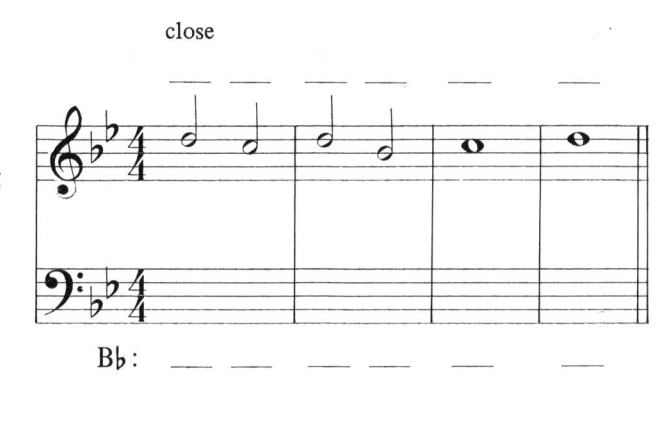

x   y

---

3 A chord of four notes built in 3rds may be constructed by superimposing another 3rd on the two existing 3rds of a triad. Chord **x** is constructed from triad **w** in this way. Copy triad **y** at **z**. Then superimpose another 3rd, making a four-note chord built in 3rds. *(no ♯'s or ♭'s.)*

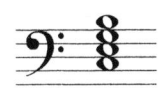

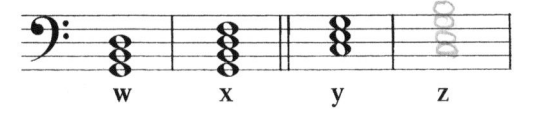

w   x   y   z

---

(1) 3–4		**1**
(2) 7–8 (3) whole tones		

1 The major scale has DST's at (1) 3-4 and (2) 7-8 and (3) whole tones. everywhere else.

2 1 2 3 4 5

2–3

Shown are the first 5 notes of the C *minor* scale. There is a DST at 2-3 and whole tones everywhere else.

3 1 2 3 4 5   1 2 3 4 5
         major   *minor*

3

The first 5 notes of the C major and C minor scales are identical, except for note 3 .

2–3

The minor scale has a DST at 2-3. (1–2 *or* 2–3

4 *or* 3–4 *or* 4–5)

5 Mark the location of the DST with a "½", and write the first five notes of the E minor scale:

  1   2   3   4   5

  1   2   3   4   5

6 Write the first 5 notes of the F minor scale:

  1   2   3   4   5

  1   2   3   4   5

1 (to note) 5

7 The minor scale has several forms. These differ in structure from note 5 to note 8 only. All forms of the minor scale have the same structure from note 1 to note 5 .

Harmonize this melody using I and V. Follow the above procedure.

open

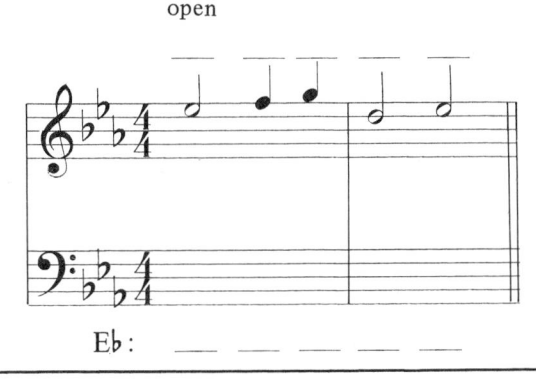

62

Eb: I V I V I

Eb: __ __ __ __ __

(1) chord

(2) 5th or more

In this example the soprano changes, but the (1) _____ remains the same. In filling in the AT it is important to avoid leaps of a (2) .... and to stay within the vocal ranges. Complete the connection.

close

63

Ab: I   I

or f#: I I   V   I

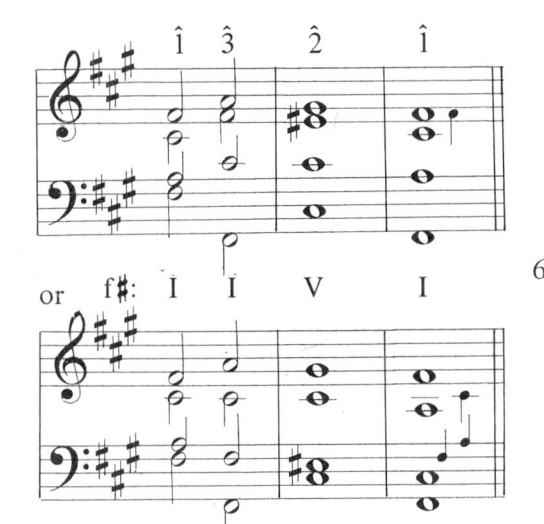

Complete this melody harmonization. Write the soprano scale degrees; write the Roman numerals; write the first chord; complete the AT connections.

64

f#: __ __ __ __

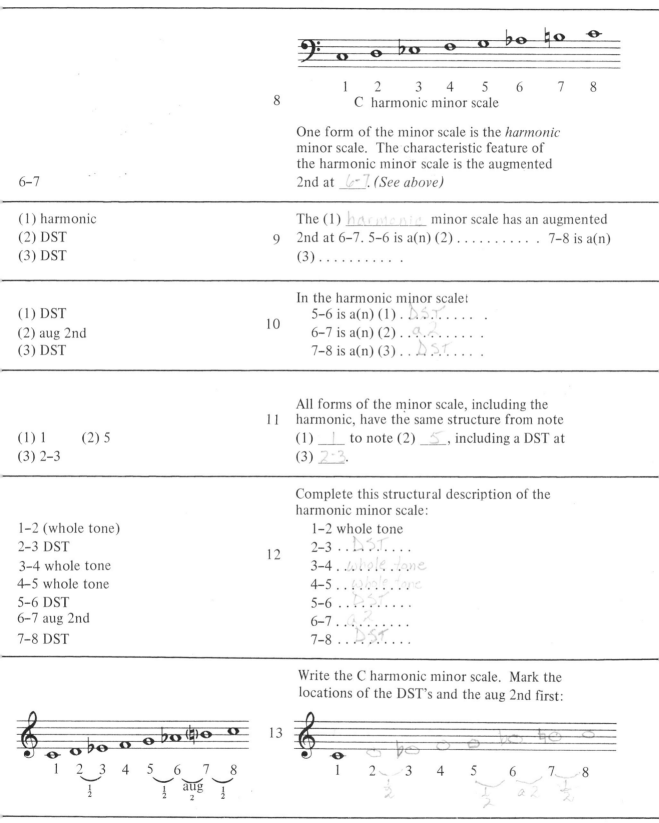

8

C harmonic minor scale

1 2 3 4 5 6 7 8

One form of the minor scale is the *harmonic* minor scale. The characteristic feature of the harmonic minor scale is the augmented 2nd at __6-7__. *(See above)*

6–7

---

(1) harmonic
(2) DST
(3) DST

9

The (1) __harmonic__ minor scale has an augmented 2nd at 6–7. 5–6 is a(n) (2) . . . . 7–8 is a(n) (3) . . . .

---

(1) DST
(2) aug 2nd
(3) DST

10

In the harmonic minor scale
5–6 is a(n) (1) . __DST__ . . . . .
6–7 is a(n) (2) . . __a2__ . . . . .
7–8 is a(n) (3) . . __DST__ . . . .

---

(1) 1 (2) 5
(3) 2–3

11

All forms of the minor scale, including the harmonic, have the same structure from note (1) __1__ to note (2) __5__, including a DST at (3) __2-3__.

1–2 (whole tone)
2–3 DST
3–4 whole tone
4–5 whole tone
5–6 DST
6–7 aug 2nd
7–8 DST

12

Complete this structural description of the harmonic minor scale:
1–2 whole tone
2–3 . . __DST__ . . . .
3–4 . __whole tone__
4–5 . . __whole tone__
5–6 . . . __DST__ . .
6–7 . . __a2__ . . . . .
7–8 . . . __DST__ . . .

Write the C harmonic minor scale. Mark the locations of the DST's and the aug 2nd first:

13

1 2 3 4 5 6 7 8
½ ½ aug 2 ½

1 2 3 4 5 6 7 8

Set 29 / I and V, harmonizing a given melody

This melody is to be harmonized with I and V.
First write the soprano scale degrees; then write
the appropriate Roman numeral for each chord
of the harmonization. *(Do not write the chords yet.)*

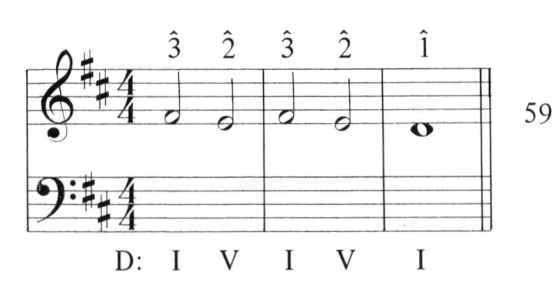

59

D: I   V   I   V   I

D: __ __ __ __ __

Continuing with the problem from the previous
frame, complete the first chord, write the bass line,
write the alto and tenor voices. *(Remember to
think of this as a chain of individual connections.)*

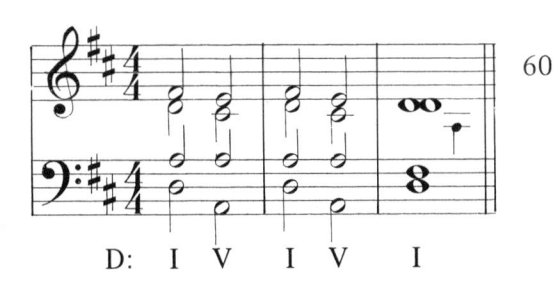

60

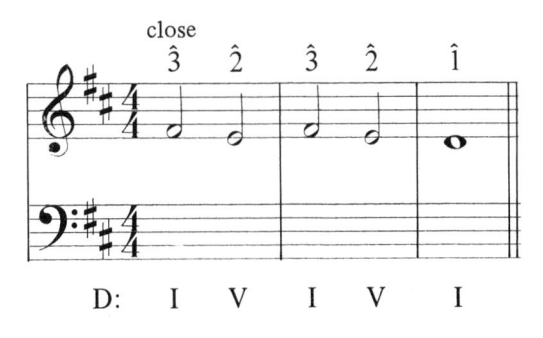

D: I   V   I   V   I

D: I   V   I   V   I

Harmonize this melody using I and V. Proceed
in this order: Write the soprano scale degrees;
write the Roman numerals; complete the first
chord; write the bass line; connect the AT of each
pair of chords:

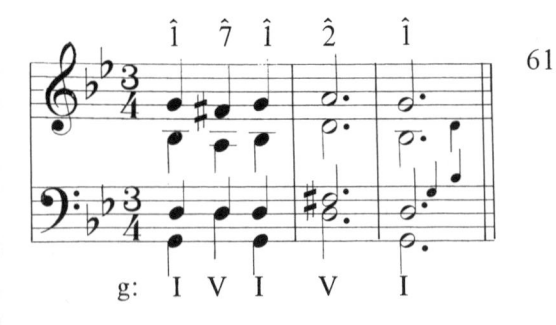

61

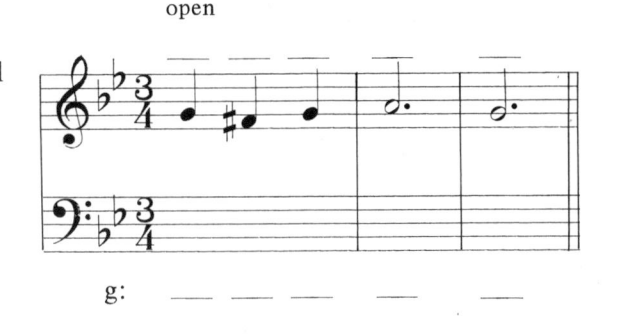

g: I   V   I   V   I

g: __ __ __ __ __

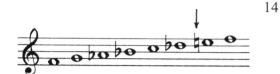

Because of the unusual nature of the aug 2nd, a sign should always be placed before note 7 in the harmonic minor scale. This is true even when the sign is a natural and technically unnecessary. Insert this sign in the F harmonic minor scale:

14

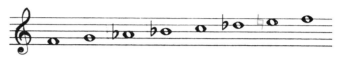

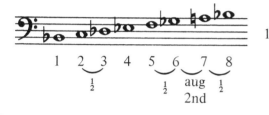

Write the B♭ harmonic minor scale. *(The locations of the DST's and aug 2nd may be marked first as a guide.)*

15

1   2   3   4   5   6   7   8

Certain harmonic minor scales contain both ♯ and ♭ signs. Write the D harmonic minor scale. *(Note numbers, etc., may be written first.)*

16

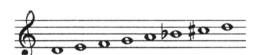

Write the G harmonic minor scale:

17

Write the A harmonic minor scale:

18

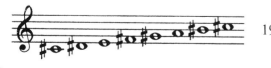

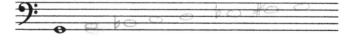

Write the C♯ harmonic minor scale:

19

Follow instructions in frame 53:

open

55

F: I   V   I

---

close

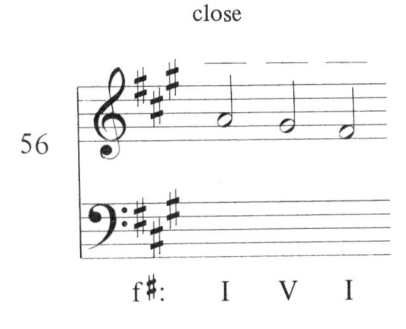

56

f♯:   I   V   I

---

close

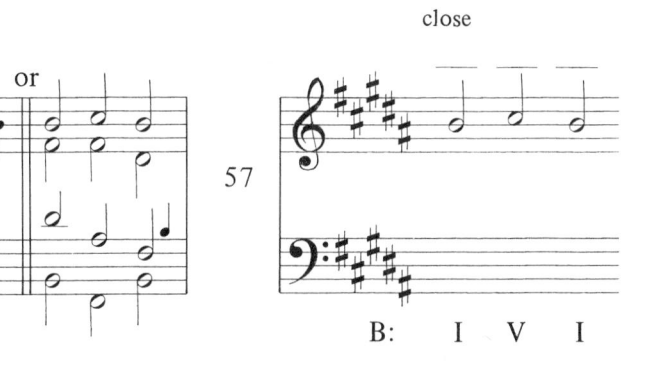

57

B: I   V   I

---

(1) 1̂ (and)
   3̂

(2) 2̂ (and) 7̂

58

A simple melody may be harmonized with I and V in root position. The soprano scale degrees which most often occur with I are (1) ____ and ____. The soprano scale degrees which most often occur with V are (2) ____ and ____.

ascending   *descending*

20

C melodic minor scales

Two other forms of the minor scale are the
melodic minor ascending, and the *melodic
minor* descending.

descending

21

As the examples in frame 20 show, the melodic
minor scales consist entirely of whole tones and
(1) . . . . DST's . . . Unlike the harmonic minor
scale, they contain no (2) . . . aug. 2nds . . .

(1) DST's
(2) aug 2nd(s)

22

All minor scales have the same structure from
note (1) __1__ to note (2) __5__ , including a DST
at (3) 2-3.

(1) 1 (2) 5
(3) 2-3

---

1 2 3 4 5 6 7 8   8 7 6 5 4 3 2 1

23

The melodic minor ascending has DST's at 2-3
and (1) 7-8. The melodic minor descending
has DST's at 2-3 and (2) 5-6.

(1) 7-8
(2) 5-6

24

The location of the DST's in the melodic
minor scales causes notes 6 and 7 to be higher
in the melodic minor (1) ascending than in the
melodic minor (2) descending.

(1) ascending
(2) descending

25

The melodic minor ascending has DST's at
2-3 and 7-8.

7-8

26

The melodic minor descending has DST's at
2-3 and 5-6.

5-6

27

The melodic minor scales, like the major
scales, consist entirely of DST's and whole tones

whole tones

See the space below for a comment on the bass line in this answer and other similar cases.

Harmonize the following soprano patterns with I V I. First, mark the soprano scale degrees and determine the types of AT connections. Then, complete the first chord, write the bass line, and complete the AT connections.

53

c♯: I V I

The bass may form a unison with the tenor. However, no bass note should be *higher than* the tenor note in the same chord. Nor should a bass note be higher than the tenor note in either of the surrounding chords. In the example below, the final bass note C♯ is higher than the preceding tenor note; this voice-leading fault, known as an *overlap*, could be corrected by writing the final bass note an octave lower.

In many cases, the solution to an exercise will have two or more correct bass lines, which differ only in the octave placement of certain notes. For the sake of simplicity, only one correct bass line will be shown for the solutions in this book. You should consider your bass line correct if it differs from the given solution only in the octave placement of notes, and if it avoids overlap of tenor and bass as described above (and, of course, if it remains within the bass range). Sometimes, in order to avoid overlap, you may need to change the octave placement of one or more bass notes that you have written after completing the upper notes of an exercise.

c♯: I V I

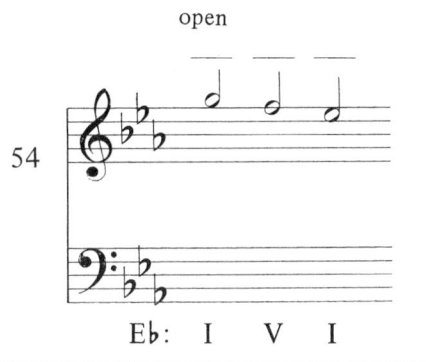

54

E♭: I V I

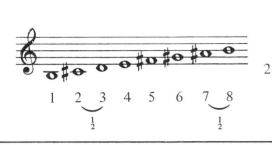

Write the B melodic minor ascending scale.
Mark the DST locations first.

28

1   2   3   4   5   6   7   8

1 2 3   4   5   6   7   8

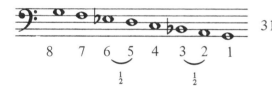

Write the A♭ melodic minor ascending scale:

29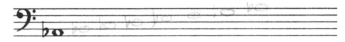

2-3 (and) 5-6

30 The melodic minor descending has DST's at
___ and ___.

Write the G melodic minor descending scale.
Mark the DST locations first.

31

8   7   6 5   4   3 2   1

8   7   6 5   4   3   2   1

Write the E♭ melodic minor descending scale:

32

2-3

33 All forms of the minor scale have a DST at ___.

3

34 The harmonic minor scale has ___ (how many?)
DST locations.

---

(1) 2-3
(2) 5-6
(3) 7-8
(4) aug 2nd
(5) 6-7

35 The harmonic minor scale has DST's at (1) ___,
(2) ___, and (3) ___, a(n) (4) ___ ___
at (5) ___, and whole tones everywhere else.

I V I

48   . . . . is the fundamental harmonic progression.

Consider the following I V I progressions to
be chains of individual connections. Connect
I V; then connect V I. For each pair of connections, determine from the soprano pattern
if an AT common tone-stepwise connection is
possible. Then, using the indicated spacing for
the first chord, complete the connections.

49

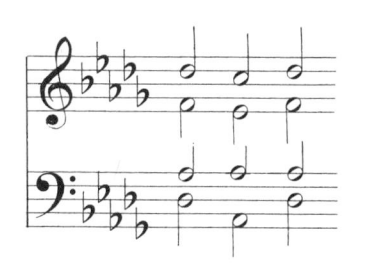

Db: I   V   I

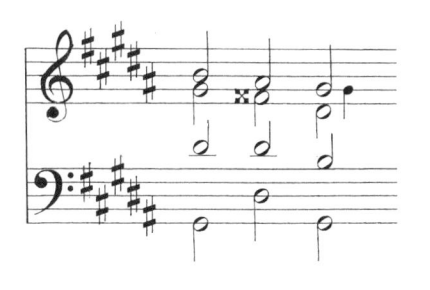

50

g♯:   I   V   I

Listed below are the three-note soprano patterns
most commonly found with I V I. Circle the
pairs of scale degrees which allow AT common
tone-stepwise connections:

51

$\hat{1}$ ⓐ $\hat{1}$ $\hat{3}$ ⓑ $\hat{3}$
$\hat{1}$ $\hat{2}$ $\hat{1}$ $\hat{3}$ ⓒ $\hat{1}$
$\hat{1}$ ⓓ $\hat{3}$ $\hat{3}$ ⓔ $\hat{1}$

$\hat{1}$ $\hat{7}$ $\hat{1}$ $\hat{3}$ $\hat{2}$ $\hat{3}$
$\hat{1}$ $\hat{2}$ $\hat{1}$ $\hat{3}$ $\hat{7}$ $\hat{1}$
$\hat{1}$ $\hat{2}$ $\hat{3}$ $\hat{3}$ $\hat{2}$ $\hat{1}$

$\hat{1}$ $\hat{2}$
(and) $\hat{2}$ $\hat{1}$

52   In the soprano patterns most commonly found
in I V I, all pairs of scale degrees allow AT
common tone-stepwise connections except ___ ___
and ___ ___.

(1) 2–3 (and) 7–8 (2) 2–3 (and) 5–6	36	The melodic minor ascending scale has DST's at (1) _2-3_ and _7-8_. The melodic minor descending scale has DST's at (2) _2-3_ and _5-6_.
F♯ G♯ A B C♯ D E♯ F♯	37	Spell the F♯ harmonic minor scale: F♯ _G♯_ _A_ _B_ _C♯_ _D_ _E♯_ F♯
D♯ E♯ F♯ G♯ A♯ B♯ C✕ D♯	38	Spell the D♯ melodic minor ascending scale: D♯ _E♯_ _F♯_ _G♯_ _A♯_ _B♯_ _C✕_ D♯
F E♭ D♭ C B♭ A♭ G F	39	Spell the F melodic minor descending scale: F _E♭_ _D♭_ _C_ _B♭_ _A♭_ _G_ F

Certain minor scales require one or two double sharps. Write the indicated scales:

40

G♯ harmonic minor

41

A♯ melodic minor ascending

Set 16 / MINOR KEY SIGNATURES (1)

signs (*or* sharps)	1	The scale of D major and the key signature of D major have the same _#'s /signs_.
D major	2	Another way of stating the same thing is: The key signature of D major corresponds to the _D_ _major_ scale.
melodic minor descending	3	The minor key signatures correspond to the *melodic minor descending* scale. Thus, the key signature of B minor contains the same signs as the B _melodic_ _minor_ _descending_ scale.

Follow instructions for frame 43.

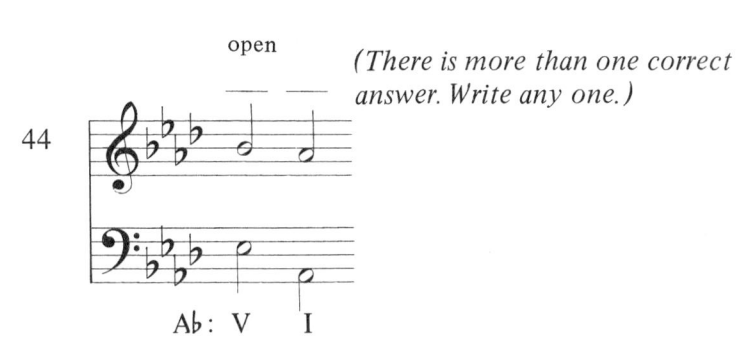

open

(There is more than one correct answer. Write any one.)

44

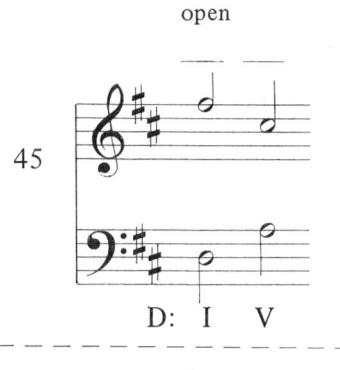

A♭: V   I

open

(Be sure to check for correct doubling in the V chord.)

45

D: I   V

close

46

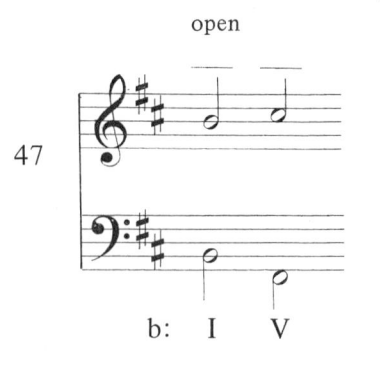

F: V   I

open

47

b: I   V

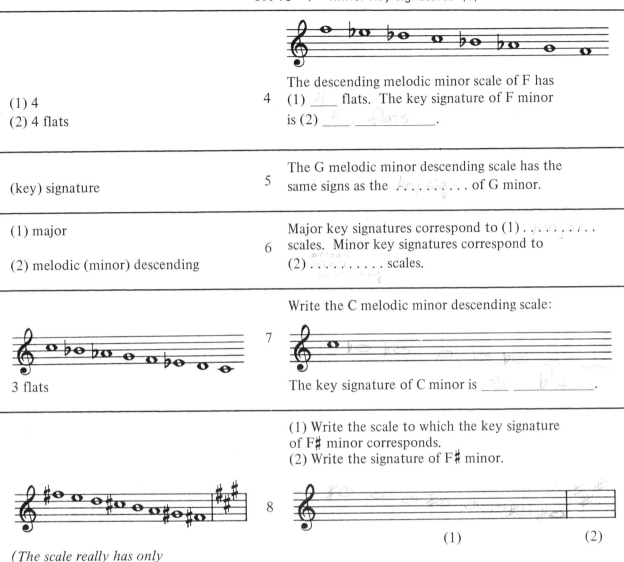

(1) 4

(2) 4 flats

4 The descending melodic minor scale of F has
(1) ___ flats. The key signature of F minor
is (2) _____ .

(key) signature

5 The G melodic minor descending scale has the
same signs as the _____ of G minor.

(1) major

(2) melodic (minor) descending

6 Major key signatures correspond to (1) ....
scales. Minor key signatures correspond to
(2) .... scales.

3 flats

7 Write the C melodic minor descending scale:

The key signature of C minor is _____ .

8 (1) Write the scale to which the key signature
of F♯ minor corresponds.
(2) Write the signature of F♯ minor.

(1)   (2)

*(The scale really has only
3 sharps, not 4; hence the signature
is 3 sharps.)*

9 E♭ major   C melodic minor
                       descending

The E♭ major scale and the C melodic minor
descending scale both contain E♭, A♭, and B♭,
other notes being ♮. These two scales have the
same _____ .

signs (*or* flats)

(1) 1̂ (or) 3̂ (2) 2̂ (or) 7̂	39	This and the following three frames contain important points for review. I V I is the fundamental harmonic progression. The most common soprano lines in I V I are those using (1) ___ or ___ with I and (2) ___ or ___ with V.
(1) 1̂ 7̂, 3̂ 2̂, 3̂ 7̂ (2) 7̂ 1̂, 2̂ 3̂	40	Many problems in chord connection involve a given soprano pattern which is to be harmonized. Some soprano patterns permit common tone-stepwise connections in the AT, and some do not. AT common tone-stepwise connections are found with the following soprano patterns: In I V, (1) ___ ___, ___ ___, ___ ___. In V I, (2) ___ ___, ___ ___.
(1) 1̂ 2̂ (2) 2̂ 1̂ (3) a 5th or more (4) ranges	41	Soprano patterns which do not allow common tone-stepwise connections are: In I V, (1) ___ ___. In V I, (2) ___ ___. In writing these connections, it is important to avoid AT leaps of (3) . . . ., to keep voices within their respective (4) _____, and to use correct spacing.
(1) root (2) third (3) fifth (4) root	42	Often in a V I connection with soprano 2̂ 1̂, the leading tone (in the alto or tenor) resolves to 1̂, resulting in a I chord with tripled (1) _____ *(chord member)*, one (2) _____ , and no (3) _____ . In all other I V and V I connections both triads have the usual doubling for root position chords: the (4) _____ is doubled.
	43	The following frames contain I V and V I connections. Follow this procedure: 1. Label soprano scale degrees. 2. Write the first chord in the indicated spacing. 3. Complete the connection. Use an AT common tone-stepwise connection if possible.

signature

10 Since the scales of E♭ major and C melodic minor descending have the same signs, the two keys of E♭ and C minor have the same key ___*sig.*___ .

Write the indicated scales:

G major   E melodic minor descending

11

(1) sign(s)

The two scales have the same (1) . . *sign* . . . . .
Therefore, the keys of G major and E minor

(2) (key) signature

have the same (2) . . . *sig* . . . . which is

(3) 1 sharp

(3) __1__ __#__ .

12 For every melodic minor descending scale there is a major scale having the same signs. Therefore, each key signature is used for one minor key and one major key. The given signature stands for

(1) G   (2) E

(1) __G__ major or (2) __E__ minor.

(1) (key) signature
(2) major
(3) minor
((2) and (3) in either order.)

13 Each (1) . . *sig.* . . . represents one (2) __major__ key and one (3) __minor__ key.

min 3rd

14 As previously shown E♭ major and C minor have the same signature. C and E♭ form a(n) *m.3* . . . . . . *(Name the interval.)*

min 3rd

15 G major and E minor have the the same signature. E and G are a(n) . *m.3* . . . . apart.

(1) Î

(2) third

Complete the following V I connections with soprano $\hat{2}$ $\hat{1}$ moving to a I chord with tripled root and no fifth. The procedure is to resolve $\hat{7}$ to (1) ____ and to complete the connection by moving the remaining voice to the (2) _____ (*chord member*) of I.

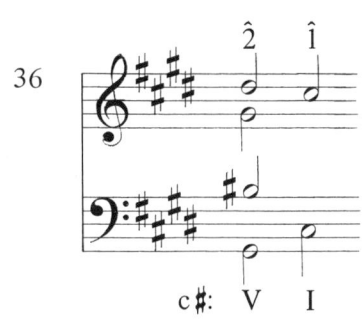

36

c#: V I

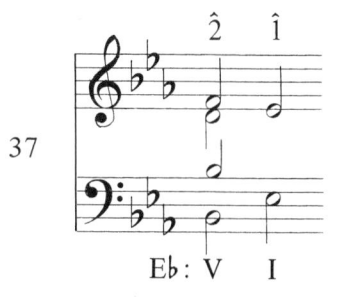

37

Eb: V I

This connection can be completed correctly in two ways. In your first solution move to a complete tonic (with doubled root, one third, and one fifth). In your second solution move to an incomplete tonic (with tripled root and no fifth).

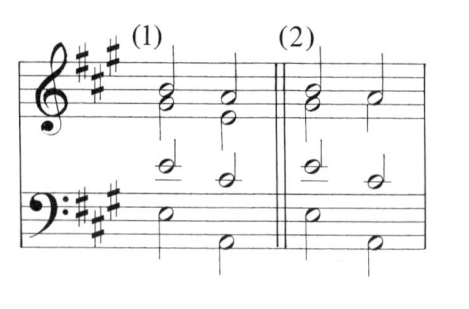

38

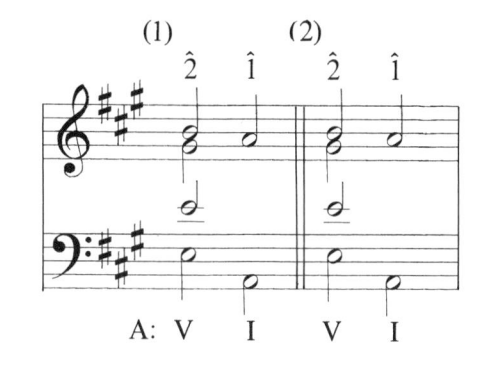

A: V I V I

(1) C (2) min 3rd	16	This "signature" (no sharps or flats) represents either the key of A minor or the key of (1) _C_ major. Again, the interval between the two tonics is a(n) (2) ..m.3..... .
D	17	The tonics of two keys represented by the same signature are always a minor 3rd apart. The *major* tonic is the *higher* of the two. F major and _D_ minor have the same signature.
(1) C♯ (2) 4 sharps	18	E major and (1) _C♯_ minor have the same signature, which is (2) _4 ♯'s_ .
(1) min 3rd (2) above	19	If two keys have the same signature the major tonic lies a(n) (1) _min._ _3rd_ (2) _above_ (above *or* below) the minor tonic.
(1) B♭ (2) 2 flats	20	(1) _B♭_ major and G minor have the same signature, namely (2) _2_ _♭'s_ .
5 flats	21	B♭ minor has a signature of _5_ _♭'s_ . *(First find the major key with the same signature.)*
no sharps or flats	22	The signature of A minor is ..n♯'s.or.♭'s
(1) major (2) min 3rd (3) minor	23	Two keys have the same signature when the (1) _major_ tonic lies a (2) _minor_ _3rd_ above the (3) _minor_ tonic.

C♭ G♭ (D♭) A♭ (E♭) B♭ F (C) A♭ E♭ (B♭) F (C) G D (A) (G) D A E B F♯ C♯ (E) B F♯ C♯ G♯ D♯ A♯	24	Complete this table:

signature	7♭'s	6♭'s	5♭'s	4♭'s	3♭'s	2♭'s	1♭	no♭
major key	C♭	G♭	D♭	A♭	E♭	B♭	F	C
minor key	A♭	E♭	B♭	F	C	G	D	A

signature	1♯	2♯'s	3♯'s	4♯'s	5♯'s	6♯'s	7♯'s
major key	G	D	A	E	B	F♯	C♯
minor key	E	B	F♯	C♯	G♯	D♯	A♯

root

Often in a V I connection with soprano $\hat{2}$ $\hat{1}$, the leading tone in the alto or tenor resolves to $\hat{1}$, resulting, as in the example below, in a tonic chord with tripled ___root___ *(chord member)*, one third, and no fifth. Such a tonic chord is referred to as *incomplete*, the *complete* tonic being the chord with doubled root, one third, and one fifth.

33

Bb: V   I

Resolve the leading tone to $\hat{1}$ in the examples below. *(Do not complete the remaining voice yet.)*

34

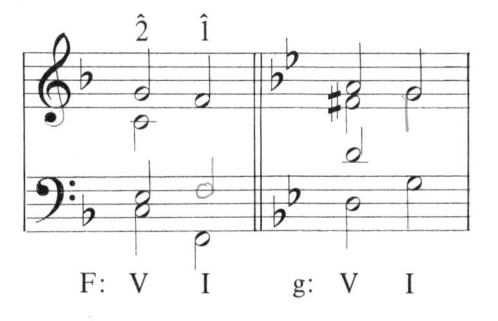

F: V   I   g: V   I

fifth

A chord for four voices with tripled root can have only one other chord member present. It is always the case in a chord with tripled root that the third is also present and the ___5ᵗʰ___ is omitted. Complete these connections, adding the third to the tonic chord:

35

F: V   I   g: V   I

(1) signature (2) relative	1	Two keys having the same signature are called *relative* keys. E♭ major and C minor have the same (1) ___sig.___. They are (2) _relative_ keys.
G minor	2	The terms *relative minor* and *relative major* are applied in this way: C minor is the relative minor of E♭ major. E♭ major is the relative major of C minor. The relative minor of B♭ major is _G___minor_.
relative major	3	C major is the ___rel.___maj___ of A minor.
D major	4	The relative major of B minor is _D___maj___.
(1) relative major (2) 2 sharps (3) 2 sharps	5	D major, the (1) _rel. ma..._ of B minor, has a signature of (2) _2___#'s___. The signature of B minor is (3) _2___#'s___.
4 sharps *(same as E major)*	6	The signature of C♯ minor is ___4___#'s___. *(First find the relative major and its signature.)*
1 flat	7	The signature of D minor is _1___b___.
5 sharps	8	G♯ minor has a signature of _5___#'s___.
	9	Write the signature of A♯ minor:
	10	Write the signature of E♭ minor:
D♯ (minor) *(The relative minor of F♯ major)*	11	What minor key has a signature of 6 sharps? _D♯_ *(First find the major key with 6 sharps.)*
A♭	12	What minor key has a signature of 7 flats? _A♭_
F♯	13	3 sharps is the signature of _F♯_ minor.

There are two correct solutions to the previous problem. Alternative solutions for this problem and problems in following frames are indicated with small notes (♩ and ♪).

Complete the following connections:

30

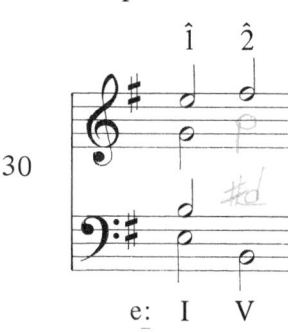

e: I V

31

D: V I

(1) alto (2) does not

According to the procedures we have discussed thus far, there is only one correct solution to the problem below. In the solution, 7̂ in the (1) _alto_ *(voice)* (2) .do̲e̲s̲ ̲n̲o̲t̲.. (does *or* does not) resolve to 1̂.

problem:

32

Bb: V I

solution:

Bb: V I

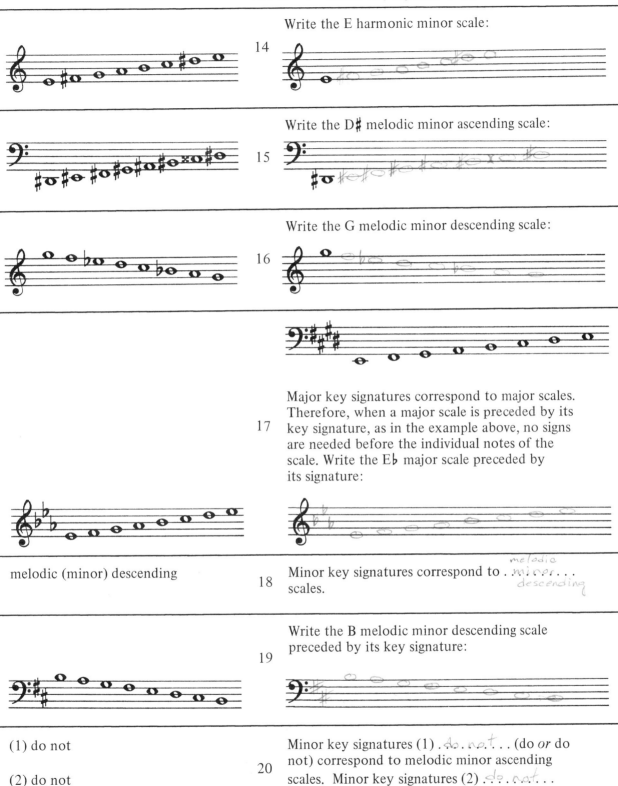

Write the E harmonic minor scale:

14

Write the D♯ melodic minor ascending scale:

15

Write the G melodic minor descending scale:

16

Major key signatures correspond to major scales.
Therefore, when a major scale is preceded by its
17 key signature, as in the example above, no signs
are needed before the individual notes of the
scale. Write the E♭ major scale preceded by
its signature:

melodic (minor) descending

Minor key signatures correspond to . *melodic* . *minor* . . .
18 scales. *descending*

Write the B melodic minor descending scale
preceded by its key signature:
19

(1) do not

Minor key signatures (1) . *do* . *not* . . . (do *or* do
20 not) correspond to melodic minor ascending
scales. Minor key signatures (2) . *do* . *not* . . .
(2) do not correspond to harmonic minor scales.

The spacing in the second chord is
incorrect; it is neither close nor open.

What is wrong with the completed connection below?
.. *spacing* .. Write a correct solution. *(Hint: Think of
the notes that are needed to complete the chord. How
can the AT move to these notes following the
principles given in frame 23?)*

27

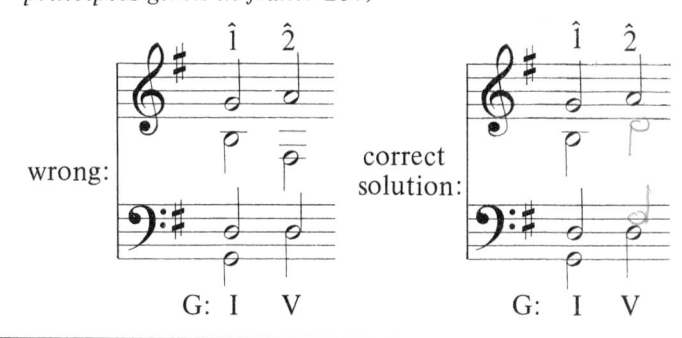

wrong: correct
                solution:

G: I   V   G: I   V

---

(1) are not

(2) leaps of a 5th or more
   (*or* large leaps)

(3) ranges   (4) root
(5) close (or) open

28

Complete the following I V connections with Î 2̂ in
the soprano and V I connections with 2̂ Î in the
soprano. These connections (1) *are not* .. (are
or are not) common tone-stepwise. In completing
the connections be sure to avoid (2) *leaps < 5th*
in the AT, to keep the voices within their respective
(3) *ranges* , to double the (4) *root* of
each chord, and to use (5) *open* or *close*
spacing in each chord.

f♯: V   I

- -

29

A♭: I   V

*See the space at the top of the
following page for an explanation
of this answer.*

When melodic minor ascending scales or harmonic minor scales are written with their key signatures, one or two signs must be inserted before the notes of the scale. Write the Eb melodic minor ascending scale, first without the key signature, then with the key signature. Check carefully to see that the two scales are identical.

21

Write the F♯ harmonic minor scale, first without the key signature, then with the key signature:

22

↑

write signature

23

(1) sharp (2) C
(3) accidentals

Signs not belonging to the key signature are called *accidentals*. In this example the natural before B and the (1) _♯_ before (2) _C_ are (3) _accidentals_.

(1) major

(2) melodic (minor) descending

24

Major key signatures correspond to (1) _maj_ scales. Minor key signatures correspond to (2) _mel. min. descending_ scales.

(1) major
(2) signs
(3) major key
(4) (key) signature

25

For every melodic minor descending scale there is a (1) _maj_ scale with the same (2) _signs_. Therefore, for every minor key there is a (3) _maj. key_ with the same (4) _sig_.

(1) y

(2) There are large
leaps in the AT.

Which of the two solutions to the problem below is correct? (1) __y__ What is wrong with the incorrect solution? (2)... *A.T. leaps too large*

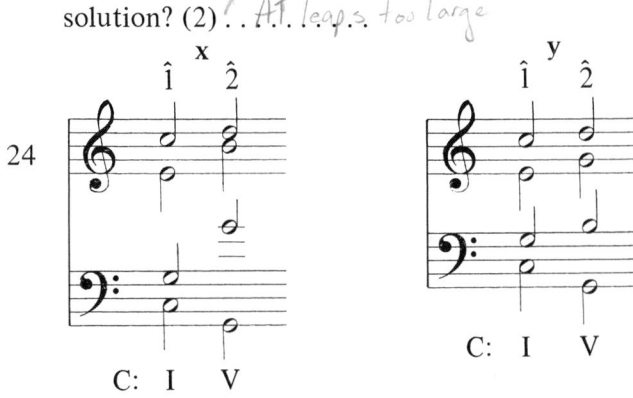

24

Both solutions are correct.

Sometimes there is more than one correct solution to a problem. Complete the problems below using the indicated spacing for the second chord. Which is/are correct solutions? ...*both*....

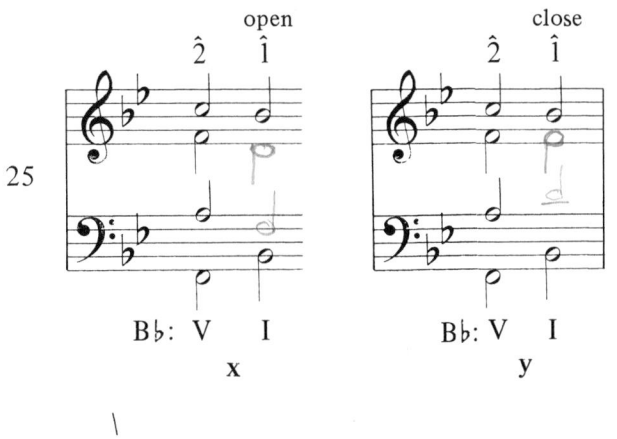

25

*(Note that solution **y** is not common tone-stepwise. Although the common tone is kept in the alto, the tenor is not stepwise.)*

(1) no

(2) The tenor exceeds its range.

Is the connection below correct? (1) *no*

If not, what is wrong? (2) *tenor out of range*

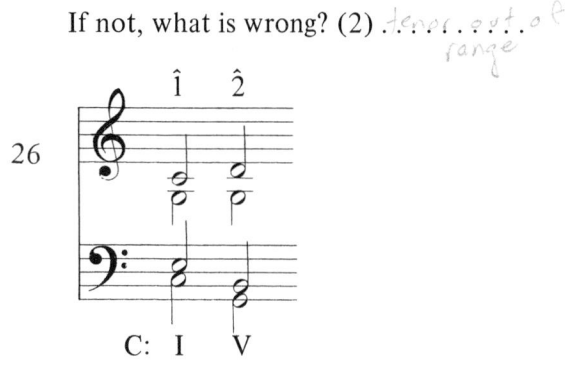

26

(1) major	26	If the tonic of a (1) ...*ma*.... key lies a
(2) minor 3rd (3) minor		(2) ..*m 3*..... above the tonic of a (3) .*min*....
(4) (key) signature		key, the two keys have the same (4) ..*sig*..... .

the same signature	27	Two keys that have ....*sig*.... are relative keys.

melodic minor ascending and harmonic minor	28	Which scales require accidentals when written with the key signature? *harm. and ascend. min.*

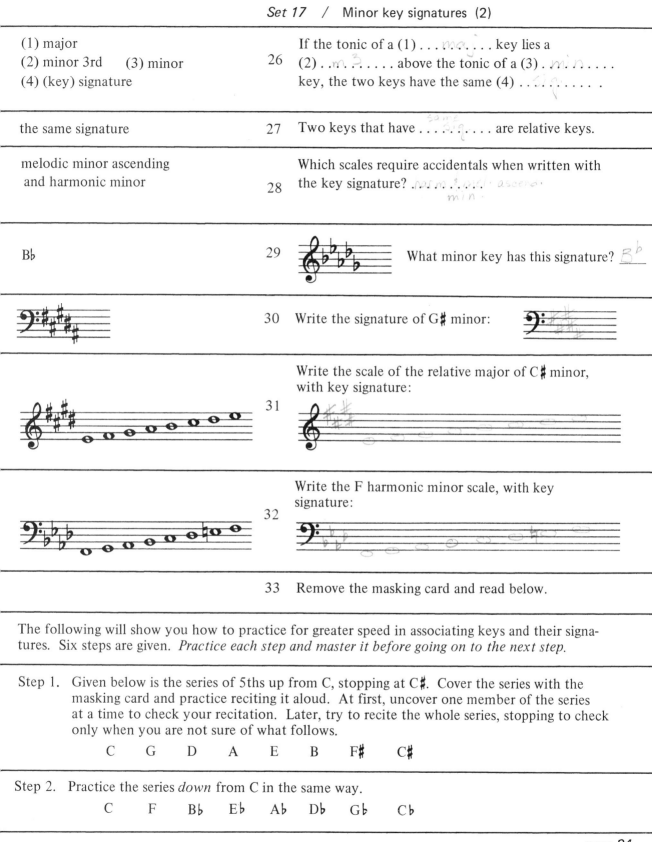

B♭	29	What minor key has this signature? *B♭*
	30	Write the signature of G♯ minor:
	31	Write the scale of the relative major of C♯ minor, with key signature:
	32	Write the F harmonic minor scale, with key signature:
	33	Remove the masking card and read below.

The following will show you how to practice for greater speed in associating keys and their signatures. Six steps are given. *Practice each step and master it before going on to the next step.*

Step 1. Given below is the series of 5ths up from C, stopping at C♯. Cover the series with the masking card and practice reciting it aloud. At first, uncover one member of the series at a time to check your recitation. Later, try to recite the whole series, stopping to check only when you are not sure of what follows.

C G D A E B F♯ C♯

Step 2. Practice the series *down* from C in the same way.

C F B♭ E♭ A♭ D♭ G♭ C♭

I V with a soprano of $\hat{1}$ $\hat{2}$ does not allow a common tone-stepwise connection. As can be seen from the example below, if a common tone-stepwise connection is attempted, the connection will be faulty because the V chord will have no _third_ *(chord member).*

third

20

Bb: I   V

Likewise, V I with a soprano of $\hat{2}$ $\hat{1}$ does not permit a common tone-stepwise connection. As can be seen from the example below, if a common tone-stepwise connection is attempted, the connection will be faulty because the I chord will have no _third_ *(chord member).*

third

21

Bb: V   I

Sometimes a given soprano does not allow an AT common tone-stepwise connection. As is illustrated in the previous two frames, this is the case in I V with a soprano of (1) _$\hat{1}$ $\hat{2}$_ and in V I with a soprano of (2) _$\hat{2}$ $\hat{1}$_.

(1) $\hat{1}$ $\hat{2}$
(2) $\hat{2}$ $\hat{1}$

22

When a common tone-stepwise connection between two chords is not possible, you must use a different procedure to complete the chord connection. Base your voice leading on the following rules:

1. Avoid AT leaps of a 5th or more.
2. Keep the voices within their respective ranges.
3. Double the root in each chord.
4. Use close or open spacing in each chord.

Remember these rules and refer to them as you complete the problems in the following frames.

23

Step 3. Now let's return to the series of 5ths *up* from C. Recite this series as a series of *major keys,* giving the signature of each key as you go along, like this:

no sharps or flats C   one sharp G   two sharps D
. . . . and so on to . . . . seven sharps C♯

Step 4. Recite the series of 5ths *down* from C as a series of major keys with signatures:

no sharps or flats C   one flat F   two flats B♭
. . . . and so on to . . . . seven flats C♭.

Step 5. Cover the bottom row of the following table with the masking card. Name aloud the major key corresponding to the first given signature (3♯). Expose the first member of the bottom row to check your answer. Complete the entire table in this way, checking each item as you go along. Then cover the *top* row and give the signatures for the major keys, one at a time. Go through the table backwards as well as forwards. Repeat these operations until speed and assurance are felt. At first you will get most of your answers by going through the series of keys, as practiced above. The more you practice, the more often you will be able to answer without the help of the series.

3♯	5♭	6♯	7♭	1♯	4♭	4♯	1♭	7♯	6♭	5♯	3♭	2♯	2♭	4♯	7♭	2♯	3♭	6♯	5♭	1♯	1♭	5♯	6♭	3♯	2♭	7♯	4♭
A	D♭	F♯	C♭	G	A♭	E	F	C♯	G♭	B	E♭	D	B♭	E	C♭	D	E♭	F♯	D♭	G	F	B	G♭	A	B♭	C♯	A♭

Step 6. The table below contains minor keys (symbolized by small letters) and their signatures. Practice as above. At first, you will rely mostly on association with the relative major keys. The more you practice, the more readily your responses will come without thinking of the relative major key.

1♯	5♭	3♯	4♭	7♯	1♭	6♯	3♭	2♯	7♭	5♯	6♭	4♯	2♭	7♯	5♭	4♯	4♭	6♯	2♭	1♯	7♭	5♯	3♭	3♯	6♭	2♯	1♭
e	b♭	f♯	f	a♯	d	d♯	c	b	a♭	g♯	e♭	c♯	g	a♯	b♭	c♯	f	d♯	g	e	a♭	g♯	c	f♯	e♭	b	d

TEST COVERING PART 3

The questions below will test your mastery of the material in Part 3. Complete the entire test, then check your answers with the correct ones on page 137. For each question that you miss, the corresponding material may be reviewed in the set whose number is given with the correct answer.

1. Fill in the blanks in the following series: C♭ G♭ D♭ <u>A♭</u> <u>E♭</u> <u>B♭</u> F C

2. The above is a . .series. .of. 5ᵗʰs

common tone-stepwise	13	Connected in the smoothest way, the alto and tenor are ..~~common-tone~~ *stepwise*... in all of the following progressions: I V with soprano $\hat{1}$ $\hat{7}$, $\hat{3}$ $\hat{2}$, $\hat{3}$ $\hat{7}$; V I with soprano $\hat{7}$ $\hat{1}$, $\hat{2}$ $\hat{3}$.
(1) $\hat{1}$ $\hat{7}$, $\hat{3}$ $\hat{2}$, $\hat{3}$ $\hat{7}$ (2) $\hat{7}$ $\hat{1}$, $\hat{2}$ $\hat{3}$ (3) the common tone in the same voice (4) the remaining voices stepwise	14	In the smoothest connections of the following progressions, the AT are common tone-stepwise: I V with soprano (1) _$\hat{1}$_ _$\hat{7}$_ , _$\hat{3}$_ _$\hat{2}$_ , _$\hat{3}$_ _$\hat{7}$_. V I with soprano (2) _$\hat{7}$_ _$\hat{1}$_ , _$\hat{2}$_ _$\hat{3}$_. The voice leading procedure is: 1. Keep (3) _common tone in same voice_ 2. Move (4) _remaining voices stepwise_
(1) DST (*or* semitone) (2) leading tone	15	In normal chord connection, the progression V I with a soprano of $\hat{7}$ $\hat{3}$ does not occur. Because of its position a (1) ..*DST*... below tonic, $\hat{7}$ is an active tone, having a strong tendency to move to $\hat{1}$ (the central, most stable tone of a key). For this reason it is called the *leading tone*. The term, (2) _leading tone_ describes the function of $\hat{7}$, which is to lead to $\hat{1}$.
$\hat{1}$	16	When $\hat{7}$ is in the soprano voice, it is imperative that the following I chord have _$\hat{1}$_ in the soprano. When $\hat{7}$ is in the alto or tenor, it is not as prominent, and although it often leads to $\hat{1}$, it need not, depending upon other voice leading considerations.
(1) does not (2) $\hat{1}$	17	In a normal chord connection, the progression V I with a soprano of $\hat{7}$ $\hat{3}$ (1) .*does not*.. occur. When $\hat{7}$ occurs in the soprano, the following I has (2) _$\hat{1}$_ in the soprano.
(1) $\hat{1}$ (or) $\hat{3}$ (2) $\hat{2}$ (or) $\hat{7}$	18	The most common soprano lines in I V I are those using (1) _$\hat{1}$_ or _$\hat{3}$_ with I and (2) _$\hat{2}$_ or _$\hat{7}$_ with V.
(1) $\hat{1}$ $\hat{7}$, $\hat{3}$ $\hat{2}$, $\hat{3}$ $\hat{7}$ (2) $\hat{7}$ $\hat{1}$, $\hat{2}$ $\hat{3}$ (3) does not occur (is not found, etc.)	19	Soprano patterns that allow common tone-stepwise connections in the AT are: In I V, (1) _$\hat{1}$_ _$\hat{7}$_ , _$\hat{3}$_ _$\hat{2}$_ , _$\hat{3}$_ _$\hat{7}$_. In V I, (2) _$\hat{7}$_ _$\hat{1}$_ , _$\hat{2}$_ _$\hat{3}$_. In normal chord connection, the soprano pattern $\hat{7}$ $\hat{3}$ (3) _doesn't occur_

3. Give the full name of each scale:

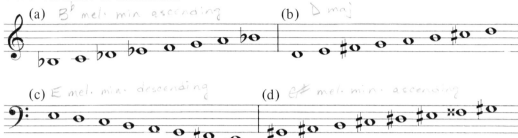

(a) B♭ mel· min ascending   (b) D maj

(c) E mel· min· descending   (d) e♯ mel· min· ascending

4. Write scales as indicated:

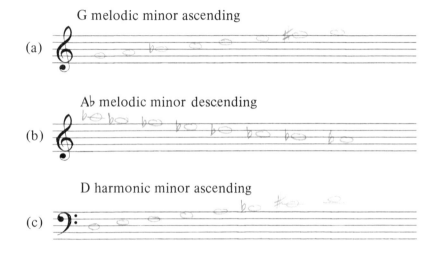

(a) G melodic minor ascending

(b) A♭ melodic minor descending

(c) D harmonic minor ascending

5. Name the major key and minor key corresponding to each of the following signatures:

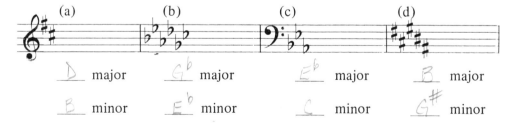

(a)   (b)   (c)   (d)

D major   G♭ major   E♭ major   B major

B minor   E♭ minor   C minor   G♯ minor

6. Write key signatures as indicated:

(a) B♭ major   (b) C♯ minor   (c) F minor   (d) F♯ major

8

Which of the above soprano patterns in I V permit common tone-stepwise movement in the *alto and tenor*? *(Give scale degrees.)*

$\hat{1}\ \hat{7},\ \hat{3}\ \hat{2},\ \hat{3}\ \hat{7}$

9

In I V progressions, soprano patterns of $\hat{1}\ \hat{7}$, $\hat{3}\ \hat{2}$, and $\hat{3}\ \hat{7}$ allow common tone-stepwise connection of the alto and tenor. Complete these connections:

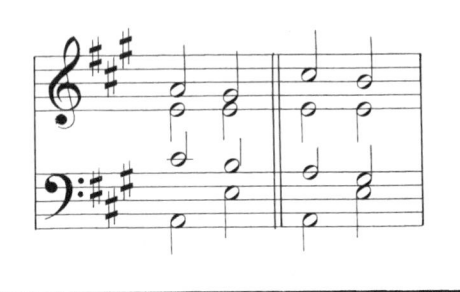

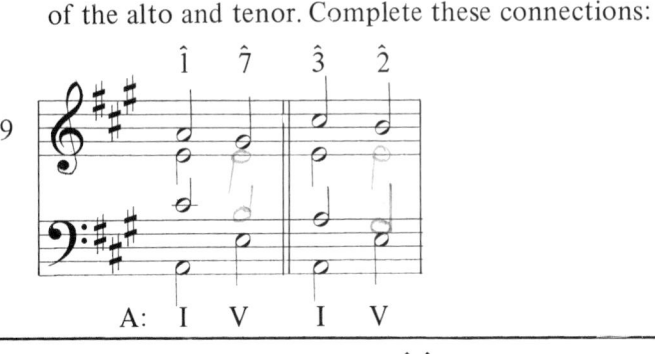

10

common tone-stepwise

Although the soprano pattern $\hat{3}\ \hat{7}$ leaps, it permits a .*stepwise*. . . connection of the alto and tenor. Complete the connection. *(Be sure to check for correct doubling in V.)*

11

$\hat{1}\ \hat{7},\ \hat{3}\ \hat{2},$ (and) $\hat{3}\ \hat{7}$

Connected the smoothest way, the alto and tenor are common tone-stepwise in I V progressions having soprano patterns of __$\hat{1}$__ __$\hat{7}$__, __$\hat{3}$__ __$\hat{2}$__, and __$\hat{3}$__ __$\hat{7}$__. *(Do not include patterns with $\hat{5}$.)*

12

(1) $\hat{7}\ \hat{1}$ (2) $\hat{2}\ \hat{3}$

The soprano patterns in this example allow common tone-stepwise connections in V I. The soprano scale degrees are: (1) __$\hat{7}$__ __$\hat{1}$__ and (2) __$\hat{2}$__ __$\hat{3}$__. Complete the connections:

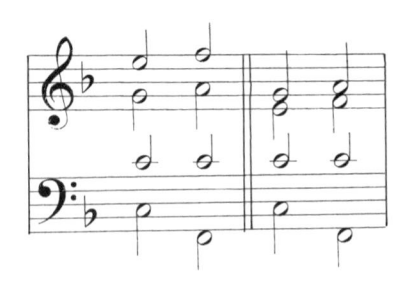

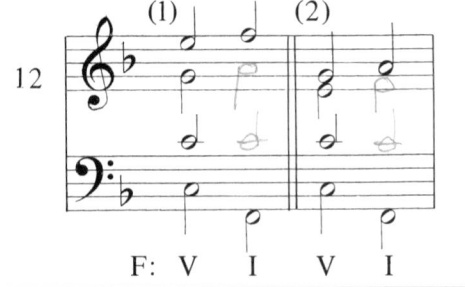

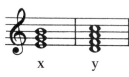

1   In traditional harmony, chords are constructed in 3rds. Chord **x** has 3 notes and consists of these two 3rds:

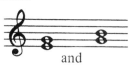

and

3

Chord **y** has 4 notes and consists of ___3___ (*how many?*) 3rds.

2   Using C as the lowest note, construct a chord of five different notes. *(Do not use sharps or flats.)*

3rds

3   Chords are constructed in ___3ʳᵈs___ .

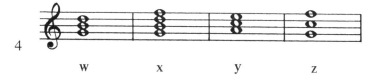

w   x   y   z

(1) y (2) triad(s)

A chord of 3 notes built in 3rds is a *triad*.
Chord w and chord (1) ___y___ are (2) ___triad___ s.

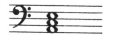

5   Write a triad with A as the lowest note. *(no sharps or flats)*

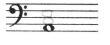

---

triad

6   If another 3rd were added above the top note E, the chord would no longer be a ___triad___ .

---

chord of three notes
(built in 3rds)

7   A triad is a ... Chord of 3 notes built in 3rd's.

---

root

8   The *root* of a chord is the note on which it is built. E♭ is the ___root___ of this chord.

---

common tone-stepwise	1	As the examples in the previous set have shown, the smoothest way of connecting I V and V I is the ..*Common tone- stepwise*.. connection.
is not		However, not all I V and V I connections are common tone-stepwise. This connection ..*is not*.. (is *or* is not) common tone-stepwise.

2	

f: V   I

soprano	3	Many problems in chord connection involve a given soprano pattern that is to be harmonized. There are some soprano patterns which permit common tone-stepwise connections and some which do not. Hence, the way in which I V or V I is connected depends upon a given *soprano* pattern.
(1) Î 3̂ 5̂ (2) 5̂ 7̂ 2̂	4	I contains scale degrees: (1) _1_ _3_ _5_. V contains scale degrees: (2) _5_ _7_ _2_.
I V I	5	The most common soprano lines in the fundamental harmonic progression, ..*I V I*.. , are those using Î or 3̂ with I and 2̂ or 7̂ with V. 5̂ is most often found in an inner voice.
(1) Î (or) 3̂ (2) 2̂ (or) 7̂	6	The most common soprano lines in I V I have (1) _1_ or _3_ with I and (2) _2_ or _7_ with V.

(1) Î 7̂ (2) Î 2̂ (3) 3̂ 2̂ (4) 3̂ 7̂	7	The most common soprano patterns in I V are illustrated. Mark the soprano scale degrees: (1) _1_ _7_ (2) _1_ _2_ (3) _3_ _2_ (4) _3_ _7_ C: I V I V I V I V

z

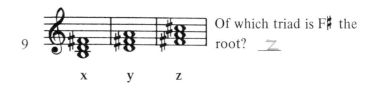

9 Of which triad is F♯ the root? _z_

x   y   z

---

(1) root

(2) third   (3) fifth

10 The note lying a 3rd above the root is called the *third*.
The note lying a 5th above the root is called the *fifth*.
In the chord shown D is the (1) _root_ , F is the
(2) _3rd_ , and A is the (3) _5th_ .

---

(1) 3rd

(2) fifth

(3) 5th

*(Except for this answer,
do not consider it wrong
if you give 3rd instead of
third, or fifth instead of 5th, etc.)*

11 *3rd* and *5th* are general names of intervals. They
also represent chord members. For clarity, this
book uses *3rd* and *5th* for interval names, *third*
and *fifth* for chord members. Thus the third lies
a (1) _3rd_ (3rd *or* third) above the root.
The interval between root and (2) _fifth_
(5th *or* fifth) is a (3) _5th_ (5th *or* fifth).

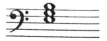

12 Construct a triad on the root E.
(no sharps or flats)

13 F is the *third* of a triad.
Complete the triad *(no
sharps or flats).*

G

14 The fifth of a triad is D. Its root is _G_ .
(Assume all notes are ♮.)

---

(1) major

(2) minor

15 In this triad the interval between
root and third is a (1) _maj_
3rd, and the interval between third
and fifth is a (2) _min_ 3rd.

---

(1) close

(2) open

When a chord is in (1) _close_ spacing, there are no gaps between SA or AT. When a chord is in (2) _open_ spacing, there is a gap of of one chord note between SA and a gap of one chord note between AT.

31

Unless otherwise indicated, instructions for close or open spacing in all exercises in this book refer only to the *first* chord of a pattern. The placement of notes in subsequent chords is determined by voice leading considerations.

Complete the first chord (AT missing) in open spacing. Then connect the indicated chords:

32

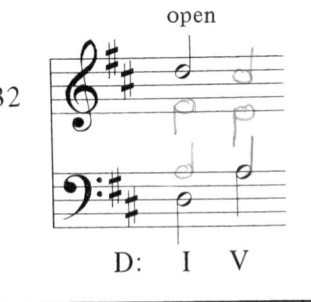

D: I V

Complete the first chord in close spacing. Connect the chords:

33

e♭: V I

(1) major 3rd (2) minor 3rd	16	This triad has a (1) ___maj___ ___3rd___ between root and third and a (2) ___min___ 3rd between third and fifth.

17 There are various structural types of triads, depending upon the specific names of the 3rds between the chord members. Both chord **x** and chord **y** have a major 3rd between root and third, and a minor 3rd between third and fifth. They are therefore . *same* . . . . (the same *or* different) in structure.

the same

different	18	The two triads are . . *diff't* . . in structure.

19 The triad structures of traditional harmony contain major and minor 3rds only. Which of the triads are *not* traditional harmonic structures? . *y . . z* . . . .

y and z

20 A triad composed of a major 3rd below a minor 3rd is a *major triad*. Chord **x** is a major triad. Chord **y** has a (1) ___maj___ 3rd below a (2) ___min___ 3rd. It (3) . . . . *is* . . . . (is *or* is not) a major triad.

(1) maj   (2) min

(3) is

major triad	21	A ___maj triad___ is composed of a major 3rd below a minor third.

(1) min (2) maj (3) is not	22	This triad has a (1) ___min___ 3rd below a (2) ___maj___ 3rd. It (3) . . *is not* . . a major triad.

Write a common tone-stepwise connection of A: I V.
*(Suggested procedure: Spell A: V. Carry out step 1.
Which notes are still needed in the SAT? Which way
must the remaining voices move? Carry out step 2.)*

27

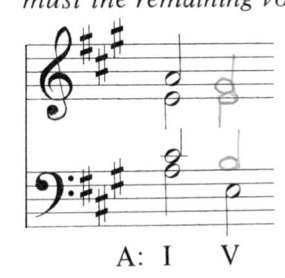

A: I   V

In the following frames write common tone-stepwise
connections:

28

a: V   I

*(Reminder: $\hat{7}$ requires an accidental in
minor keys.)*

29

c♯: I   V

30

E: V   I

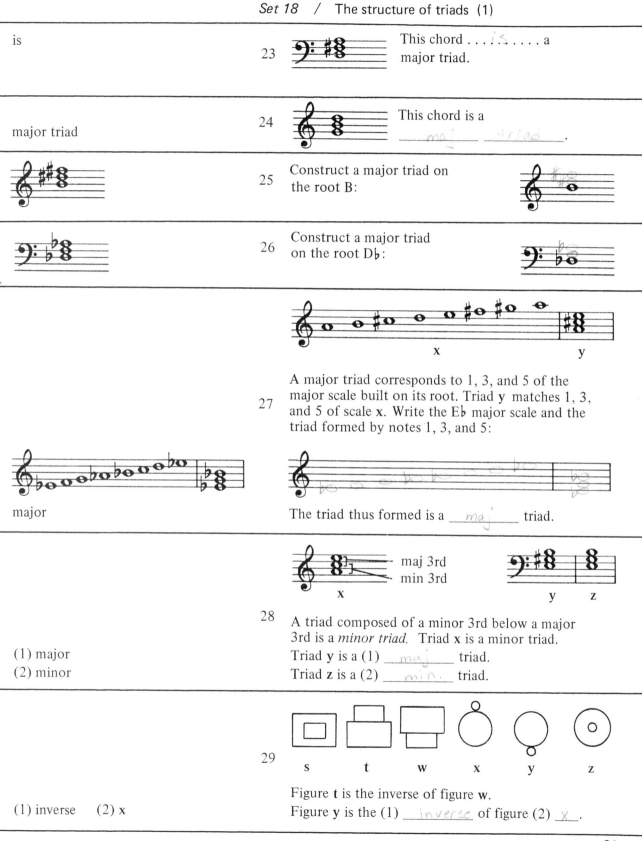

is

23 This chord . . . . *is* . . . . a major triad.

major triad

24 This chord is a ___*maj* *triad*___ .

25 Construct a major triad on the root B:

26 Construct a major triad on the root D♭:

27 A major triad corresponds to 1, 3, and 5 of the major scale built on its root. Triad **y** matches 1, 3, and 5 of scale **x**. Write the E♭ major scale and the triad formed by notes 1, 3, and 5:

major

The triad thus formed is a ___*maj*___ triad.

28 A triad composed of a minor 3rd below a major 3rd is a *minor triad*. Triad **x** is a minor triad.

(1) major Triad **y** is a (1) ___*maj*___ triad.
(2) minor Triad **z** is a (2) ___*min*___ triad.

29 Figure **t** is the inverse of figure **w**.

(1) inverse (2) x Figure **y** is the (1) ___*inverse*___ of figure (2) ___*x*___ .

y

Chord connections may be spoken of in degrees of smoothness. The less motion, the smoother the connection. Which is smoother, **x** or **y**? _y_

22

b: I V I V

x

In general, the greatest possible smoothness is desirable in chord connection. Which is smoother, **x** or **y**? _x_

23

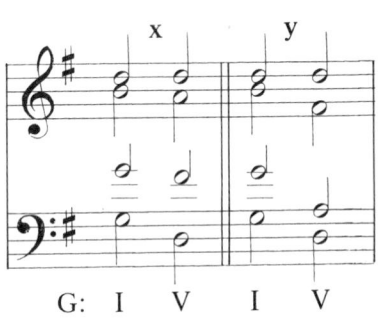

G: I V I V

common tone-stepwise connection

24

The smoothest way to connect two triads having a common tone is the common tone-stepwise connection. The smoothest way to connect I and V is the .*Common . tone- stepwise connection*

smoothest

25

The common tone-stepwise connection is the _smoothest_ connection between I and V.

(1) Keep the common
    tone in the same voice.
(2) Move the remaining
    voices stepwise.

26

Give the procedure for the smoothest connection of root position triads that have a common tone:
1. (1) *keep common tone in same voice*
2. (2) *move remaining voices stepwise*

When this procedure is followed, defects of voice leading, such as faulty parallel motion and AT leaps of a 5th or more, are automatically avoided.

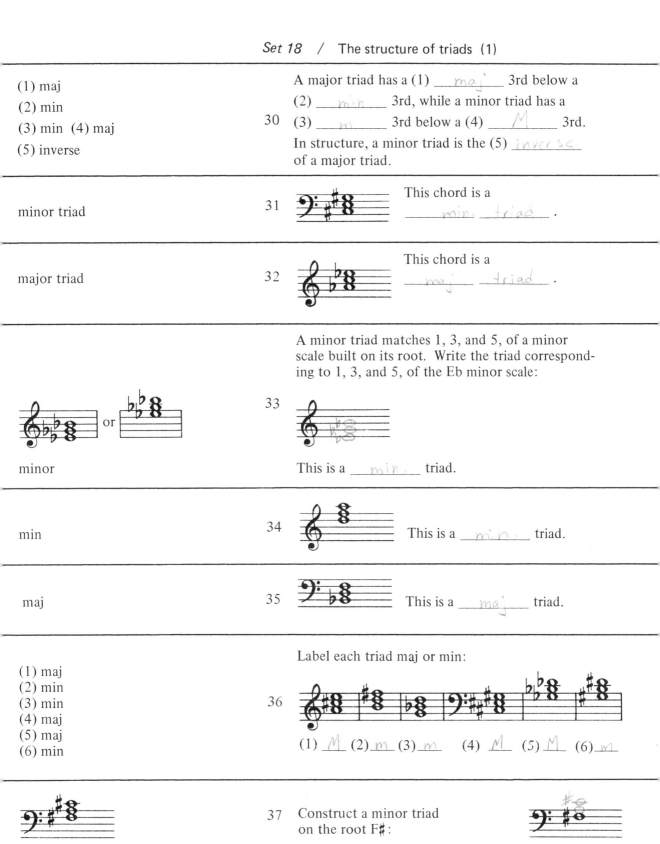

(1) maj

(2) min

(3) min (4) maj

(5) inverse

30 A major triad has a (1) ___maj___ 3rd below a (2) ___min___ 3rd, while a minor triad has a (3) ___m___ 3rd below a (4) ___M___ 3rd. In structure, a minor triad is the (5) _inverse_ of a major triad.

---

minor triad

31 This chord is a ___min. triad___ .

---

major triad

32 This chord is a ___maj triad___ .

---

33 A minor triad matches 1, 3, and 5, of a minor scale built on its root. Write the triad corresponding to 1, 3, and 5, of the Eb minor scale:

This is a ___min.___ triad.

minor

---

min

34 This is a ___min.___ triad.

---

maj

35 This is a ___maj___ triad.

---

(1) maj
(2) min
(3) min
(4) maj
(5) maj
(6) min

36 Label each triad maj or min:

(1) _M_ (2) _m_ (3) _m_   (4) _M_ (5) _M_ (6) _m_

---

37 Construct a minor triad on the root F#:

Now let's continue with the problem begun above. So far there is only one note, G, in the SAT of the second chord. What two notes of C: I are still missing from the SAT of the second chord?

C (and) E

_C_ and _E_. *(Do not write the notes yet.)*

17

C: V   I

In the example in the previous frame the SA can be moved *by step* to the missing notes C and E. The SA must both move _____up_____ (up *or* down) to reach C and E by stepwise motion.

18

up

Write C and E in the second chord by moving the SA of the first chord by step:

19

C: V   I

The missing SAT of the second chord were arrived at by following these two main steps:

20

(1) common tone

(2) step

1.   Keep the (1) _common tone_ in the same voice.
2.   Move the remaining voices by (2) _step_.

Keeping the common tone in the same voice and moving the remaining (S, A, or T) voices stepwise is an extremely frequent kind of connection. We will refer to it as *common tone-stepwise*. The connection just completed above is a _Common tone-stepwise_ connection.

21

common tone stepwise
(You may abbreviate CTS.)

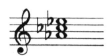

38 Construct a minor triad
on the root A♭:

---

minor triad with root D

39 The expression *C major triad* denotes a major
triad with root C. Similarly, the expression
D minor triad denotes a . min. triad on
root D

*(In all answers of this kind
the entire chord may be
written an octave higher or
lower than shown.)*

40 Write an F maj triad:

---

41 Write a D♯ min triad:

Give the root and type of each triad:

(1)   (2)   (3)   (4)   (5)

42

(2) C♭ maj
(3) C min
(4) E♭ maj
(5) E♯ min

Example: (1) C   maj
(2) C♭   maj
(3) C   min
(4) E♭   maj
(5) E♯   min.

43 Suppose A♯ is the *third* of
a major triad. Write the
complete triad:

---

44 Suppose A♭ is the *third*
of a minor triad. Write
the complete triad:

The notion of "common tone" refers to note spellings not absolute pitches. In the example, no two pitches are exactly the same, but the two chords have a common tone. The common tone is _f_ .

F(*or* $\hat{5}$)

13

Bb: V   I

In this example the SAT of the second chord will be spelled _C_ _E_ _G_ . (*Do not write the second chord yet.*)

C E G

14

C: V   I

The common tone in C: V I is (1) _G_ . In the first chord of the example below, the common tone is in the (2) _tenor_ (*which voice?*).
Write the common tone in the *same voice* in the second chord. (*Do not complete the chord yet.*)

(1) G

(2) tenor

15

C: V   I

In a root position triad with correct doubling, all three chord members are present in the . S.A.T. . . . (*which voices?*).

SAT

16

	45	Suppose F is the fifth of a major triad. Write the complete triad:	

	46	Suppose E is the fifth of a minor triad. Write the complete triad:	

Set 19 / THE STRUCTURE OF TRIADS (2)

unlike

1 Since a major triad contains a major 3rd and a minor 3rd, we may say that it has two *unlike* 3rds. A minor triad also contains a major 3rd and minor 3rd (though not in the same relative position). A minor triad has two ___unlike___ thirds.

unlike

2 Both major triads and minor triads are composed of two ___unlike___ 3rds.

Construct the indicated triads:

C major triad   C minor triad

3

(1) perfect
(2) perfect

Examination of these two triads shows that a major triad has a(n) (1) ___perf___ 5th between root and fifth. A minor triad has a(n) (2) ___perf___ 5th between root and fifth.

unlike

4 Triads with two ___unlike___ 3rds have a perfect 5th between root and fifth.

perf 5th

5 maj 3rd + min 3rd = ___perf___ ___5th___

fundamental harmonic	In studying I V I, the *fundamental harmonic* progression, it is easiest to begin by considering 6 separately the movement from I to V (symbolized: I V) and the movement from V to I (symbolized: V I).

E	A C major triad is spelled C E G. A G major triad is spelled G B D. There is one note that occurs in both 7 triads, the note G. Such a note is called a common note, or *common tone*. What is the common tone in these two triads: A C♯ E and E G♯ B? _E_

common tone (*or* common note)	8 F♯ is the *common tone* in these two triads: B D F♯ and F♯ A♯ C♯.

(1) E♭ G B♭ (2) B♭ D F (3) B♭	E♭: I is spelled (1) _E♭_ _G_ _B♭_ 9 E♭: V is spelled (2) _B♭_ _D_ _F_ The common tone in E♭: I V is (3) _B♭_.

scale degrees	When placed above a numeral, the symbol ⌃, called a caret, means "scale degree." Thus, the symbol 1̂ means scale degree 1, etc. As in the following example, these symbols often refer to the soprano voice. Here, the symbols indicate that the soprano consists of *scale degrees* 3, 2, and 1.

10

d: I   V   I

(1) 1̂ (2) 7	The tonic note, no matter what its octave placement, is referred to as scale degree 1, symbolized 11 (1) _1̂_. There are (2) _7_ different degrees in a scale.

(1) 1̂ 3̂ 5̂ (2) 5̂ 7̂ 2̂ (3) 5̂	The scale degrees in I are: (1) _1̂_ _3̂_ _5̂_. The scale degrees in V are: (2) _5̂_ _7̂_ _2̂_. 12 The scale degree designation for the common tone between I and V is (3) _5̂_.

like	6	This triad contains two _____ (like *or* unlike) 3rds.
like	7	This triad contains two _like_ (like *or* unlike) 3rds.
(1) min (2) dim (3) maj (4) aug	8	Triad **x** has two (1) _min_ (major *or* minor) 3rds and a(n) (2) _dim_ 5th between root and fifth. Triad **y** has two (3) _maj_ (major *or* minor) 3rds and a(n) (4) _aug_ 5th between root and fifth.
(1) dim 5th (2) aug 5th	9	min 3rd + min 3rd = (1) _dim_ _5th_ maj 3rd + maj 3rd = (2) _aug_ _5th_
(1) unlike (2) like	10	Triads with two (1) _unlike_ (like *or* unlike) 3rds have a perfect 5th between root and fifth. Triads with two (2) _like_ (like *or* unlike) 3rds do not have a perfect 5th between root and fifth.
(1) dim (2) aug	11	Triads with two *like* 3rds take their names from the interval between root and fifth. Since triad **x** has a diminished 5th between root and fifth, it is a *diminished triad*. Triad **y** is a(n) (1) _dim_ triad. Triad **z** is a(n) (2) _aug_ triad.
root (and) fifth	12	Diminished and augmented triads take their names from the interval between _root_ and _5th_ .

tonic

The term *tonic* refers to the function of the I chord. The chord below has ___tonic___ function.

1

G: I

dominant

The term *dominant* refers to the function of the V chord. The chord below has ___dominant___ function.

2

G: V

(1) tonic
(2) dominant

Chords **x** and **z** have (1) ___tonic___ function.
Chord **y** has (2) ___dominant___ function.

3

Bb: I V I

closing tonic

4 I V I is the *fundamental harmonic progression* in Western tonal music. The I chord which opens the progression is referred to as the *opening* tonic; the I chord which closes the progression is referred to as the ___closing___ ___tonic___.

(1) I V I
(2) opening

5 The fundamental harmonic progression in Western tonal music is (1) ___I V I___ . . . . . . It is the most basic way of moving from an (2) ___opening___ tonic to a closing tonic.

(1) dim

(2) aug

13

Chord **x** is a(n) (1) ___dim___ triad.

Chord **y** is a (n) (2) ___aug.___ triad.

x   y

Write the following triads:

14 dim triad on the root A:

15 A aug triad:

16 D♯ dim triad:

17 D♭ aug triad:

---

(1) 3rds
(2) triad

18 A chord of three notes built in (1) ___3rds___ is a (2) ___triad___.

---

t   w   x   y   z

19 Which of the chords do(es) *not* belong to the chords of traditional harmony? .t. ; .y. . . . .

t and **y** *(t is built in 4ths;*
y contains an aug 3rd.)

Show the structure of major and minor triads by filling in the blanks:

20

min	maj
perf	perf
maj	min

major triad   *minor triad*

Indicate the voices involved and the errors in the
following. If a given connection is correct, mark
it correct.

SB, parallel octaves

56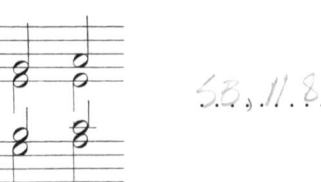

SB, ll. 8's

*(Hint: Note the specific quality of the intervals
in this problem.)*

Correct
*(The 5th in the 2nd
chord is dim.)*

57

correct

AB, parallel octaves and
TB, parallel perfect 5ths

58

AB, ll. 8's
TB, ll p5's

SB, parallel perfect 5ths

59

SB, ll. p5's

TB, consecutive perfect 5ths

60

TB, consec. p5's

Fill in the blanks:

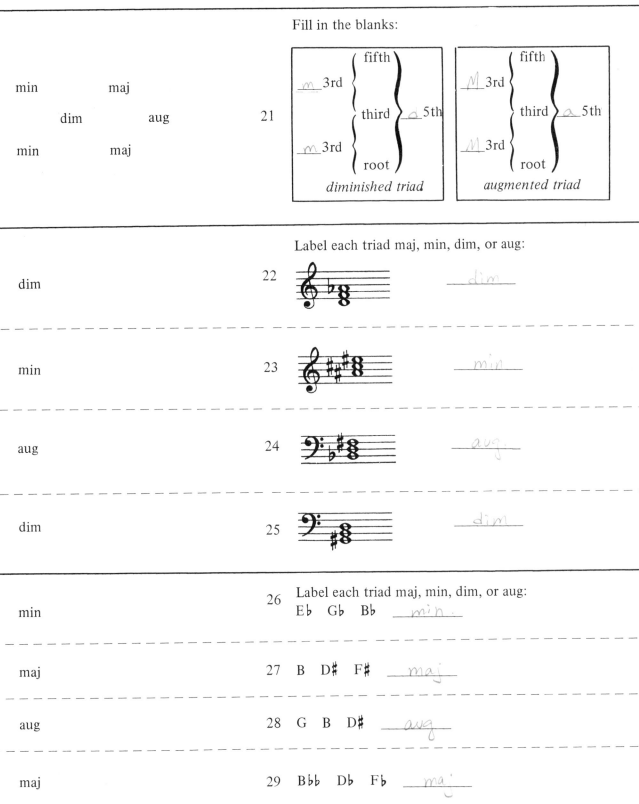

min   maj

    dim   aug

min   maj

21

_m_ 3rd { fifth

{ third } _d_ 5th

_m_ 3rd { root

diminished triad

_M_ 3rd { fifth

{ third } _d_ 5th

_M_ 3rd { root

augmented triad

Label each triad maj, min, dim, or aug:

dim

22

dim

---

min

23

min

---

aug

24

aug.

---

dim

25

dim

---

min

26   Label each triad maj, min, dim, or aug:
Eb Gb Bb   _min._

---

maj

27   B   D♯   F♯   _maj_

---

aug

28   G   B   D♯   _aug_

---

maj

29   B♭♭   D♭   F♭   _maj_

(1) perfect 5th

(2) dim 5th   (3) is not

The interval between the AT in chord **x** is a
(1) . . p.5 . . . . The interval between the AT in
chord **y** is a (2) . . d 5 . . . . . . This (3) . . is not . . .
(is *or* is not) a case of parallel perfect 5ths. Only
parallel *perfect* 5ths are to be avoided; therefore,
this is not faulty movement.

53

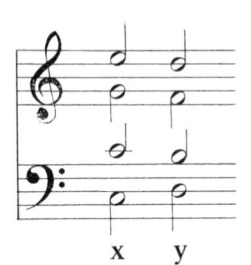

x   y

---

(1) octave   (2) octave

(3) perfect 5th

54

The rules governing parallel motion may be summarized
as follows:

1. Two voices may not move from a prime or
    (1) _octave_ or double (2) _octave_ , etc. to
    another such interval.

2. Two voices may not move from a (3) . . . p.5 . . . .
    or corresponding compound interval to another
    such interval.

AB and TB

It is very easy (but very incorrect) to write chord
connections containing faulty parallels. In the
(horrible) example given here, the following pairs
of voices produce faulty parallels: AB., TB. . .

55

Write the indicated triads:

30 C♯ min triad:

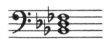
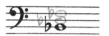

31 B♭ dim triad:

F A C♯

32 Spell an F aug triad: F A C♯

A♭ C E♭

33 Spell an A♭ maj triad: A♭ C E♭

Write the four different types of triad, using E as the *root* in each case:

maj   min   aug   dim

34

maj   min   aug   dim

Write the four different types of triad, using E♯ as the *third* in each case:

maj   min   aug   dim

35

maj   min   aug   dim

Write the four different types of triad, using F as the *fifth* in each case:

maj   min   aug   dim

36

maj   min   aug   dim

(1) SB
(2) perfect 5ths

Like consecutive octaves, consecutive perfect 5ths
are avoided. Considering the perfect 5th and its
corresponding compound intervals as a group, two
voices may not move from one member of the
group to another. Here the (1)...*S.B.*....*(voices)*
produce consecutive (2) .*p.5.ths*.......

49

In checking for both parallel and consecutive perfect
5ths the procedure to follow is: Locate the perfect
5th (if there is one) in a chord. Does it move to a perfect 5th in the next chord? If so, the connection is
faulty.

Follow this procedure for the examples below. If the
connection is faulty, indicate the voices involved and
describe the error. If the connection is correct, mark
50 it correct.

TB, parallel perfect 5ths

T.B., // p.5's

SB, consecutive perfect 5ths   51

SB, consec p5's

SB, parallel perfect 5ths   52

SB, // p.5's

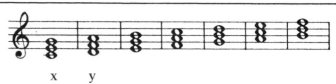

x   y

1   These are the seven triads derived from the C major
scale. The tonic is the root of triad **x**. Note 2 is the
root of triad **y**. Each note of the scale is used, in turn,
as the ____root____ of a triad.

root

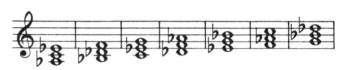

2   These triads are derived from the __A♭ major__
__scale__.

A♭ major

scale

Shown below is one of the triads derived from
the G major scale. Write the other triads derived
from the G major scale. Do not use a key signature.

3

Since major key signatures correspond to
__major__ __scales__, the triads derived from a

4   major scale may be written with a key signature and
no accidentals. The triads derived from the D major
scale are shown in this way above. Write the key signature for B♭ major and the triads derived from the B♭
major scale:

major scales

(1) TB
(2) parallel perfect 5ths

Parallel *perfect* 5ths are to be avoided. In this chord connection the (1) . .T.B. . . . . .*(voices)* incorrectly make (2) _parallel_ _perfect_ _5ths_.

46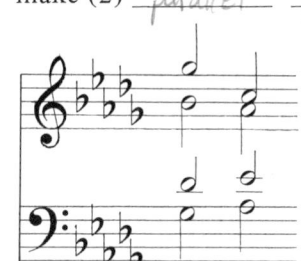

(1) AB
(2) parallel perfect 5ths

In this faulty chord connection the (1) . .A.B. . . . . *(voices)* make (2) _11_ _p_ _5ths_.

47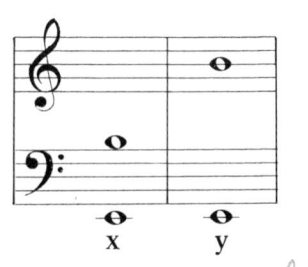

Just as compound intervals corresponding to the octave are avoided in parallel motion, so are compound intervals corresponding to the perfect 5th (such as intervals **x** and **y**) avoided in parallel motion.

x   y

AB

48 In case **z** below the . .A.B. . . . *(voices)* are faulty, producing parallel perfect 5ths. *(Compound intervals corresponding to the perfect 5th are generally referred to as perfect 5ths.)*

z

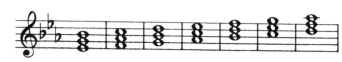

5 The seven triads derived from a scale are the
diatonic triads in the corresponding key. Shown
above are the seven (1) _diatonic triads_
in the key of (2) _Eb major_ .

(1) diatonic triads
(2) Eb major

scale

6 Diatonic triads are derived from a _scale_ .

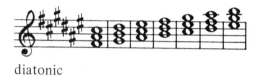

diatonic

7 These are two of the seven _diatonic_ triads in the
key of F♯ major. Write the other five.

scale degree 4

8 Notes of a scale are referred to numerically as scale
degrees. The expression, scale degree 2, means note
2 of a scale. The note C♯ is scale degree 3 of the A
major scale. The note Eb is _scale 4_ of the
Bb major scale.

9

(1) diatonic
(2) A major

Above are the seven (1) _diatonic_ triads
in the key of (2) _A major_ .

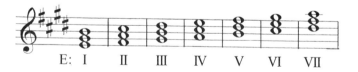

E: I II III IV V VI VII

10

6

Roman numerals corresponding to scale
degrees are used to indicate roots of diatonic
triads. Shown above are the seven diatonic triads
in E major and their Roman numeral symbols.
The triad whose root is scale degree _6_ has the
symbol VI.

You will need to learn to spot parallel octaves and primes and consecutive octaves quickly. A good procedure to use is the following: Locate the octave or prime (if there is one) in a chord. Does it move to an octave or prime in the next chord? If so, the connection is faulty.

Follow this procedure for the examples below. If the connection is faulty, indicate the voices involved and describe the error. If the connection is correct, mark it correct.

42

TB, parallel primes

T.B., // primes

SB, parallel octaves 43

S.B., // octaves

correct 44

correct

SB, consecutive octaves 45

S.B. /consec. octaves

scale degree 5

V

11 The root of this chord, D, is ___scale___ ___degree___ ___5___ of the G major scale. Write the chord symbol under the chord.

G:

IV

12 Write the chord symbol:

Ab: *IV*

---

diatonic

13 Roman numerals symbolize ___diatonic___ triads.

F: VII

x   D: I

y   *F: VI*

14 When used as a key symbol, C means C major, C♯ means C♯ major, etc. Major keys are symbolized by capital letters. Thus, the complete symbol for chord **x** is D: I. Chord **y** is in the key of F major. Write the complete chord symbol under chord **y**.

Write the proper symbol under each of the following chords. In each case assume the major key corresponding to the given signature.

Eb: II

15   *Eb: II.*

B: III

16   *B: II*

A: V

17   *A: V*

Db: I

18   *Db: I*

C♯: IV

19   *C♯: IV*

SB

Which pair of voices is at fault in this example?
..*SB*..... The term *consecutive octaves* is
commonly used to describe cases such as this ·
where 2 voices move from one octave (or compound) to another in contrary motion.

39

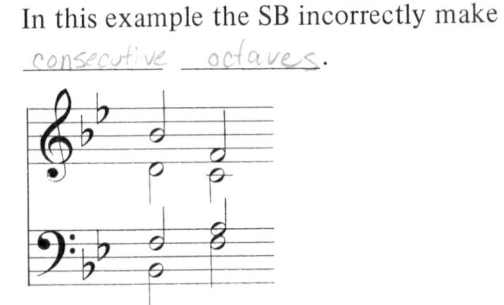

consecutive octaves

In this example the SB incorrectly make
consecutive octaves.

40

(1) are not
(2) are not
(only the bass moves)

For faulty parallel motion to exist, *both* voices
must actually move. In case **x** the SA (1) *are not*
(are *or* are not) faulty. In case **y** the TB (2) *are not*
faulty.

41

diatonic	20	Triads derived from a scale are ___diatonic___ triads.

degrees	21	Notes of a scale are referred to numerically as scale ___degrees___ .

(1) diatonic triad (2) scale degree 4 (*or* note 4) (3) C major	22	The symbol C: IV stands for a (1) ___diatonic___ ___triad___ built on (2) ......4.... in the key of (3) ___C___ ___major___ .

23 Write C: I:

(In all answers of this kind the entire chord may be written an octave higher or lower than shown.)

Write the indicated triads, using the appropriate key signature in each case:

24 Bb: II

25 D: III

26 Eb: VII

27 Ab: V

28 A: V

The interval of a 15th (interval **x**, for example) may be called a *double octave.* Similarly, the 22th (interval **y**, for example) may be called a

triple octave

<u>*triple*</u>   *octave* .

36

x   y

(1) SB

(2) parallel (double) octaves

Like parallel octaves, parallel double octaves and parallel triple octaves, etc. are avoided. Here the (1) . *SB* . . . . . *(voices)* incorrectly make (2) *parallel (double) octaves*

(For convenience, compound intervals corresponding to the octave are generally referred to as octaves.)

37

(1) prime

(2) octave

(3) contrary

In addition to avoiding parallel primes, octaves, and compound octaves, two voices may not move from one interval of this group to another. In the example, the TB move from a(n) (1) . *prime* . . in chord **x** to a(n) (2) . *octave* . . . . in chord **y**. This is faulty even though the TB move in (3) *contrary* motion.

38

x   y

Write the indicated triads *without key signatures:*

29 F: I

30 F: II

31 E: III

32 G♭: VI

33 F♯: VI

F   A♭   C   34   Spell D♭: III: _E A♭ C_

G♯ B   D♯   35   Spell B: VI: _G♯ B D♯_

maj   36   C: I is a ___major___ triad.
                         (What structural type?)

min   37   The structural type of C: II is
                         minor.

Give the structural types of the other five diatonic triads in C:

38

I	II	III	IV	V	VI	VII
maj	min	min	maj	maj	min	dim

III IV V VI VII
min maj maj min dim

(1) parallel

In this example, no pair of voices moves in (1) _parallel_ motion. In their relative motion the four voices are *independent*. It is neither desirable nor possible to avoid *all* parallel motion, but certain types of parallel motion are avoided because they destroy the impression of four (1) _independent_ voices.

(2) independent
(*or* separate, etc.)

32

---

(1) SB
(2) parallel

Parallel octaves and parallel primes are avoided. In this faulty chord connection the (1) ....*SB*... (*which pair of voices?*) make (2) _parallel_ octaves.

33

---

(1) TB
(2) primes

Here the (1) ..*TB*......(*voices*) incorrectly make parallel (2) _primes_ .

34

---

(1) octaves
(2) primes

   (*either order*)

35

Parallel (1) _octaves_ and parallel (2) _primes_ are avoided.

scale	39 Diatonic triads are derived from a _scale_ .

	40 All major scales have the same structure. Therefore, a diatonic triad from one major scale (or key) has the same structure as the corresponding diatonic triad from another scale (or key). C: I is a major triad. G: I is a major triad. D: I is a major triad, etc.
major	In *any* major key, I is a(n) _ma_ triad.

(1) minor	41 Since C: II is a(n) (1) _min_ triad, II is
(2) minor	a(n) (2) _min_ triad in any major key.

Complete the structural description of diatonic triads in major keys:

	I	maj	
	II	min	
III min	III	_m_	
IV maj	IV	_ma_	42
V maj	V	_ma_	
VI min	VI	_mi_	
VII dim	VII	_dim_	

(Hint: Remember the form of the previous item: "Since C: II is a minor triad. . . . . .")

(1) IV (and) V	In any major key, I, (1) _V_ , and _V_ , are
(2) II, III, (and) VI	43 major triads; (2) _II_ , _III_ , and _VI_ , are minor
(3) VII	triads; and (3) _VII_ is a diminished triad.

Set 21 / DIATONIC TRIADS IN MINOR

	1 Authorities differ on the question of which minor scales are diatonic scales, and which triads are diatonic triads in the minor keys. But one thing seems certain: In the minor keys the vast majority of triads correspond to the *harmonic* minor scale. It is therefore convenient to define diatonic triads in minor as triads derived from the harmonic minor scale. In the major keys, diatonic
(1) major	triads are derived from the (1) . . _maj_ . . . . scale.
	In the minor keys, diatonic triads are derived from
(2) harmonic minor	the (2) _har. min._ . . scale.

parallel perfect
5ths

28

In the foregoing examples of parallel motion, the general name of the interval between the voices remained the same. In some cases of parallel motion, the specific name is also maintained. In case **x** the voices move in parallel minor 3rds. In case **y** the voices move in _parallel_ _perfect_ _5ths_.

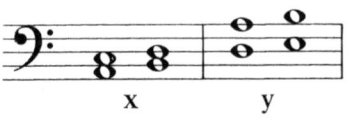

x   y

---

parallel perfect octaves

29

The TB move in _parallel_ _perfect_ _octaves_.

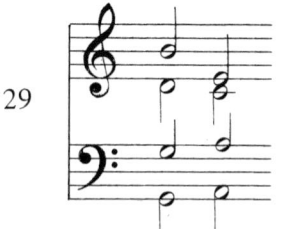

---

parallel major 10ths (*or* 3rds)

30

The ST move in _parallel_ _major_ _10ths_.

---

(1) AT
(2) major 3rds

31

The (1) ..._AT_..... *(which pair of voices?)* move in parallel (2) _major_ _3rds_.

---

diatonic	2	Triads derived from the C harmonic minor scale are the _diatonic_ triads in C minor.
E minor	3	Minor keys are symbolized by small letters. e:I means I in the key of _E minor_.

Write the proper symbol beneath each of the following chords. In each case assume the minor key corresponding to the given signature.

4

c: II

c: II

5

d: IV

d: IV

6

f♯: V

f♯: V

7

f: VII

f: VII

do not	8	Harmonic minor scales _do not_ (do or do not) correspond to the minor key signatures.

Write the signature of D minor followed by the D harmonic minor scale:

accidental	10	A sign not belonging to the key signature is a(n) _accidental_.
(1) 7 (2) raised	11	When a harmonic minor scale is written with key signature, scale degree (1) _7_ must be (2) _raised_ (raised or lowered) by an accidental.

Write the Ab minor harmonic scale, with key signature:

12

Motion by two voices in opposite directions is called *contrary motion.* Cases x and (1) _z_ show (2) _contrary_ _motion_.

(1) z
(2) contrary motion

23

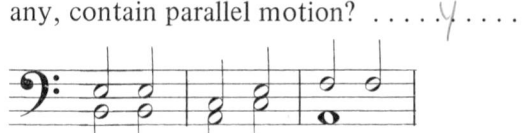

One stationary voice and one moving voice make *oblique motion.* Name the type of motion in each example:

(1)   (2)   (3)   (4)   (5)

24

(1) oblique
(2) similar
(3) contrary
(4) oblique
(5) contrary

(1) _oblique_
(2) _similar_
(3) _contrary_
(4) _oblique_
(5) _contrary_

Parallel motion is a special kind of similar motion. In parallel motion the two voices maintain an interval of the same general name. In case x the voices move from one 3rd to another. They move in parallel 3rds. In case y the voices move in _parallel_ 6ths.

parallel

25

Here the voices move in _parallel_ _5ths._

parallel 5ths

26

When neither voice changes pitch, there is *no* motion, parallel or otherwise. Which cases, if any, contain parallel motion? ..... _y_ ....

y

27

(1) diatonic (2) harmonic minor	**13** In the minor keys, (1) _diatonic_ triads are derived from the (2) _harm. min._ scale.

(1) 7 (2) raised (3) 7 (4) raised	**14** When the harmonic minor scale is written with key signature, scale degree (1) _7_ must be (2) _raised_. Therefore, when diatonic triads in minor keys are written with key signature, scale degree (3) ____ must be (4) _____ in those triads containing it.

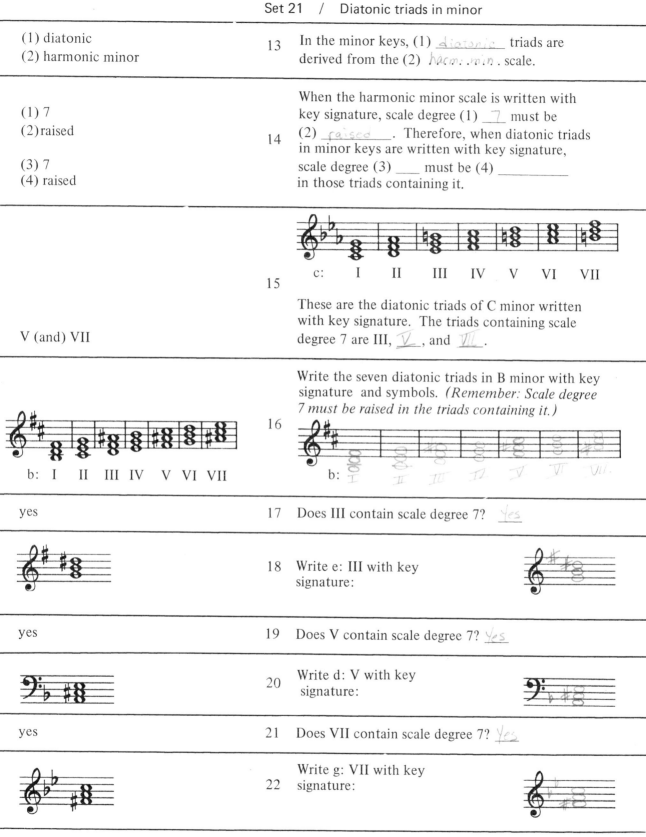

15

c: I   II   III   IV   V   VI   VII

These are the diatonic triads of C minor written with key signature. The triads containing scale degree 7 are III, _V_ , and _VII_ .

V (and) VII

16 Write the seven diatonic triads in B minor with key signature and symbols. *(Remember: Scale degree 7 must be raised in the triads containing it.)*

b: I   II   III   IV   V   VI   VII

b: I   II   III   IV   V   VI   VII

yes	**17** Does III contain scale degree 7? _Yes_

	18 Write e: III with key signature:

yes	**19** Does V contain scale degree 7? _Yes_

	20 Write d: V with key signature:

yes	**21** Does VII contain scale degree 7? _Yes_

	22 Write g: VII with key signature:

Fill in the AT using the indicated spacing:

19

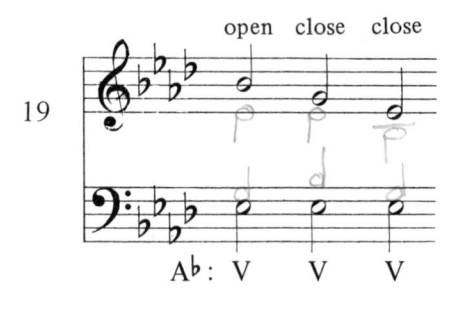

A♭: V   V   V

When the chord remains the same, the bass need not
repeat; it may sustain its note, or it may rise or fall
(1) sustains   an octave. In example **x** the bass (1) _sustains_ its
note. In example **y** the bass rises an octave, but the
(2) chord   (2) _chord_ remains the same.

20

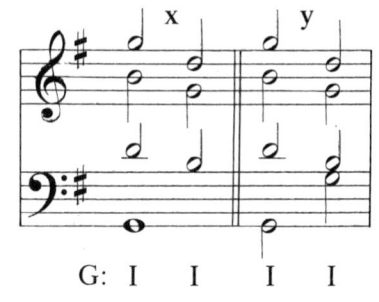

G: I   I   I   I

Complete example **y**. Write a different solution
for example **z**.

21

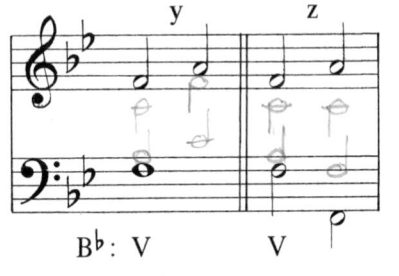

B♭: V   V

(AT either order)

Motion by two voices in the same direction is
called *similar motion*. In case **x** both voices move
(1) y   up. In case (1) _y_ both voices move down. Cases
(2) similar   **x** and **y** show (1) _similar_ motion.

22

x   y   z

Write the indicated triads, with key signature:

23

f#:   III

24

bb: V

25

g#:   VII

26   The triads *not* containing scale degree 7
are Ⅰ, Ⅱ, Ⅳ, Ⅵ .

I, II, IV, and VI

Write the indicated triads with key signatures:

27

c#:   I

28

eb: II

29

ab: IV

30

a: VI

31

f: III

Case **w** is incorrect because the tenor goes out of range to A♯. (*A♮ is the highest note of the tenor range.*)

Case **z** is incorrect because the tenor goes out of range *and* because the AT have large leaps.

Which of the four solutions is/are incorrect, and why? w./.T.range. z/T range, AT leap
(If a connection has two defects, give both.)

16

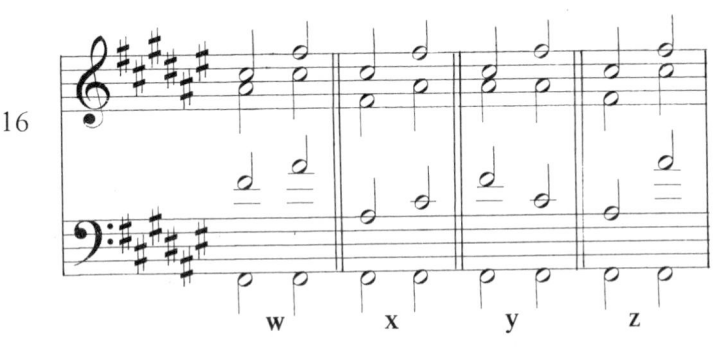

w   x   y   z

Write *all* of the *correct* solutions to the given problem. (Copy the SB for the second and any further correct solutions.)

17

(*either order*)

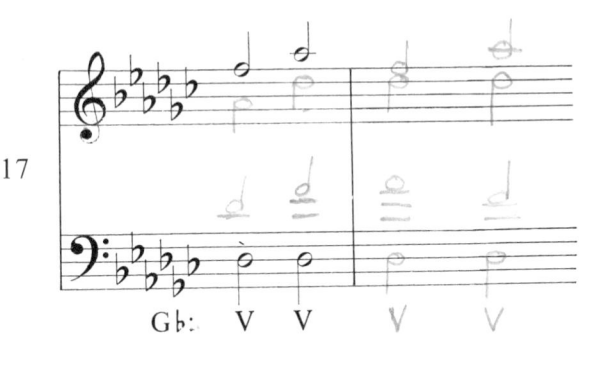

G♭:   V   V   V   V

Fill in the AT for all chords using the indicated spacing. *(First connect chords* **x** *and* **y**, *then chords* **y** *and* **z**.)

18

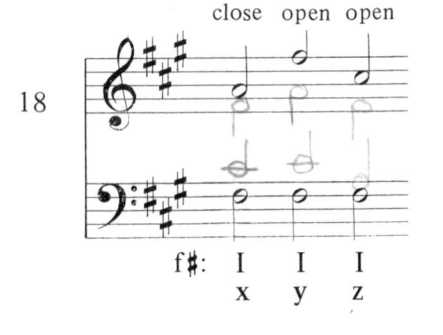

close open open

f♯:   I   I   I
      x   y   z

Write indicated triads with key signatures:

32 d: VII

33 d♯: VI

34 a♯: V

35 Write b♭: V, without key signature:

36 Write g♯: IV, without key signature:

D   F   A   **37** Spell d: I: D   F   A

B   D♯   F♯   **38** Spell e: V: B   D♯   F♯

min   **39** A diatonic triad from one major scale has the same structure as the corresponding diatonic triad from another major scale. For example, in any *major* key VI is a(n) ___min___ triad.

(1) min
(2) min
(3) min
   40 Similarly, a diatonic triad from one harmonic minor scale has the same structure as its counterpart from any other harmonic minor scale.

a: I is a(n) (1) ___min___ triad.

e: I is a(n) (2) ___min___ triad, etc.

In *any* minor key, I is a(n) (3) ___min___ triad.

dim   **41** From a: II we can see that II in any minor key is a(n) ___dim___ triad.

Complete the connection:

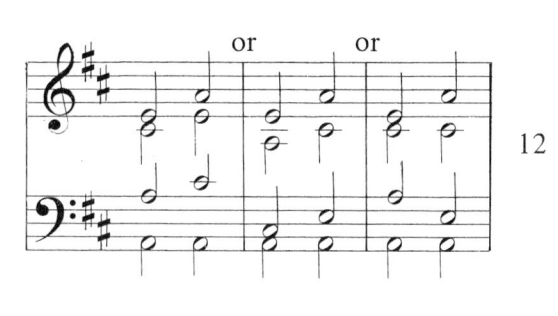

or   or

12

D: V   V

S   A   T   B

Write the ranges of the four voice parts:

13

S   A   T   B

---

(1) x
(2) tenor

Both case **x** and case **y** are free of large AT leaps. However, case (1) _x_ is unacceptable, because the (2) _tenor_ *(which voice?)* exceeds its range.

14

x   y

No. *(Open spacing in the second chord puts the tenor out of range.)*

Complete the connection. Is there more than one correct solution? _No_

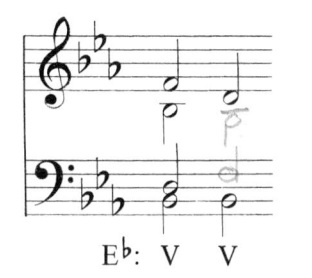

15

E♭: V   V

42 Write a: III:

---

aug

43 From a: III we can see that
III is a(n) _____ *aug* _____ triad in
any minor key.

Complete the structural description of diatonic
triads in minor keys:

I	min
II	dim
III	aug
IV	*min*
V	*maj*
VI	*maj*
VII	*dim*

44

IV min
V maj
VI maj
VII dim

---

one (VII)

45 Of the seven diatonic triads in the *major* keys,
how many are diminished triads? _____ *I (VII)*

---

46 Of the seven diatonic triads in the *major* keys,
how many are augmented triads? _____ *none*

---

(1) I, IV, and V
(2) II, III, and VI
(3) VII

47 In any *major* key the major triads are
(1) *I, IV, V*...; the minor triads are
(2) *II, III, VI*.; and the diminished triad is
(3) *VII*.

---

(1) V VI
(2) I IV
(3) II VII
(4) III

48 List the diatonic triads in the *minor* keys according to structural type:
major: (1) *V, VI*.....
minor: (2) *I, IV*.....
diminished: (3) *II, VII*.....
augmented: (4) *III*.....

---

no
*(I is a major triad in the major
keys and a minor triad in the
minor keys.)*

49 Does I have the same structure in the major keys
as in the minor keys? *No*

Complete the second chord as directed in examples
x and **y** below:

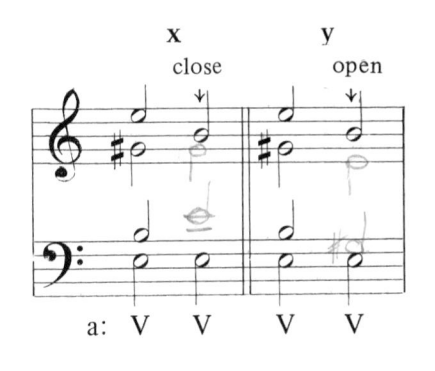

9

(1) yes

(2) yes *(In **x** the ♯ need not appear
before the second G in the alto. In
y the ♯ should appear before the
tenor G♯ because it lies in a different
octave.)*

Does the spacing indicated in example **x** produce
a correct solution? (1) _yes_. Does the spacing indicated in example **y** produce a correct solution? (2) _yes_ .

Fill in the AT of the second chord, following this
procedure: First think of the notes to be added. Then
choose either close or open spacing for the second
chord, depending upon which avoids AT leaps
of a fifth or more. If both close and open spacing
produce correct solutions, write either.

(only one correct solution)

10

e♭: V   V

Complete the first chord of this problem. Then
follow the procedure outlined in the previous frame
to complete the connection. *(Remember, the root
must be doubled in both chords.)*

(only one correct solution)

11

g♯: V   V

II no	50	Does II have the same structure in the major keys as in the minor keys?	No
III no	51	Does III?	No
IV no	52	IV?	No
V yes	53	V?	Yes
VI no	54	VI?	No
VII yes	55	VII?	Yes

TEST COVERING PART 4

The questions below will test your mastery of the material in Part 4. Complete the entire test, then check your answers with the correct ones on page 138. For each question that you miss, the corresponding material may be reviewed in the set whose number is given with the correct answer.

1. Label each triad *maj, min, dim,* or *aug*:

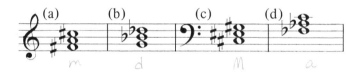

       m   d   M   a

2. Write the indicated triads:

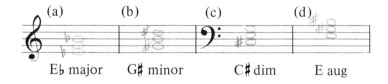

   Eb major   G♯ minor   C♯ dim   E aug

3. The seven triads derived from a major or harmonic minor scale are the ___diatonic___ triads in the corresponding key.

4. (1) ___Roman___ numerals corresponding to scale degrees are used to indicate (2) ___roots___ of diatonic triads.

Correct solutions to problems such as the one in the previous frame must 1) avoid AT leaps of a 5th or more, and 2) use either close or open spacing in the second chord. Sometimes there is only one correct solution to a problem; sometimes either close or open spacing in the second chord will produce a correct solution.

Which of the solutions below is/are correct? (1) ⨉..⋎.....
Solution (2) ⋎ uses open spacing for the second chord. Solution (3) ⨉ uses close spacing for the second chord.

(1) x and y*

(2) y

(3) x

(Solution z is incorrect because the AT contain large leaps, and the spacing in the second chord is neither close nor open.)

6

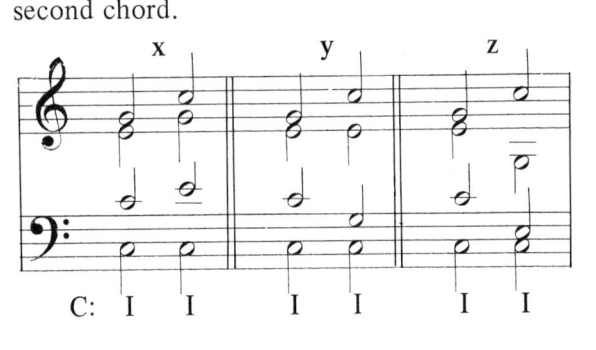

C: I   I   I   I   I   I

---

(1) 5th or more

(2) AT

(3) close (or) open

7 Correct solutions must avoid leaps of a (1) . 5th or more in the (2) .. AT ..... *(voices)*, and use either (3) __close__ or __open__ spacing.

---

(1) close

(2) open

(3) no

(4) yes

Consider problem **w** below and two proposed solutions **x** and **y**. Solution **x** uses (1) __close__ spacing in the second chord. Solution **y** uses (2) __open__ spacing in the second chord. Is solution **x** correct? (3) __no__ *(Does it avoid AT leaps of a 5th or more?)* Is solution **y** correct? (4) __yes__

8

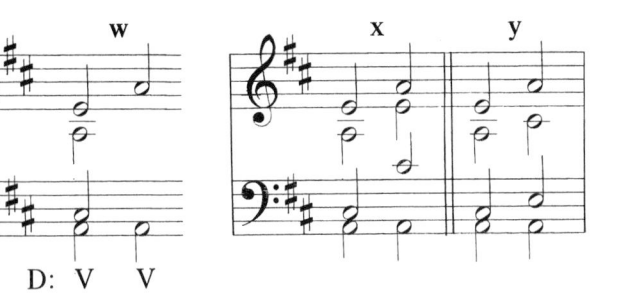

D: V   V

5. Complete the table, showing the correspondence between root and type for diatonic triads in major and minor keys:

	TRIAD TYPE			
	maj	min	dim	aug
major keys	I IV V	II , III , VI	VII	————
minor keys	V, VI	I , IV	II , VII	III

6. Under each chord, write the symbols for key and root (for example C: I). In each case assume the major key corresponding to the given signature.

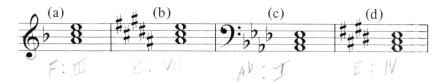

(a) F: III   (b) B: VII   (c) Ab: I   (d) E: IV

7. Follow the same instructions as for question 6, but assume the minor key corresponding to the given signature in each case.

(a) e: V   (b) c: VII   (c) g: III   (d) f#: IV

8. Construct triads, using the signature of the indicated key in each case:

(a) C: II   (b) c: V   (c) F#: III   (d) f#: III   (e) A: VI   (f) bb: IV

A chord may be repeated with a change of soprano, often accompanied by a change of alto and/or tenor.
In this example the . .*SA*. . . . . .*(which voices?)* move, but the chord remains the same.

SA

2

E♭: I   I

In its role as chief bearer of melodic interest, the soprano sometimes makes large leaps of a 5th or more. In order not to detract from the melodic effect of the soprano, leaps of a *5th or more* are avoided in the AT. In the example, the largest leap in the soprano is a (1)___*m 6*___ . The largest leap in the alto is a (2)___*M 3*___. The largest leap in the tenor is a (3)___*p 4*___ .

(1) 6th

(2) 3rd

(3) 4th

3

(1) 5th

(2) AT

4

Leaps of a (1) ___*5th*___ or more are avoided in the (2) . .*A.T.*. . . . .*(voices)*.

This example is a fundamental type of problem in chord connection. The task is to fill in the alto and tenor voices of the second chord. What are the two notes that are missing in the second chord?
___*E*___ and ___*G*___ *(Do not fill in the notes.)*

E (and) G

5

C: I   I

1

If the G in chord **x** is transposed up an octave, chord **y** results. Write the chord which results when the D in chord **x** is transposed down an octave.

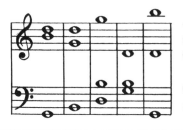

G B D

2   Chords do not lose their identity or change their spelling when one or more notes are transposed up or down an octave. Chords **x** and **y** are different forms of G B D. Chord **z** is still another form of
. .G. .B. .D. . . . .

By transposing one or more notes of this chord one or more octaves we can obtain a very large number of chords, a few of which are shown below.

(1) G B D

3

All of these chords are spelled (1) _G_ _B_ _D_ Octave transposition simply results in different chords with the same

(2) spelling (*or* notes)

(2) _spelling_ .

4   All members of a chord keep their original names —root, third, and fifth—regardless of octave transpositions. In all of the chords shown in frame 3,

(1) third
(2) fifth

G is the root, B is the (1) ___third___ , and D is the
(2) ___fifth___ .

5   It follows that chords with the same spelling have the same root (and third and fifth). The root of

C

any chord spelled C E G is _C_ .

Write B:VI, third in the soprano, open spacing, with key signature:

or

62

Write f:V, root in the soprano, open spacing, with key signature:

63

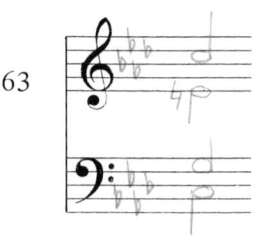

Set 27 / VOICE LEADING

The term *voice leading* is used to refer to both the melodic movement of a single voice and to the combined movement of two or more voices.
Melodic movement may be by *step* or by *leap*.

1 A melodic interval of a 2nd is a step.
A melodic interval of a 3rd or more is a leap. Label each of the following intervals step or leap.

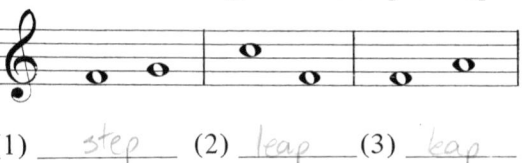

(1) step   (2) leap   (3) leap

(1) ___step___   (2) ___leap___   (3) ___leap___

(1) spelling	6	Chords with the same (1) _spelling_ have the same
(2) root		(2) _root_ .

x   y

	7	
(1) B		It is obvious that the root of chord **x** is (1) _B_ . Since chords **x** and **y** are spelled the same, the root
(2) B		of chord **y** is also (2) _B_ , but this might not be obvious if chord **x** were not present for comparison. It is easier to find the root of chord **x** than the root of chord **y**, because chord **x** is arranged in 3rds and
(3) arranged in 3rds		chord **y** is not (3) _arranged in 3rds_ .

no	8	Is this chord arranged in 3rds? _No_

z	9	Chord **w** may be arranged in 3rds by trying each note in turn as the lowest note until the 3rds show up. Chord _z_ shows how chord **w** may be arranged. in 3rds.

A	10	Chord **y** is an arrangement in 3rds of chord **x**. The root of chord **x** is _A_ .

57

(1) III, V, (and) VII

(2) 7

Since diatonic triads in the minor keys are derived from the harmonic minor scale, some triads in the minor keys require an accidental when written with key signature. These triads are (1) III , V , and VII *(Roman numerals)*, in which scale degree (2) 7 must be raised by means of an accidental.

58

Using the given SB's, write the indicated triads: g: V, open spacing *(Hint: An accidental is required.)*

59

E♭: II, close spacing

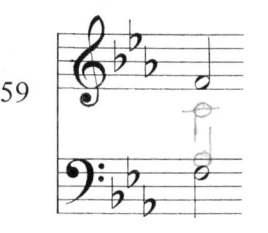

60

Using the given bass, write D: I, third in the soprano, close spacing:

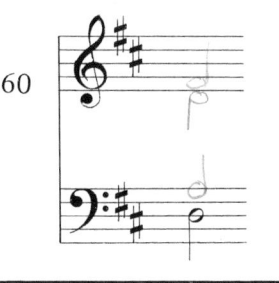

or

61

Write e: I, fifth in the soprano, close spacing, *with key signature:*

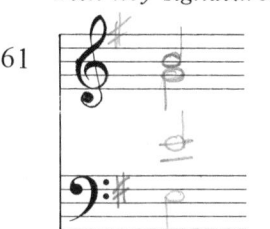

or

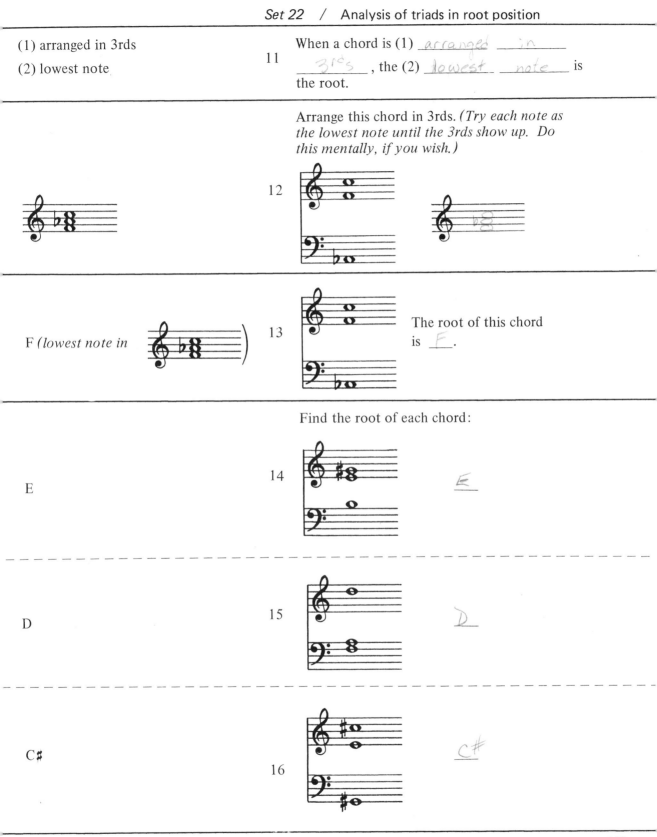

(1) arranged in 3rds

(2) lowest note

11 When a chord is (1) _arranged_ _in_ _3rds_ , the (2) _lowest_ _note_ is the root.

12 Arrange this chord in 3rds. *(Try each note as the lowest note until the 3rds show up. Do this mentally, if you wish.)*

F *(lowest note in* 〔 〕 13 The root of this chord is _F_.

Find the root of each chord:

E 14 E

D 15 D

C♯ 16 C♯

Write a D♭ major triad in root position, root in the soprano, close spacing:
(Write the bass, then the SAT. There are several correct answers.)

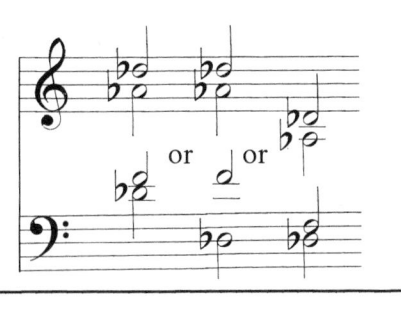
or 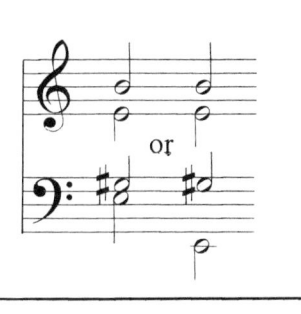 or

52

Write an E major triad in root position, fifth in the soprano, open spacing:

or

53

Write a B minor triad in root position, third in the soprano, open spacing:

correct | incorrect (tenor out of range)

54

(1) major

(2) harmonic minor

55

In major keys, diatonic triads are derived from the (1) ..major... scale. In minor keys, diatonic triads are derived from the (2) harm. minor. scale.

(1) do

(2) do not

56

Major scales (1) ..do...... (do *or* do not) conform to major key signatures. Harmonic minor scales (2) .do. not... (do *or* do not) conform to minor key signatures.

Find the root of this chord:

B

17

B

---

(1) arranging (the chord) in 3rds

(2) lowest

18

When a chord root is not obvious, it may be found by (1) .*arranging*.*chord.in.3rds* The root will then be the (2) _*lowest*_ note.

G

19

Octave doubling does not affect the names of chord members. _*G*_ is the root of all chords shown.

B min

20

The structural type of a triad is not affected by octave transpositions or doublings. All of these chords are _*B*_ _*min*_ *(root and type)* triads.

A min

21

This chord is a(n) _*A*_ _*min*_ triad.

Give the root and type of this triad:

D aug

22

_*D*_ _*aug*_

Write root position triads in open spacing,
using the given SB's and types:

48

minor

49

major

B

The third of a G major triad is __B__ .
Using the given bass, write a G major triad with
the third in the soprano, close spacing. *(First write
the soprano note within the appropriate range.)*

50

Using the given bass, write an E minor triad with
the root in the soprano, close spacing. For the
soprano note, either the high E or the low E may
be written. Hence, there are two correct solutions.
Write either one:

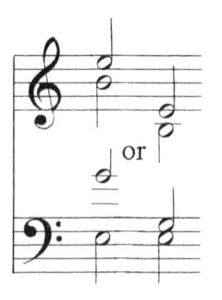

51

Give the root and type of each triad:

A dim

23

A dim (handwritten)

A♭ major

24

A♭ maj (handwritten)

25

x   y

(1) is not

(2) is

It should be clear that the lowest note of a
chord may or may not be the root. The low-
est note of chord **x** (1) ...*is not*... (is *or* is not)
the root. The lowest note of chord **y**
(2) ....*is*.... the root.

26   s   t   w

x   y   z

(1) **w** (and) **y**

(2) root position

When the lowest note of a chord is the root,
the chord is in *root position*. Chords **s**, (1) *w* ,
and *y* are in (2) __root__ __position__ .

Write the indicated triads in close spacing:

44

E augmented

45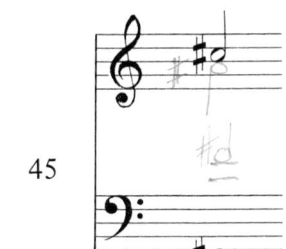

F♯ major

Using the given SB, write a C major triad in *open* spacing.
(Write the alto, then the tenor, skipping one chord note between SA, and one between AT.)

46

Using the given SB, write a D minor triad in open spacing. *(As a check of your finished work, make sure that all three chord notes are present in the SAT.)*

47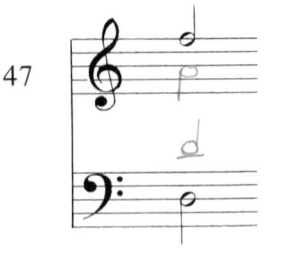

no

27 Is this chord in root position? _No_

no

28 Is this chord in root position? _No_

(1) lowest (2) root

29 A chord is in root position when the
(1) _lowest_ note is the (2) _root_ .

is

30 This chord . . . _is_ . . . . in root position.

is not

31 This chord . . . _is not_ . in root position.

Roman

32 _Roman_ numerals are used as symbols for diatonic triads.

root

33 A Roman numeral indicates the scale degree that is the _root_ of a triad.

(1) x
(2) y
(3) (perfect) prime

There are no size limits to the TB interval, except those created by the voice ranges themselves. The TB interval may be large, as in chord (1) __x__ (**x** *or* **y**), or small, as in chord (2) __y__ (**x** *or* **y**). It may even be a(n) (3) ...*prime*.., as in chord **z**.

40

x   y   z

---

root (*or* bass)

41

Close and open spacing insure correct doubling. When close or open spacing is used, a triad in root position automatically has a doubled __root__.

Using the given SB, write an F major triad in close spacing. (*Spell the chord. Write the alto, then the tenor, leaving no gaps between SA or AT.*)

42

(*Reminder: ST stems are up. AB stems are down.*)

Using the given SB, write the indicated triad in close spacing:

43

C minor

G: I   II   III

root

34   Up to this point, Roman numerals have been used only for triads with all three notes within the range of a 5th, such as those shown. Such triads are, of course, in ___root___ position.

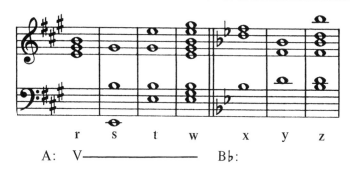

         r   s   t   w   x   y   z

35   A: V————————— B♭:

(1) z   (2) I

The same system of numerals is used for all diatonic triads in root position. Triads **r, s, t,** and **w,** all have the symbol A: V. Triad **x** and triad (1) _z_ both have the symbol B♭: (2) _I_.

The remaining frames are exercises in writing symbols for root position triads. The Roman numeral(s) should be preceded by a key name, making the complete symbol C: I or C: II, not simply I or II. In the next three frames assume the major key corresponding to the signature. Write the chord symbol:

36

G: II

G: II

A chord with no gaps between SA or AT is in *close spacing*. The SAT chord notes are as close together as possible. Chords x and (1) _y_ are in (2) _close_ _spacing_.

(1) y
(2) close spacing

35

x   y   z

---

(1) no gaps
(2) SA (or) AT

36

In close spacing there are (1) _no_ _gaps_ between (2) ..*SA*..... or ...*AT*..... .

When there is a gap of *one* available chord note between SA, and a gap of *one* available chord note between AT, the chord is in *open spacing*. Chords x and (1) _z_ are in (2) _open_ _spacing_.

(1) z

(2) open spacing

37

x   y   z

---

(1) one

(2) one

38

In open spacing the number of available chord notes skipped between SA is (1) _one_, and the number of available chord notes skipped between AT is (2) _one_.

---

(1) close

(2) SA (and) AT

39

The terms open and close refer to the spacing among the upper three voices. In close spacing the SAT are as (1) _close_ together as possible with no gaps; in open spacing there is a gap between both (2) ..*SA*.....*(voices)* and ..*TA*.....*(voices)* of one available chord note.

Write the chord symbol:

37

F: V

F: V

38

Ab: VI

Ab: VI

In the next three frames assume the minor key corresponding to the signature. Write the chord symbols:

39

c: V

c: V

40

b: III

b: III

41

g#: II

g#: II

C♯

This chord is spelled AC♯E. What chord note would fill the gap between SA? _C♯_

31

---

(1) G B♭ D

(2) gap

This chord is spelled (1) _G B♭ D_. There are no available chord notes between AT. Therefore, there is no (2) _gap_ between AT.

32
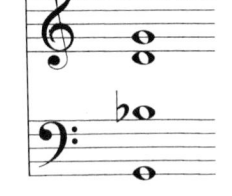

---

(1) F A♭ C
(2) yes

This chord is spelled (1) _F A♭ C_.
Is there a gap between AT? (2) _yes_.

33

---

no

Is there a gap between SA? _no_

34

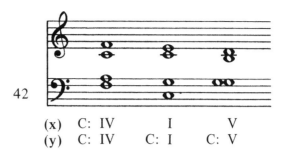

42

(x) C: IV   I   V
(y) C: IV   C: I   C: V

The key symbol is not repeated for successive
chords in the same key. This example is properly
analyzed as in __X__. (x *or* y)

x

Write the chord symbols:

43

I IV V I

E: I   IV   V   I

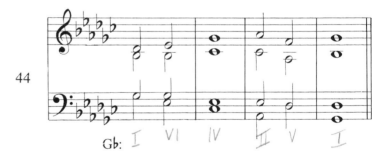

44

I VI IV II V I

Gb: I   VI   IV   II   V   I

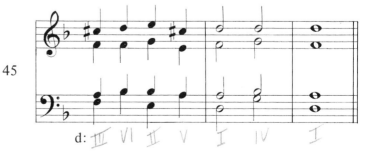

45

III VI II V I IV I

d: III VI II V   I   IV   I

(1) root (2) bass	26 In triads in root position the (1) __root__ (root, third, *or* fifth) is doubled. It follows that in root position triads the note in the (2) __bass__ *(which voice?)* is doubled.
(1) AB (2) soprano (3) tenor	27 In this chord the root is doubled in the (1) .*AB*...... *(which 2 voices?)*. The third is in the (2) __sop__. The fifth is in the (3) __ten.__ .
    SAT (*or* upper three parts)	28 If the bass and one other part are doubled, as in the example in the previous frame, it follows that no two of the upper three parts have the same chord member. SAT each have different chord members. In other words, all three chord members of a root position triad are present in the .*SAT*...... .
x and y	29 Shown are several root position triads. In which triads is the doubling correct? .*X, y*.....
(1) x (2) y	30 Chord **x** is spelled GBD. If all the available chord notes are filled in between the SB of chord **x**, we have chord **y**. Chord (1) __X__ has gaps. Chord (2) __y__ has no gaps.

(1) F
(2) A   (3) C

In all of these chords, the root is (1) _F_ *(pitch)*,
the third is (2) _A_, and the fifth is (3) _C_.

1

---

root position

2   When the lowest note of a chord is the root, the
chord is in __root__ __position__.

---

third

Chord **x** is in root position. When the root of
chord **x** is transposed up an octave, chord **y** is
formed. The lowest note of chord **y** is the
__third__ (root, third, *or* fifth).

3

x   y

---

(1) third
(2) first inversion

When the lowest note of a chord is the third, the
chord is in *first inversion.* The lowest note of the
chord below is the (1) __third__. The chord
is, therefore, in (2) __1st__ __inversion__.

4

---

(1) root

(2) third

5   When the lowest note of the chord is the
(1) __root__, the chord is in root position.
When the lowest note of the chord is the
(2) __third__, the chord is in first inversion.

---

(1) first inversion
(2) third

This triad is in (1) __1st__ __inversion.__ The
(2) __third__ is the lowest note.

6

For each triad, tell which member (root, third, *or* fifth) is doubled:

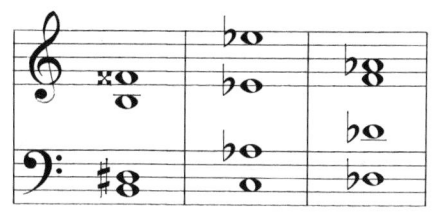

21

(1) root (2) fifth (3) root

(1) _root_ (2) _fifth_ (3) _root_

As a rule, the root is doubled in root position triads. Which triads, if any, have correct doubling?

. . . . 𝑦 . . . .

y

22

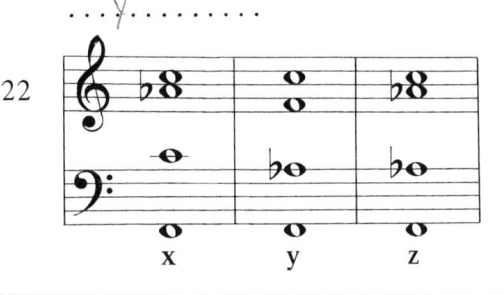

x   y   z

---

root

23 In root position triads the _root_ is doubled.

Rewrite the chord with correct doubling, changing only the alto note:

24

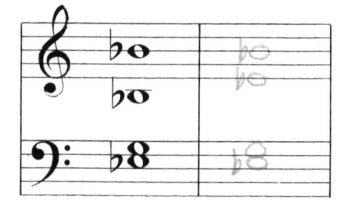

Rewrite the chord with correct doubling, changing only the soprano note:

25

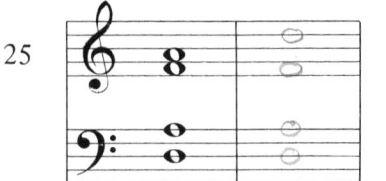

third	A triad is in first inversion whenever the lowest note is the ___third___ . The notes above the lowest note may be in any arrangement. However, in the exercises in this set and the following set, the notes will be written as close together as possible without octave transpositions, as in the example below:

7

root
fifth
third

---

first inversion	This triad is in ___1st___ ___inversion___. Label the chord members (root, third, fifth):

8

root
fifth
third

root
fifth
third

---

root position	Be careful *not* to confuse the term *root* with *lowest note*. Only when a triad is in ___root___ ___position___ is the root the lowest note.

9

---

(1) D♯	The root of this triad is (1) ___D♯___ *(pitch)*.
(2) third	The lowest note is the (2) ___third___ *(chord*
(3) first inversion	*member).* The triad is in (3) ___1st___ ___inversion___.

10

---

(1) E	The root of this triad is (1) ___E___ *(pitch)*.
(2) root	The lowest note is the (2) ___root___ *(chord*
(3) root position	*member).* The triad is in (3) ___root___ ___position___.

11

---

root position	This triad is in ___root___ ___position___. Construct the first inversion of the triad. *(In all construction exercises notes are to be written as close together as possible.)*

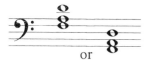

or

(In all answers of this kind the entire chord may be written in a different octave.)

12

Unisons between SA and TB involving stemmed
notes are notated as shown in example **x**. Assume
that examples **y** and **z** are four voice chords, and
add stems to the noteheads:

17   

Bb

A triad contains only three chord members. When
a triad is written for four voices, two of the voices
must have the same chord member. One of the
three chord members of the triad is *doubled.* In
triad **x**, D is doubled. In triad **y**, _Bb_ *(note name)*
is doubled.

18

doubled

G is _doubled_ in this triad.

19   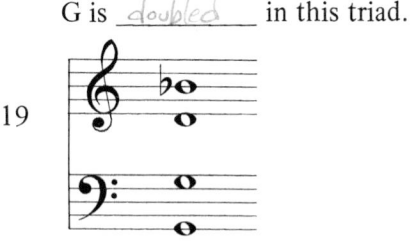

doubled

20   Since G is the root of the triad in the previous
frame, we may say that the root is _doubled_ .

Construct the first inversion of these triads:

13

14

(1) G
(2) B
(3) D
(4) D
(5) fifth

15

In all of these chords, (1) _G_ is the
root, (2) _B_ is the third, (3) _D_ is the
fifth. The lowest note of chord **y** is
(4) _D_ , which is the (5) _fifth_ (*chord
member*) of the triad on G.

x   y   z

fifth

16

Chord **x** is in root position. When both
the root and the third of chord **x** are
transposed up an octave, chord **y** is formed.
The _fifth_ (*chord member*) of chord **y**
is the lowest note.

x   y

(1) second inversion
(2) fifth

17

When the lowest note of the chord is
the fifth, the chord is in *second inversion*. This triad is in (1) _2nd
inversion_. The (2) _fifth_ is
the lowest note.

(1) third
(2) fifth

18

A triad is in first inversion when the lowest
note is the (1) _third_ . A triad is in second
inversion when the lowest note is the (2) _fifth_ .

(1) second inversion
(2) fifth

third
root
(fifth)

19

This triad is in (1) _2nd inversion_. The
lowest note is the (2) _fifth_ (root, third, *or*
fifth). Label the other chord members:

third
root
fifth

Even when AT have the same
pitch, as in this example, the
alto is written on the

(1) treble (*or* upper)

(2) bass (*or* lower)

13   (1) ___treble___ staff, and the
tenor is written on the

     (2) ___bass___ staff.

---

y

Another convention in writing four parts on two
staves concerns the direction of stems: ST stems
are written up, AB stems are down. There are no
exceptions. Which is correct, **x**, **y**, or **z**? _y_

14

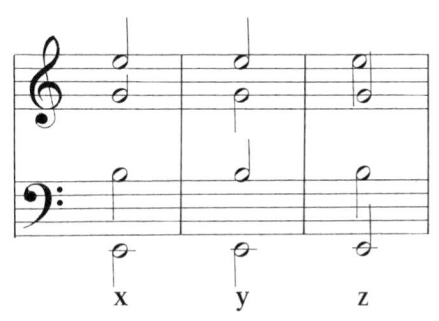

Put a stem onto each notehead:

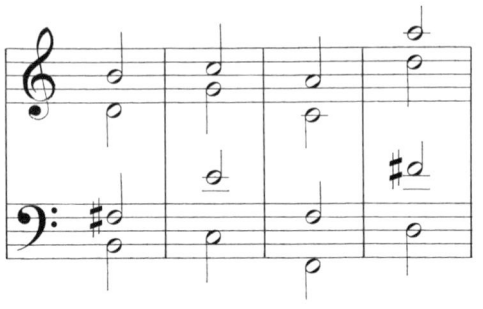

15

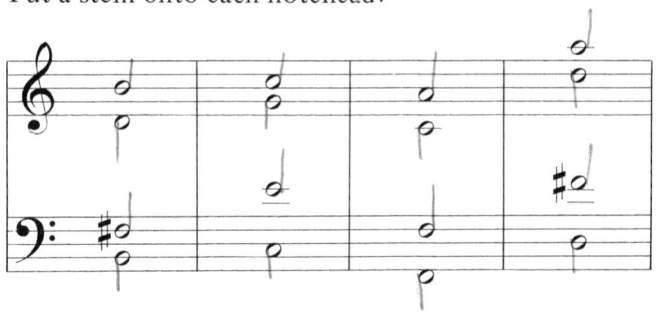

Example **x** demonstrates the way whole note unisons
between SA and TB are notated. Write a whole note
unison between TB in example **y**:

16

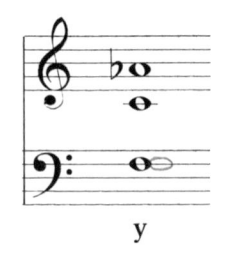

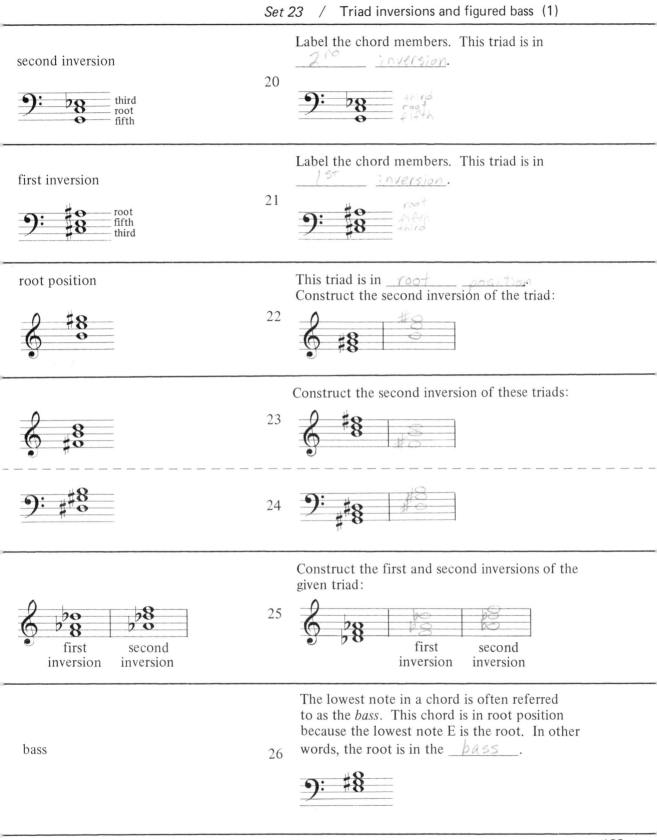

second inversion

third
root
fifth

20 Label the chord members. This triad is in
___2ⁿᵈ___ inversion.

third
root
fifth

---

first inversion

root
fifth
third

21 Label the chord members. This triad is in
___1ˢᵗ___ inversion.

root
fifth
third

---

root position

22 This triad is in ___root___ position
Construct the second inversion of the triad:

---

23 Construct the second inversion of these triads:

24

---

first
inversion

second
inversion

25 Construct the first and second inversions of the
given triad:

first
inversion

second
inversion

---

bass

26 The lowest note in a chord is often referred
to as the *bass*. This chord is in root position
because the lowest note E is the root. In other
words, the root is in the ___bass___.

Crossing of voices in a chord is to be avoided.
For example, the soprano should not be lower
than the alto, nor the bass higher than the tenor.

(1) tenor

Chord **x** is faulty because the (1) ___*tenor*___

(2) alto

is higher than the (2) ___*alto*___ .

9

x

10

In speaking of combinations of the four voice
parts, as, for example, soprano and alto, or soprano,
alto, and tenor, it is convenient to abbreviate. SA
means soprano and alto. SAB means *sop./alto/bass*

soprano, alto, and bass

11

When four voice parts are
written on two staves, SA
are written on the treble
staff, TB on the bass staff.
There are no exceptions to
this practice, regardless of
the number of ledger lines
necessary. Which is correct,
x or y? ___*y*___

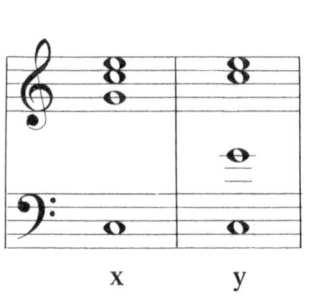

x   y

y

These chords are not written correctly
for four voices. Rewrite each chord correctly
(without changing any pitches):

12

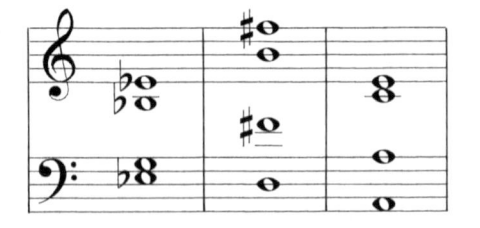

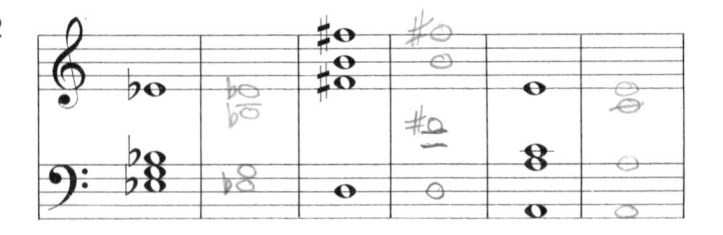

third

27 Do not confuse the terms *root* and *bass*. Only when a chord is in root position is the root in the bass. When a chord is in first inversion the ___third___ *(chord member)* is in the bass.

C

28 The bass of this chord is G. The root is _C_.

(1) F♯ (2) D

29. The bass of this chord is (1) _F♯_. The root is (2) _D_.

(1) root position
(2) 5th   *(either*
(3) 3rd   *order)*

30 When the bass of a chord is the root, the chord is in (1) __root__ ___position___. The intervals above the bass are a (2) __3rd__ and a (3) __5th__ .

(1) first inversion
(2) 6th
(3) 3rd

31 This chord is in (1) __1st__ ___inversion___. The intervals above the bass, as marked in the example, are a (2) __6th__ and a (3) __3rd__ . *(Give the general names of the intervals.)*

(1) first inversion
(2) 6th
(3) 3rd

32 This chord is in (1) __1st__ ___inversion___. The intervals above the bass are a (2) __6th__ and a (3) __3rd__ .

(1) second inversion
(2) 6th
(3) 4th

33 This chord is in (1) __2nd__ ___inversion___. The intervals above the bass are a (2) __6th__ and a (3) __4th__ .

Write the ranges of the four voice parts (without checking above, if possible):

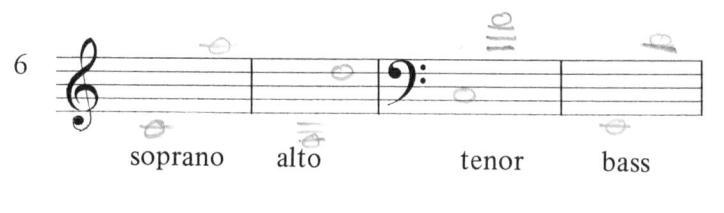

6

soprano   alto   tenor   bass

Inspect each of the following chords to see whether the four voice parts are within their respective ranges. If all four voices are in range, label the chord *correct*. If not, tell which voice or voices are out of range.

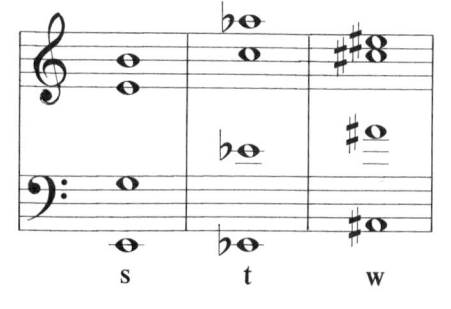

7

s t w

s correct
t bass *(The lowest note of the bass range is E♮).*
w tenor

correct   *bass*   *tenor*

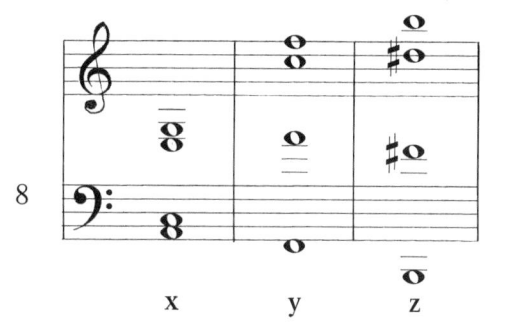

8

x y z

x soprano and alto
y correct
z soprano, alto, and bass

alto/sop.   *correct*   *bass/alto/sop.*

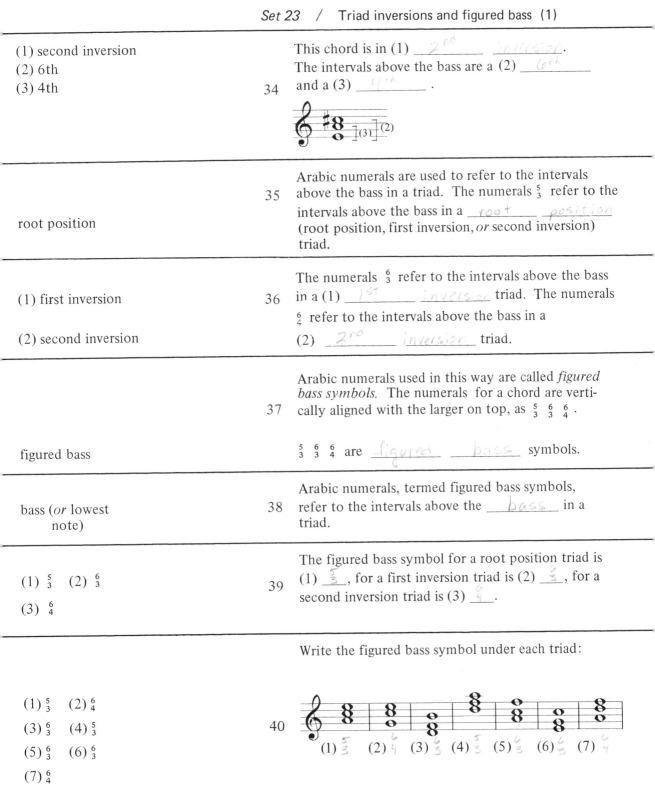

(1) second inversion
(2) 6th
(3) 4th

34   This chord is in (1) __2ⁿᵈ__ *inversion*.
The intervals above the bass are a (2) __6th__
and a (3) __4th__ .

---

root position

35   Arabic numerals are used to refer to the intervals above the bass in a triad. The numerals $\frac{5}{3}$ refer to the intervals above the bass in a __root__ __position__ (root position, first inversion, *or* second inversion) triad.

---

(1) first inversion

(2) second inversion

36   The numerals $\frac{6}{3}$ refer to the intervals above the bass in a (1) __1st__ *inversion* triad. The numerals $\frac{6}{4}$ refer to the intervals above the bass in a (2) __2ⁿᵈ__ *inversion* triad.

---

figured bass

37   Arabic numerals used in this way are called *figured bass symbols.* The numerals for a chord are vertically aligned with the larger on top, as $\frac{5}{3}$ $\frac{6}{3}$ $\frac{6}{4}$.

$\frac{5}{3}$ $\frac{6}{3}$ $\frac{6}{4}$ are __figured__ __bass__ symbols.

---

bass (*or* lowest
    note)

38   Arabic numerals, termed figured bass symbols, refer to the intervals above the __bass__ in a triad.

---

(1) $\frac{5}{3}$ (2) $\frac{6}{3}$

(3) $\frac{6}{4}$

39   The figured bass symbol for a root position triad is (1) __$\frac{5}{3}$__, for a first inversion triad is (2) __$\frac{6}{3}$__, for a second inversion triad is (3) __$\frac{6}{4}$__ .

---

(1) $\frac{5}{3}$ (2) $\frac{6}{4}$

(3) $\frac{6}{3}$ (4) $\frac{5}{3}$

(5) $\frac{6}{3}$ (6) $\frac{6}{3}$

(7) $\frac{6}{4}$

40   Write the figured bass symbol under each triad:

(1) $\frac{5}{3}$ (2) $\frac{6}{4}$ (3) $\frac{6}{3}$ (4) $\frac{5}{3}$ (5) $\frac{6}{3}$ (6) $\frac{6}{3}$ (7) $\frac{6}{4}$

y *(Chord **w**, spelled*
  GBDF, is a 7th chord,
  not a triad.)

The connection of chords in traditional harmony is best approached through the study of four-part vocal writing. Chord __y__ (**w, x, y,** *or* **z**) is a *triad* arranged for four parts.

1

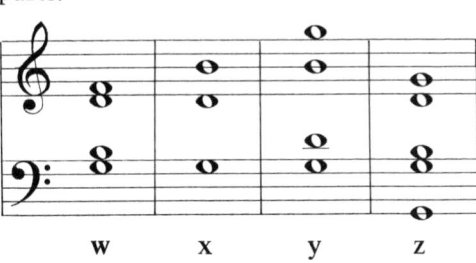

  w   **x**   **y**   **z**

---

(1) major 13th
(2) major 13th
(3) minor 14th

For the sake of uniformity we will adopt vocal ranges as shown below. The soprano range covers a major 13th. The alto range covers a(n) (1) __major__ __13th__. The tenor range covers a(n) (2) __major__ __13th__. The bass range covers a(n) (3) __minor__ __14th__.

2

  soprano   alto   tenor   bass

Study these voice ranges carefully.

---

octave

3

The tenor range is a(n) __octave__ *(what interval?)* below the soprano range.

---

octave

4

If the lowest note of the bass range were F instead of E, the bass range would be a(n) __octave__ below the alto range.

---

(1) A
(2) D

5

The upper note of the soprano and tenor ranges is (1) __A__. The upper note of the alto and bass is (2) __D__.

---

root
position

41 A chord in root position is sometimes termed a $\frac{5}{3}$ (read "five three") chord. However, chords in root position are most commonly referred to as root position chords. A $\frac{5}{3}$ chord is a ___root___ ___position___ chord.

$\frac{6}{4}$

42 A chord in first inversion is often termed a $\frac{6}{3}$ (read "six three") chord. Similarly, a second inversion chord may be referred to as a $\frac{6}{4}$ chord.

43 Construct $\frac{6}{3}$ chords over these given bass notes. Do not use ♯'s or ♭'s. *(First write a 3rd above the bass; then write a 6th above the bass.)*

(1) first
(2) second

44 $\frac{6}{3}$ chords are (1) ___1st___ inversion chords.
$\frac{6}{4}$ chords are (2) ___2nd___ inversion chords.

45 Construct $\frac{6}{4}$ chords above these given bass notes:

Set 24 / TRIAD INVERSIONS AND FIGURED BASS (2)

is

1 The structural type (maj, min, dim, aug) of a triad ___is___ (is *or* is not) the same regardless of which chord member is in the bass.

(1) major
(2) minor

(3) diminished
(4) augmented

2 Give the structural type of each group of triads:

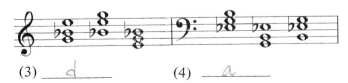

(1) ___M___   (2) ___m___

(3) ___d___   (4) ___a___

2. Construct the indicated triads:

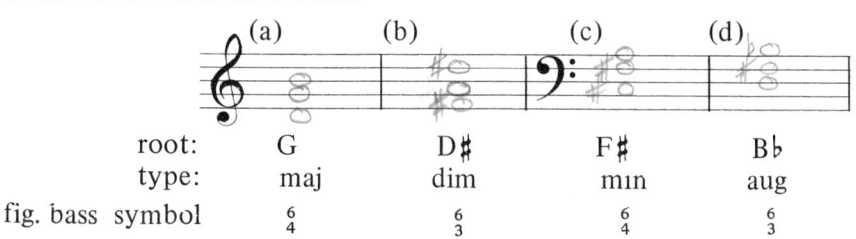

root:	G	D♯	F♯	B♭
type:	maj	dim	min	aug
fig. bass symbol	$^6_4$	$^6_3$	$^6_4$	$^6_3$

3. Construct triads as indicated above the given bass notes:

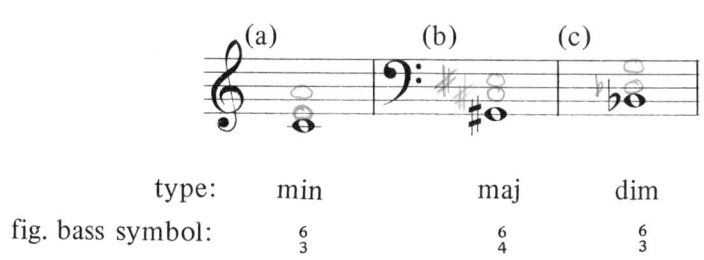

type:	min	maj	dim
fig. bass symbol:	$^6_3$	$^6_4$	$^6_3$

4. Give the root, type, and complete figured bass symbol for each chord. The first item is completed as a sample.

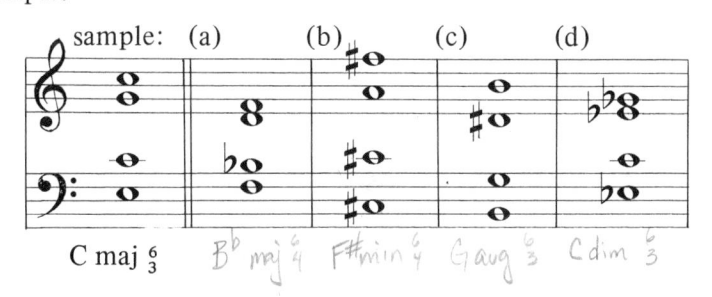

C maj $^6_3$ B♭ maj $^6_4$ F♯min $^6_4$ G aug $^6_3$ C dim $^6_3$

5. Write the appropriate symbols beneath each chord (Roman numerals for all chords, ^{6} or $^6_4$ for inversions).

(a)

(b)

(1) C♯ dim
(2) E♭ maj
(3) B min
(4) A♭ aug

3 Give the root and structural type of each triad:

(1) C♯d. (2) E♭M. (3) B.m. (4) A♭a.

A C♯ E

4 Spell an A major triad in root position:
A C♯ E. Construct an A major triad in first inversion:

5 Construct an E minor triad in first inversion.
(First mentally spell an E minor triad in root position; then write it in first inversion.)

6 Construct a B♭ major triad in second inversion:

7 Construct an A♭ minor $^6_3$ chord:

8 Construct a D major $^6_4$ chord:

B D F

9 Spell a B dim triad in root position: B D F.
Construct a B dim triad in first inversion:

10 Construct a G♯ dim $^6_3$ chord:

Write the chord symbols:

52

I IV⁶ V⁶ I   A: I IV⁶ V⁶ I

53

I IV⁶₄ I V⁶₄ I⁶ II⁶ V I   a: I IV⁶₄ I V⁶₄ I⁶ II⁶ V I

54

I VI⁶ II VII⁶ III I⁶ IV V I   D: I VI⁶ II VII⁶ III I⁶ IV V I

TEST COVERING PART 5

The questions below will test your mastery of the material in Part 5. Complete the entire test, then check your answers with the correct ones on page 139. For each question that you miss, the corresponding material may be reviewed in the set whose number is given with the correct answer.

1. Complete the following table by filling in the boxes:

chord position	chord member in bass	complete fig. bass symbol	abbrev. fig. bass symbol
root position	root	$\begin{smallmatrix}5\\3\end{smallmatrix}$	symbol omitted
1st inversion	(1) third	(2) $\begin{smallmatrix}6\\3\end{smallmatrix}$	(3) 6
2nd inversion	(4) fifth	(5) $\begin{smallmatrix}6\\4\end{smallmatrix}$	no abbrev. symbol

A C♯ E♯

Spell an A aug triad in root position: *A C♯ E♯*.
Construct an A aug $^6_3$ chord:

11

12

Spell the following triads. Name the bass first,
then the note lying a 3rd or 4th above the bass
(for $^6_3$ and $^6_4$, respectively), and finally the note
lying a 6th above the bass.

B	D	G	G maj $^6_3$: *B D G*
A♭	D	F	13 D dim $^6_4$: *A♭ D F*
D♭	G♭	B♭♭	14 G♭ min $^6_4$: *D♭ G♭ B♭♭*
A	C	F♯	15 F♯ dim $^6_3$: *A C F♯*
G	B	E♭	16 E♭ aug $^6_3$: *G B E♭*
F♯	B	D♯	17 B maj $^6_4$: *F♯ B D♯*
G✕	C♯	E♯	18 C♯ aug $^6_4$: *G✕ C♯ E♯*
F♭	A♭	D♭	19 D♭ min $^6_3$: *F♭ A♭ D♭*

F	20 If A is the third of a major triad, the root is *F*.
G	21 If D is the fifth of a minor triad, the root is *G*.
B	22 If D♯ is the bass of a major $^6_3$ chord, the root is *B*.
C♭	23 If G♭ is the bass of a minor $^6_4$ chord, the root is *C♭*.

Construct the major $^6_3$ chord having a bass of G♯.
*(First determine the root of the chord and mentally
spell the triad.)*

24

Construct the minor $^6_3$ chord having a bass of F:

25

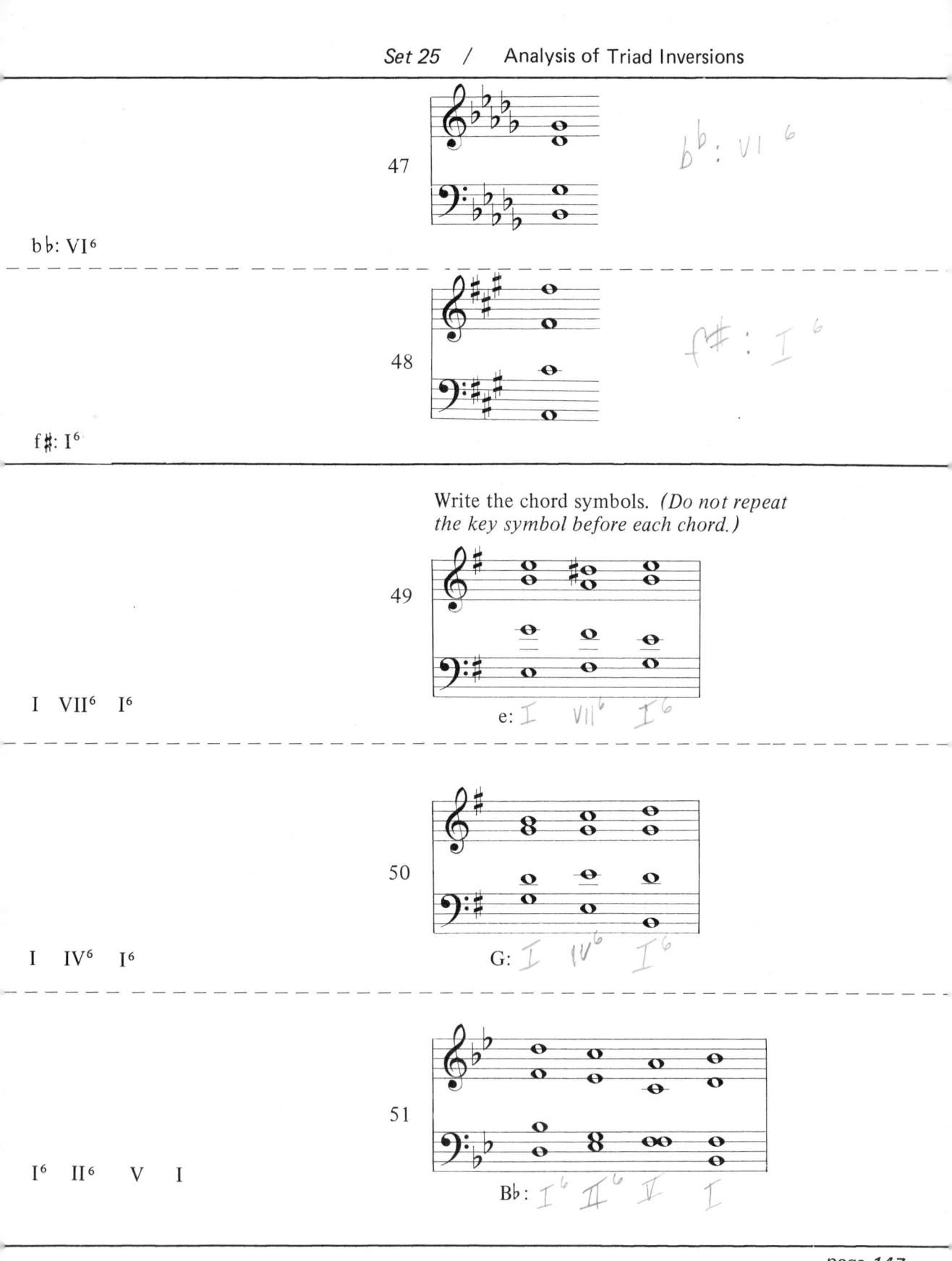

47   bb: VI⁶

bb: VI⁶

48   f#: I⁶

f#: I⁶

Write the chord symbols. *(Do not repeat the key symbol before each chord.)*

49

I   VII⁶   I⁶   e: I   VII⁶   I⁶

50

I   IV⁶   I⁶   G: I   IV⁶   I⁶

51

I⁶   II⁶   V   I   Bb: I⁶   II⁶   V   I

Construct the major $^6_4$ chord having a bass of A♭:

26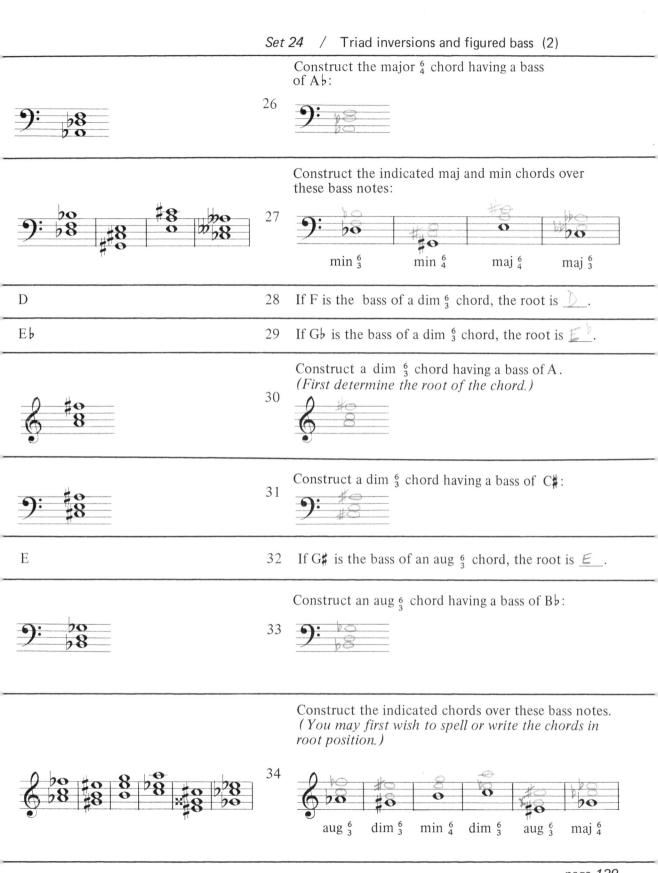

Construct the indicated maj and min chords over these bass notes:

27

min $^6_3$ min $^6_4$ maj $^6_4$ maj $^6_3$

D   28   If F is the bass of a dim $^6_3$ chord, the root is _D_ .

E♭   29   If G♭ is the bass of a dim $^6_3$ chord, the root is _E♭_ .

Construct a dim $^6_3$ chord having a bass of A.
(First determine the root of the chord.)

30

Construct a dim $^6_3$ chord having a bass of C♯:

31

E   32   If G♯ is the bass of an aug $^6_3$ chord, the root is _E_ .

Construct an aug $^6_3$ chord having a bass of B♭:

33

Construct the indicated chords over these bass notes.
(You may first wish to spell or write the chords in root position.)

34

aug $^6_3$ dim $^6_3$ min $^6_4$ dim $^6_3$ aug $^6_3$ maj $^6_4$

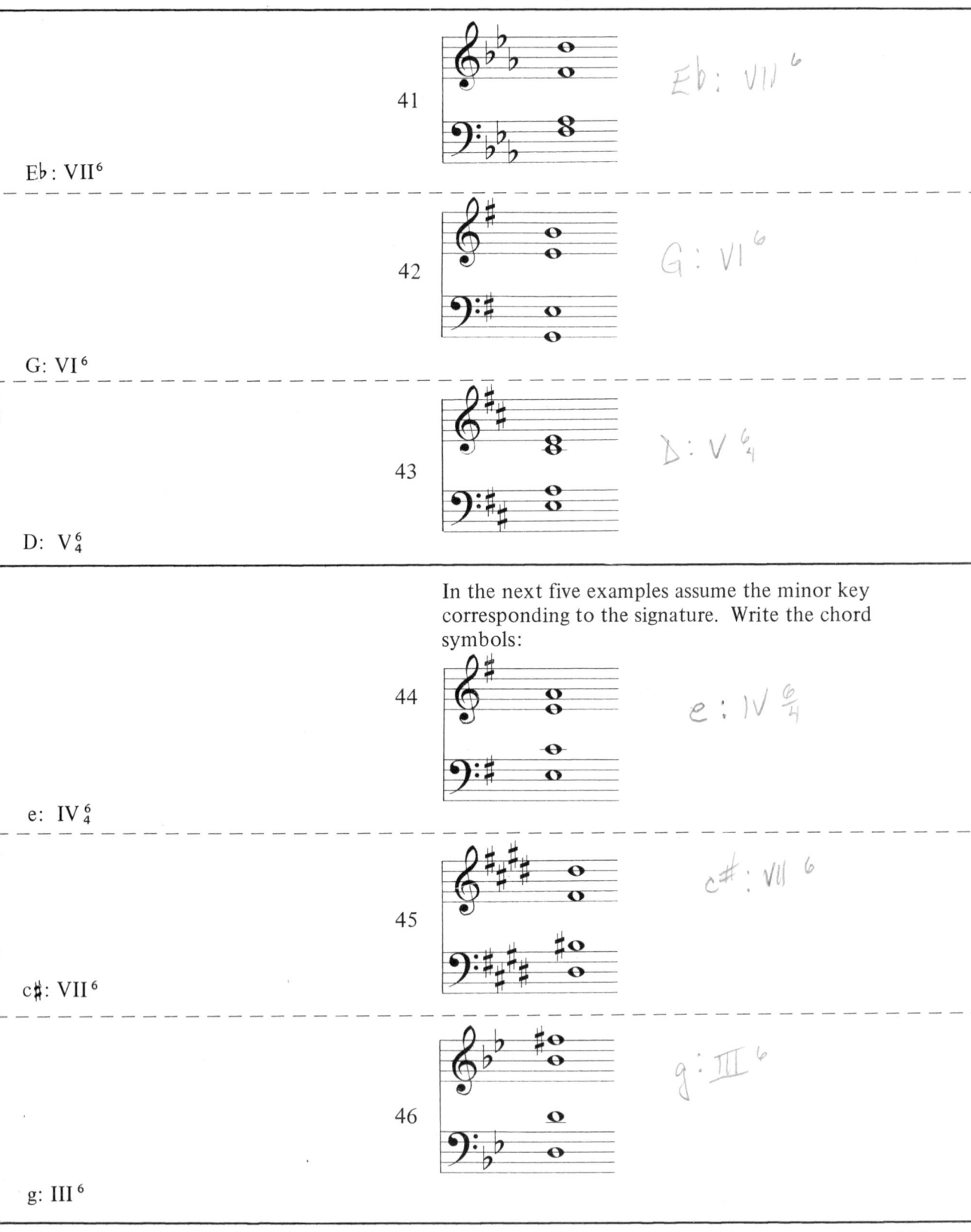

41   Eb: VII⁶

Eb: VII⁶

42   G: VI⁶

G: VI⁶

43   D: V⁶₄

D: V⁶₄

In the next five examples assume the minor key corresponding to the signature. Write the chord symbols:

44   e: IV⁶₄

e: IV⁶₄

45   c#: VII⁶

c#: VII⁶

46   g: III⁶

g: III⁶

Construct the indicated chords:

Dim $^6_3$ with *bass* of C:

35

Min $^6_4$ with *root* of E♭:

36

Aug $^6_3$ with *bass* of F♯:

37

Maj $^6_4$ with *root* of G♯:

38

You may sometimes find it helpful to check your construction of triads in inversion by calculating the specific intervals between chord members. Label the intervals in the following:

39

perf 4th   perf 4th
    min 6th   maj 6th
min 3rd   maj 3rd

C maj $^6_3$ C min $^6_3$

Show the structure of major and minor $^6_3$ chords by filling in the blanks:

40

perf   perf
   min   maj
min   maj

MAJOR $^6_3$ MINOR $^6_3$

Label the intervals in the following:

41

maj 3rd   min 3rd
   maj 6th   min 6th
perf 4th   perf 4th

C maj $^6_4$ C min $^6_4$

(1) is not

(2) A♭: IV⁶

g: I⁶₄

G♭: II⁶

F♯: IV⁶₄

The position or inversion of a chord (1) .is not.... (is *or* is not) affected by doublings or by octave transposition of notes above the lowest note. The complete symbol for each of the chords below is (2) A♭: IV. .

37

The complete symbol for both of these chords is g: .I.⁶₄ .

38

The remaining frames are exercises in writing symbols for chords. In the following five examples assume the major key corresponding to the signature, and write the chord symbol for each chord. Be sure to include the key name as part of the symbol.

39

G♭: II⁶

40

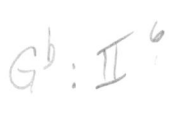

F♯: IV⁶₄

Show the structure of major and minor $^6_4$ chords
by filling in the blanks:

maj   min

    maj   min

perf   perf

42

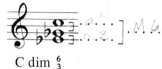

MAJOR $^6_4$

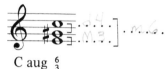

MINOR $^6_4$

This procedure may be used for dim and aug $^6_3$
chords as well. (Dim and aug $^6_4$ chords are rare.)
Label the following intervals:

aug 4th   dim 4th

    maj 6th   min 6th

min 3rd   maj 3rd

43

C dim $^6_3$ C aug $^6_3$

Write the four different types of triad in $^6_3$ position
using F♯ as the *bass*:

44

maj $^6_3$ min $^6_3$ dim $^6_3$ aug $^6_3$

Write the four different types of triad in $^6_3$ position
using E♭ as the *root*:

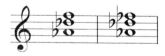

45

maj $^6_3$ min $^6_3$ dim $^6_3$ aug $^6_3$

Write major and minor $^6_4$ chords using A♭ as the *bass:*

46

maj $^6_4$ min $^6_4$

Write major and minor $^6_4$ chords using B as the *root:*

47

maj $^6_4$ min $^6_4$

Construct Bb: II⁶. *Hint: First mentally spell Bb: II. Then write it in first inversion. (Remember that in all construction exercises notes are to be written as close together as possible.)*

26

Write the indicated triads, using the appropriate key signature in each case:

27

c: IV⁶

28

Db: VI⁶₄

29

Ab: VII⁶

30

d: I⁶₄

31

G: III⁶₄

Spell the following triads. Name the bass first, then the note lying a 3rd or 4th above the bass (for ⁶₃ or ⁶₄, respectively), and finally the note lying a 6th above the bass. *(You will find it helpful to first spell the triad in root position.)*

B E G♯	32	A: V⁶₄:	B E G♯
C E♭ A	33	g: II⁶:	C E♭ A
F♯ B D♯	34	f♯: IV⁶₄:	F♯ B D
C E A	35	C: VI⁶:	C E A
G B♭ E	36	F: VII⁶:	G B♭ E

---

(1) A
(2) major
(3) $\frac{6}{3}$

1

The root of this triad is (1) _A_ .
The structural type is (2) _Maj_ .
The figured bass symbol is (3) ___ .

F min $\frac{6}{4}$

2

Give the root, type, and figured bass symbol for each
triad:
_F_ _min_ _$\frac{6}{4}$_

E dim $\frac{6}{3}$

3

_E_ _dim_ _$\frac{6}{3}$_

A aug $\frac{6}{3}$

4

_A_ _aug_ _$\frac{6}{3}$_

B min

5

The position or inversion of a chord is not affected
by doublings or by octave transposition of notes
above the lowest note. All of these chords are
_B_ *(root)* _min_ *(type)* $\frac{6}{3}$ chords.

---

(1) third
(2) first

6

The lowest note in each of these chords is the
(1) _third_ *(chord member)*. Both chords are,
therefore, in (2) _1st_ inversion.

---

b: V⁶

	Write the *minor* key symbol and complete chord symbol under this chord:
19	b : V. ⁶

6

20 When combined with a Roman numeral, the figured bass symbol for a first inversion chord is abbreviated to ___ .

$^6_4$

21 The figured bass for a second inversion chord is $^6_4$.

(1) $^6_4$

(2) E: III$^6_4$

22 When a chord is in second inversion, the complete figured bass, (1) $^6_4$, is used with the Roman numeral symbol. The complete symbol for this chord is (2) E: III $^6_4$. (Assume the major key.)

IV

23 When a chord is in root position, a figured bass symbol is *not* used with the Roman numeral label. Therefore, when there is no figured bass symbol with a Roman numeral, "$^5_3$" is assumed. III is an abbreviation for III$^5_3$, and IV is an abbreviation for IV$^5_3$.

D: II

24 Write the major key symbol and chord symbol under this chord:

D : II

(1) are not

(2) ⁶

(3) $^6_4$

25 In summary, there are three important points to remember concerning the use of figured bass symbols in combination with Roman numeral labels:
1. For root position chords, figured bass symbols (1) are not (are *or* are not) used.
2. For first inversion chords, the symbol (2) ⁶ is used with the Roman numeral.
3. For second inversion chords, the symbol (3) $^6_4$, is used with the Roman numeral.

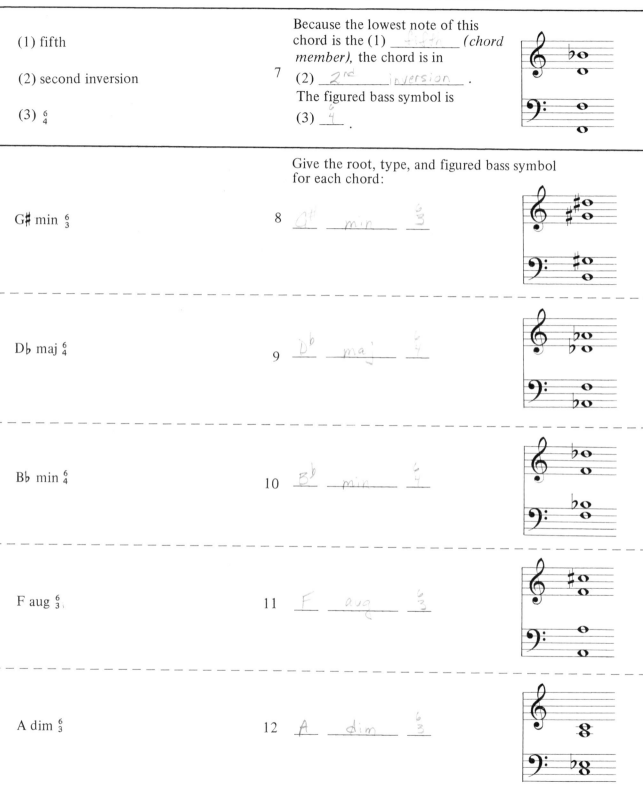

(1) fifth

(2) second inversion

(3) $\frac{6}{4}$

Because the lowest note of this chord is the (1) ___fifth___ *(chord member),* the chord is in

7 (2) ___2ⁿᵈ___ *inversion* .

The figured bass symbol is

(3) ___$\frac{6}{4}$___ .

Give the root, type, and figured bass symbol for each chord:

G♯ min $\frac{6}{3}$ 8 ___C♯___ ___min___ ___$\frac{6}{3}$___

D♭ maj $\frac{6}{4}$ 9 ___D♭___ ___maj___ ___$\frac{6}{4}$___

B♭ min $\frac{6}{4}$ 10 ___B♭___ ___min___ ___$\frac{6}{4}$___

F aug $\frac{6}{3}$ 11 ___F___ ___aug___ ___$\frac{6}{3}$___

A dim $\frac{6}{3}$ 12 ___A___ ___dim___ ___$\frac{6}{3}$___

Give root, type, and figured bass symbol:

Gb maj $\frac{6}{4}$

13 Gb   maj $\frac{6}{4}$

Roman

14 _Roman_ numerals are used to indicate the roots of diatonic triads.

---

(1) degree (*or* note)
(2) root

15 A Roman numeral indicates the number of the scale
(1) _degree_ that is the (2) _root_ of the triad.

---

16 Write the major key symbol and Roman numeral under this chord:

Eb: V

Eb : V

---

(1) 2   (2) root
(3) second inversion

17 In the analysis of chords in first and second inversion, figured bass symbols are combined with Roman numerals. In the symbol $\frac{6}{3}$, the "I" part indicates that $\hat{1}$ is the root of the chord, and the "$\frac{6}{3}$" part indicates that the chord is in first inversion. In the symbol II$\frac{6}{4}$, the "II" part indicates that scale degree (1) _2_ is the (2) _root_, and the "$\frac{6}{4}$" part indicates that the chord is in (3) _2nd_ _inversion_ (root position, first inversion, *or* second inversion).

F: IV^6

18 When combined with a Roman numeral, the figured bass symbol for a $\frac{6}{3}$ chord is usually abbreviated to $\frac{6}{}$. In our analysis of triads in inversion we will follow this convention.

The complete chord symbol for chord **x** is C: II$\frac{6}{}$.
Write the major key symbol and complete chord symbol for chord **y**: _F: IV^6_

x   y

Turn the book upside down now and continue to work on right-hand pages.

1. diatonic semitone (Set 2)

2. chromatic (Set 2)

3. whole tone (Set 3)

4. (a) CST (b) whole tone (c) whole tone (d) DST (Sets 2 and 3)

5.

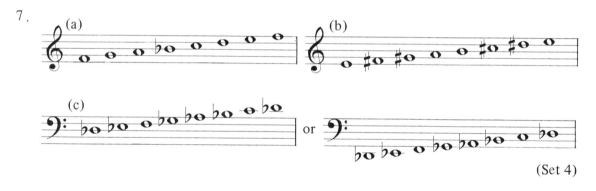

(Sets 2 and 3)

6. B major scale (Set 4)

7.

(D major)

8.

(Set 4)

9. z (Set 4)

1. the relationship between two pitches (Set 5)

2. (1) double   (2) specific   (3) general (Set 6)

3. prime (and) octave (Set 5)

4. (1) simple (2) compound (Set 11)

5. (1) 14th (2) 9th (Set 11)

6. (1) major (2) minor (3) augmented (4) diminished (5) perfect (Set 7)

7. (1) min min maj aug   (2) dim perf aug (Sets 7 and 9)

8. (1) 2nds, 3rds, 6ths, and 7ths
   (2) primes, 4th, 5ths, and octaves   (Set 6)

9. (1) major (2) perfect (Sets 6 and 9)

10. simple (Set 11)

11. transpose (Set 10)

12. (Set 11)

13. (1) y and z   (2) dissonant (Set 11)

14. minor 3rd (Set 11)

15. (a) dim 5th (Set 9)   (b) maj 2nd (Sets 6 and 7)   (c) min 6th (13th) (Set 11)
    (d) perf 4th (Set 9)   (e) maj 3rd (Sets 6 and 7)   (f) min 7th (Sets 6 and 7)

16.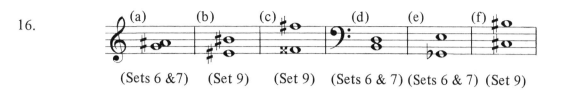

    (Sets 6 &7)   (Set 9)   (Set 9)   (Sets 6 & 7) (Sets 6 & 7) (Set 9)

ANSWERS TO TEST COVERING PART 3

1. Cb Gb Db Ab Eb Bb F C   (Set 12)

2. series of 5ths   (Set 13)

3. (a) Bb melodic minor ascending   (b) D major
    (c) E melodic minor descending   (d) G♯ melodic minor ascending   (Sets 4 and 15)

4. (a)

    (b)

    (c)

        (Set 15)

5. (a) D major   (b) Gb major   (c) Eb major   (d) B major
      B minor   Eb minor   C minor   G♯ minor   (Sets 13, 16, and 17)

6.

      (a)   (b)   (c)   (d)
           (Sets 13, 14, 16, and 17)

1. (a) min (b) dim (c) maj (d) aug   (Sets 18 and 19)

2. 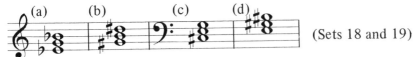   (Sets 18 and 19)

3. diatonic (Sets 20 and 21)

4. (1) Roman (2) roots (Sets 20 and 21)

5.

	TRIAD TYPE			
	maj	min	dim	aug
major keys	I IV V	II III VI	VII	
minor keys	V VI	I IV	II VII	III

6. (a) F: III (b) B: VII (c) A♭: I (d) E: IV   (Set 20)

7. (a) e: V (b) c: VII (c) g: III (d) f♯: IV   (Set 21)

8.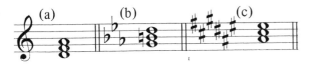

   (Sets 20 and 21)

1. (1) third   (2) $\frac{6}{3}$ (3) 6   (4) fifth   (5) $\frac{6}{4}$ (Sets 23 and 24)

2.

(Sets 23 and 24)

3.

(Sets 23 and 24)

4. (a) B♭ maj $\frac{6}{4}$ (b) F♯ min $\frac{6}{4}$ (c) G aug $\frac{6}{3}$ (d) C dim $\frac{6}{3}$ (Sets 22 and 25)

5. (a) I   II⁶   I$^6_4$ V   I

   (b) I   V$^6_4$ I⁶   V⁶   IV$^6_4$ I   (Sets 22 and 25)

ANSWERS TO TEST COVERING PART 6

1. major-minor (Set 30)

2. root (Set 30)

3. $\hat{7}$ resolves to $\hat{1}$
   (either order)
   $\hat{4}$ resolves to $\hat{3}$ (Set 31)

4. (1) a (bass), e (SB)   (Sets 26 and 27)

   (2) c (2nd chord), d (AT)   (Set 27)

   (3) f (soprano), b (2nd chord)   (Set 31)

   (4) e (TB)   (Set 27)

5.

(Sets 28 and 29)

6.

(Sets 28 and 29)

7.

(Sets 30-32)

8.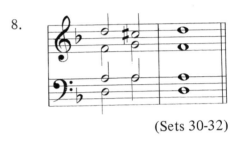

(Sets 30-32)

9.

(Sets 30-32)

10.

(Sets 30-32)

ANSWERS TO TEST COVERING PART 7

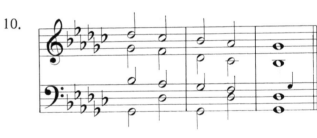

1. (1)
   (2)
   (3)
   (4)
   (5)   (Set 33)

2. (1)
   (2)
   (3)
   (4) + +   (Set 34)

3. (1) 16
   (2) 8
   (3) 7 (Sets 33 and 34)

4.  (Set 34)

5. (1) undotted
   (2) two
   (3) dotted
   (4) three (Sets 35 and 36)

6. (1) the number of
       beats in a measure
   (2) the note value
       of the beat
                        (Set 35)

7. (1) the number of divisions
       of the beat in a measure
   (2) the note value of the
       division   (Set 36)

8. ♩, ♩, ♪
   (any order)
   (Set 35)

9. ♩., ♩., ♪.
   (any order)
   (Set 36)

10. quadruple   (Set 36)

11. (1) compound
    (2) 𝅗𝅥.   (Set 36)

12. (1) simple
    (2) duple
    (3) 𝅗𝅥
    (4) compound
    (5) triple
    (6) ♩.
    (7) compound
    (8) duple
    (9) ♪.
    (10) simple
    (11) quadruple
    (12) ♩   (Sets 35 and 36)

13. (1) ♩.
    (2)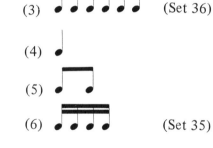
    (3)   (Set 36)
    (4) ♩
    (5)
    (6)   (Set 35)

14.    (Set 35)

anacrusis *or* pickup

15.  (Set 36)